ROLLS-ROYCE
& BENTLEY

HAYNES CLASSIC MAKES SERIES

ROLLS-ROYCE & BENTLEY

SPIRIT OF EXCELLENCE

JONATHAN WOOD

First published in 2001
Reprinted 2002

British Library Cataloguing in Publication Data:
A catalogue record for this book is available from the British Library

ISBN 1 85960 692 X

Library of Congress catalog card no. 2001132565

Haynes Publishing, Sparkford, Yeovil, Somerset BA22 7JJ, UK
Tel: 01963 442030 Fax: 01963 440001
Int. tel: +44 1963 442030 Fax: +44 1963 440001
E-mail: sales@haynes-manuals.co.uk
Web site: www.haynes.co.uk

Haynes North America, Inc.
861 Lawrence Drive, Newbury Park,
California 91320 USA

Printed in Great Britain by J. H. Haynes & Co. Ltd, Sparkford.

contents

Introduction

The dual qualities of discreet luxury and mechanical refinement make the Rolls-Royces and Bentleys of the post-war years unlike any other cars of their day. To understand why, it is necessary to take a look at how that remarkable company was created and the extraordinary individual who dominated it for the first 28 years.

Seventy-year-old Sir Frederick Henry Royce died on Saturday 22 April 1933, but not before he had overseen the concept of the V12-powered Phantom III, which was to be the last Rolls-Royce to be designed regardless of cost. Such was Royce's towering influence that it was not until four years after his death that the company began belatedly to address the all-important matter of how it engineered and manufactured its cars. Thankfully there was a crucial shift in design philosophy following the appointment, in 1936, of Ernest Hives as works manager. However, the full effects of his radical initiatives would not be felt until Rolls-Royce restarted car production in 1946.

In the 30 years between Henry Royce beginning work on his first car in Manchester in 1903 and his death, this former electrical engineer had endowed every car, from the 10hp Royce of 1904 to the complex Phantom III, with his own indelible perfectionist stamp.

A meeting in the city, probably on 4 May 1904, between Royce, whose father had been a country miller, and

The Hon Charles Rolls, whose social status and connections ensured that his name appeared prior to Royce's, at the wheel of a 1906 30hp six-cylinder Rolls-Royce. (Rolls-Royce)

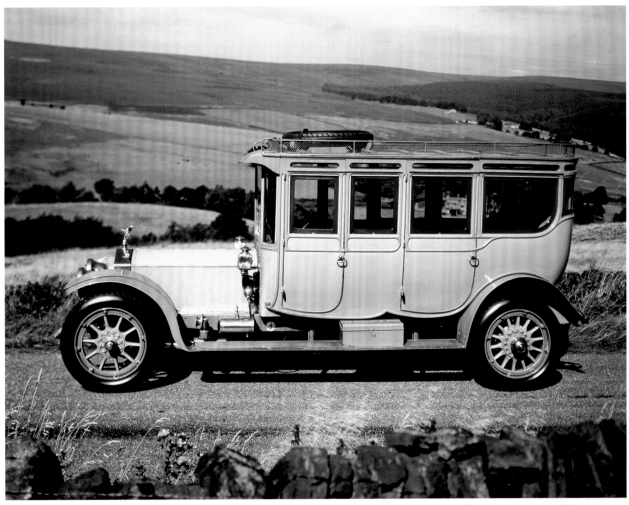

This Silver Ghost dates from 1912. Its Barker Double Pullman body was precisely the type of coachwork which permitted its wealthy owner and his retinue to motor down to the French Riviera. (LAT)

the Hon Charles Stewart Rolls, third son of Lord Llangattock, resulted in the creation of the Rolls-Royce car. The well-connected motor agent would sell the vehicles produced at Royce's factory in the Hulme district of Manchester and the founding triumvirate was completed later that year by the arrival of Claude Johnson, who was already in the employ of Rolls, and has since been dubbed 'the hyphen in Rolls-Royce'.

Johnson was a man of cultural and artistic sensibilities and these were coupled with a flair for organisation and administration. He was to hone and refine the Rolls-Royce mystique, an initiative that was sealed, in 1906, by the arrival of the 7-litre six-cylinder 40/50hp, the car which today we know as the Silver Ghost. Destined to become Rolls-Royce's sole model

until 1922, its levels of refinement, silence, reliability and sheer beauty placed it head and shoulders above its contemporaries. Such was its impact that Rolls-Royce owner Alfred Harmsworth, founder of *The Daily Mail*, could describe it, without equivocation, as being "The Best Car in the World."

As with practically all of its contemporaries, Rolls-Royce only produced its cars in chassis form. Owners would then commission a reputable coachbuilder, such as Barker, Hooper or H. J. Mulliner, to produce a body of an excellence that was in keeping with the quality of the mechanicals. This arrangement would continue throughout the inter-war years although by 1939 Rolls-Royce was one of a rapidly diminishing number of British car companies to

An artist's impression of Henry Royce at work on a 10hp Rolls-Royce in his factory at Cooke Street, Manchester. Note the classically inspired radiator on the right, which appeared late in 1904, and has, in essence, graced every Rolls-Royce since then. The luckless employee on the left is holding a bowl of porridge in the hope that Royce would eat it. He seldom did! (Rolls-Royce)

second fiddle to the Kestrel, Buzzard and, above all, the Merlin – to the extent that in 1939 cars accounted for a mere six per cent of Rolls-Royce's £1.2 million profits.

Ironically, in 1910 Charles Rolls, planes having become his latest passion, became the first Englishman to die in an aeronautical accident. Royce, meanwhile, suffered a collapse in his own health in 1911 and subsequently underwent a major operation, followed by a second in 1912, from which he thankfully recovered. However, his state of health was thereafter precarious and it was only through the attentions of nurse Ethel Aubin that he survived until his 70th year.

He left Derby, only returning on one subsequent occasion, and thereafter continued his design work first at Crowborough, Sussex, and, then, to benefit from the mild south-coast climate, at St Margaret's Bay, Kent. Subsequently, in 1917, Royce and his retinue found a new home at West Wittering and he continued to live in this West Sussex village, 150 miles (241km) from the Rolls-Royce factory, until his death. From 1912, the First World War years excepted, during the winter months Royce and his small team of some six designers occupied a drawing office at his villa at Le Canadel on the western end of the French Riviera.

This turn of events was, in truth, a blessing in disguise because the perfectionist Henry Royce was a difficult and demanding engineer-in-chief who found it impossible to reconcile himself to the fact that many of his employees were unable to match his own invariably unattainable standards.

But he continued to produce a succession of designs that followed in the Silver Ghost's distinguished wheel tracks. In 1922 came the 20hp with its 3.1-litre overhead-valve engine, the newcomer being a noticeably smaller and cheaper car than its invariably chauffeur-driven Edwardian stablemate, and thus ideal for the less prosperous although still comfortably-off twenties' owner-

perpetuate this costly practice.

Burgeoning demand for the 40/50hp meant that the company was soon outgrowing its cramped Manchester factory and in1908 it moved to a purpose-built works in Nightingale Road, Derby. This was destined to be the home of Rolls-Royce cars until 1939, and the firm's aero engines, the first of which appeared in 1915, are still manufactured there.

Aviation was in decline in the early twenties, but demand for Rolls-Royce power units progressively increased to the extent that by the early thirties their contribution to corporate coffers began to exceed that of the cars. As demand soared, chassis sales played

Rolls-Royce's secondary line of smaller cars began in 1922 with the 3.1-litre Twenty. This is a 1925 example, supplied to one A. J. Taylor, and carries a Hooper 'Standardised Saloon' limousine body. (Author's collection)

driver. The 'Twenty' paved the way for the even more successful 3.6-litre 20/25hp of 1929 that, with 3,827 sold, became the most popular Rolls-Royce of the inter-war years. It was followed in 1936 by the 4.2-litre 25/30hp.

By this time Rolls-Royce possessed a second make, it having in 1931 acquired the Bentley company. The firm had produced an impressive range of sports cars and had won the Le Mans 24-hour race on no fewer than five occasions. However, its magnificent 8-litre of 1930 was a direct challenge to the newly introduced Phantom II and, in the face of a possible Bentley take-over by Napier, Derby's one-time competitor, Rolls-Royce ruthlessly eliminated a potential rival by buying the business.

Production was transferred to Derby and the 3½-litre 'Silent Sports Car' of 1933 was a civilised, finely engineered product that was derived from the 20/25hp in the same way as its 4¼-litre successor of 1936 was

based on the 25/30hp.

In the meantime the large Rolls-Royce line had continued to evolve although demand for such expensive cars was gradually declining. In 1925 the Silver Ghost was replaced by the 7.3-litre 'New Phantom' which in 1929 was retrospectively named the Phantom I on the arrival of its Phantom II replacement. In 1935 came the Phantom III, its 7.3-litre V12 engine reflecting this configuration's growing popularity amongst luxury car makers on both sides of the Atlantic. The first Derby product to feature

independent front suspension, this superbly engineered car unfortunately suffered from a number of niggling faults on account of its being put into production too early.

With Royce's death in 1933, car design was once again centred on Derby, for the first time since 1911, and it became integrated with aero-engine developments with engineers moving, as the work demanded, from one project to another.

However, by 1936 works manager and director Arthur Wormald, who was steeped in corporate traditions having joined Royce in 1904, was suffering from ill-heath, and that year he retired. He died soon afterwards. His place was taken by 50-year-old Ernest Hives, who in 1937 also filled Wormald's seat on the board. As a former long-serving head of the experimental department, he was the first to recognise that the company needed to address the all-important matter of Henry Royce's legacy, namely its escalating engineering costs and the need to rationalise the Rolls-Royce and Bentley lines.

It was not unusual for the smaller Rolls-Royces to be bodied as shooting-brakes – either originally or as a rebodying exercise after the Second World War. This is a 20hp, and is not without charm. (LAT)

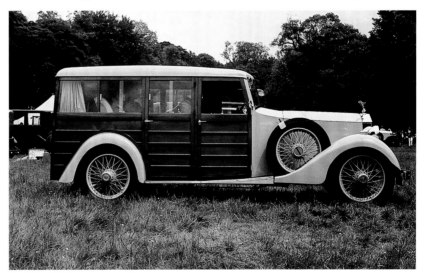

Before Rolls-Royce bought Bentley in 1931, the Cricklewood firm was a challenger to Derby's carriage-trade pre-eminence. This 6½-litre car was delivered to E. Bullivant in August 1929: Freestone & Webb was responsible for the drophead coupé body. The quick-release radiator cap was an unusual fitment. (Author's collection)

Hives believed that the company was being outclassed by the motor industry both in Britain and the United States and, in January 1937, he informed his fellow directors that he considered the Americans were building "quieter, smoother and better performing cars."[1] Hives had also recently driven a Rover Twenty, which sold for £450, a fraction of the price of the 25/30hp, and reported that he found it "excellent."

As far as Derby was concerned, its manufacturing processes had barely changed over the years, half the company's machine tools were over 20 years old, and production managers had rarely visited rival car factories. Royce had taken all the decisions regarding design policy and his long-serving engineers were never in the position of accepting responsibility. In consequence, declared Hives, "we make more mistakes than we should do." To its

credit the board gave the new works manager carte blanche to attempt to right these wrongs.

After much soul-searching, Hives decided to separate Rolls-Royce's aero engines from its chassis design. Taking effect from June 1937, the Aero Engine Division was headed by Royce's long time deputy, Albert Elliott, whilst the all-important post of chief engineer of the Chassis Division went to the capable but introverted Robert Harvey-Bailey, who had joined the company in 1910 and was at the time chief technical production engineer.

In his place as head of the Experimental Department, Hives appointed his deputy of many years' standing, the forceful William (Roy) Robotham. In 1934, soon after Royce's death, Robotham had made a fact-finding visit to America, as did Elliott, and in 1937 the Chassis Division's production engineer, Robert

Coverley, also crossed the Atlantic. All these sorties confirmed the thrust of the Hives prognosis: whilst the company's worldwide reputation was untarnished, its cars were unacceptably heavy, complicated and expensive.

Later in 1937 Robotham pointed out that the engine components of the six-cylinder engine of the F-series

Oldsmobile, which Rolls-Royce had purchased, covered a mere 15 pages of documentation. This compared with the manual for the power unit of the Wraith, the 25/30hp's impending successor, which comprised no fewer than 50 pages...

The answer was to reduce costs by adopting what the company described as the Rationalised Range

This 1933 20/25hp carries restrained 'D-back' coachwork by Hooper. Cars such as this offered cheap transport to many an impecunious motorist in the late fifties and early sixties. (LAT)

The original Continental was a Phantom II Rolls-Royce, and not a Bentley: this 1931 model originally carried four-seater open coachwork by Freestone & Webb, but was subsequently rebodied by the Carlton Carriage Company. (LAT)

The Engineering Team

The principal engineers concerned with the design of the Rolls-Royce and Bentley models of the immediate post-war years had, William Robotham (Rm*) excepted, worked directly under Sir Henry Royce (R).

The design and development of the cars were initially undertaken at Derby under the direction of chief engineer of the Chassis Division Robert Harvey-Bailey (By). Work continued throughout hostilities at the Clan Foundry which, from 1943 onwards, was under the control of Robotham. In 1946 he took over from Harvey-Bailey (1876–1962), the latter having retired at the end of 1945 at the age of 67.

Although he spent practically all his working life in the motor industry, Harvey-Bailey's degree, from King's College, London, was in civil engineering. An early advocate of front-wheel drive, he joined Rolls-Royce in 1910 from the Pilgrim Motor Company of Farnham, Surrey. He initially worked with Royce at Derby and, later, at Le Canadel. During the First World War he designed, to Royce's brief, the V12 Falcon aero engine, and after the war he contributed to the servo-assisted four-wheel brakes fitted to all Rolls-Royces from 1925 onwards. He then became chief technical production engineer and a further brief was running the Detail Drawing Office, a demanding role which involved interpreting Royce's drawings emanating from West Wittering.

William Robotham (1899–1980) had originally entered the army and he joined Rolls-Royce in 1919 as a premium apprentice, his parents having paid a £250 fee. Working in the experimental department under Ernest Hives (Hs) from 1923, he was responsible in the following year for setting up a small corporate testing station at Châteauroux to the south of Paris. In 1930 Robotham became

chief experimental chassis engineer and took over as head of the experimental department in 1937. He became chief engineer in 1946 and in 1950 took over the oil-engine division – diesels to mere mortals – which he ran until his retirement in 1963.

Chassis design was in hands of Bernard Incledon Day (1879–1956), who after a technical education at Birmingham Municipal Technical School and Sheffield University, subsequently became, from 1908 to 1913, chief engineer of the Sheffield-Simplex company which was attempting to challenge the supremacy of the Silver Ghost. He arrived at Derby in 1913 and during the First World War took charge of the Airship Design Office. After the war, Day (Da) switched to chassis design and in 1921 he joined Royce at West Wittering, where he remained until the latter's death in 1933.

The bespectacled Charles L. Jenner (Jr) was Royce's engine designer. Having serving an apprenticeship with the Phoenix Motor Company, from 1909 he worked with Harvey-Bailey when the latter was with Pilgrim in Farnham. Subsequently Harvey-Bailey offered him a job at Derby, and he joined Rolls-Royce in 1911. In 1918 he moved to West Wittering to work on aero engines where he effectively become assistant to Elliott (E). When Elliott returned to Nightingale Road in 1931 he took Jenner with him, and he was responsible for the design of the rationalised four-cylinder, six-cylinder and eight-cylinder F-head engines used in the post-war cars – although much work was undertaken by his junior, Alec Mitchell. Appointed car engine project designer in 1951, Jenner had overall responsibility for the design of Rolls-Royce's long-running V8 engine, but the work was undertaken by a team led by Jack Phillips. This was

completed just before Charles Jenner's untimely death in 1955 at the age of 62.

Coachwork was the responsibility of Ivan Evernden (1896–1980), who had attained a BSc in engineering, as did Harvey-Bailey, from King's College, London. He joined Rolls-Royce in 1916 and from 1921 until 1933 worked at West Wittering where his brief was styling and liaising with coachbuilders; he was one of Henry Royce's favourites. After Sir Henry's death Evernden (Ev) was attached to Rolls-Royce's London-based sales department but returned to Derby in 1935 as project designer, taking over the coachwork portfolio with the creation of the Chassis Division.

The forte of Donald Bastow (1909–1989) was suspension. He graduated from University College, London, with a BSc in engineering, went from there to Daimler, and in 1932 joined Royce at West Wittering, where he worked under Bernard Day on chassis design. Following Royce's death, Bastow (DB) moved to Derby where he laid out the independent front suspension system used on the Phantom III, an important commission for an engineer only in his late twenties. He was subsequently responsible for the systems used on the Wraith and the Bentley Mark V and later employed on the Mark VI and Silver Wraith. He left Rolls-Royce in 1944 to join W. O. Bentley at Lagonda and thus has the distinction of having worked for two of Britain's outstanding automobile engineers of the inter-war years. He accordingly wrote W O Bentley – Engineer (Haynes, 1978) and Henry Royce – mechanic (Rolls-Royce Heritage Trust, 1989), to which this author readily acknowledges a debt.

*This personnel reference system was introduced by Henry Royce and is still used by the company.

Another remodelled PII, this ambulance started out as a Barker landaulette but was rebodied by ambulance specialist H. J. Lomas, for war service. With so many Rolls-Royce estates and hearses rebodied as open tourers, all the more credit goes to the owner of this car for restoring it in this form. (LAT)

of cars. Robotham as its principal advocate saw it as embracing not only Rolls-Royce's traditional medium and large car lines but also an entry into the 8hp market, the medium 12hp to 14hp sector and even the 2 ton to 5 ton (2.03 to 5.08 tonnes) truck business!

But the more immediate problem was replacements for the Phantom III, Wraith and Bentley 4¼-litre. All had been designed at different times and bore little mechanical relationship to one another. In 1937 work thus began on a family of related four-cylinder, six-cylinder and eight-cylinder overhead-inlet-and-side-exhaust engines (see box). The 'six' was completed first, and examples were fitted to experimental Rolls-Royces and Bentleys from early in 1939.

A similar programme was also underway on rationalising chassis production, and Ivan Evernden in the car project office devised a set of dies which made it possible economically to vary the wheelbase of chassis frames to accommodate any length of car.

The 'Silent Sports car', Rolls-Royce's first Bentley, the 20/25-based 3½-litre. This car, with a body by Vanden Plas, was delivered to its first owner, Ian M. Service, in October 1935. (LAT)

Ernest Walter Hives 1886–1965

The stocky, and – in his latter years – bespectacled figure of Ernest Hives was employed by Rolls-Royce for close on 50 years and from 1950 until his retirement in 1957 he was the company's chairman. Berkshire-born Hives began his career as a bicycle mechanic in a Reading cycle shop, but fate played a hand when in 1903 he met the Hon Charles Rolls and became his chauffeur.

Hives subsequently joined Rolls's London motor agency, later moved to Napier, and it was from there that he went to Rolls-Royce in 1908. He became a tester and in 1914 was made head of the experimental department, a post he occupied for the next 23 years. His appointment early in 1937 as works manager and as a director was of immense significance and marked the start of a transition away from Henry Royce's perfectionist philosophy to a more realistic engineering environment.

During the Second World War Hives worked tirelessly, often sleeping at Rolls-Royce's Derby factory, to ensure that the production of Rolls-Royce aero engines was maintained. Crucially, output rose significantly during the dark days of 1940 when Hurricanes and Spitfires, powered by Rolls-Royce Merlins, triumphed in the Battle of Britain. By this time the V12 was also being produced at two new shadow factories, at Glasgow and Crewe, for which Hives was also responsible. He was made a Companion of Honour in 1943 and in 1946 replaced Sir Arthur Sidgreaves (knighted 1945) as managing director. In 1950 he was elevated to the peerage as Baron Hives of Hazeldene and, at the end of the year, he became Rolls-Royce's chairman. Lord Hives retired in 1957 at the age of 70, having made an immeasurable contribution to the affairs of Rolls-Royce on land and air.

The Division addressed the problem of the multifarious coachbuilt bodies fitted to the company's products by standardising body design. It was able to effect this through its ownership, from 1938, of Park Ward. In consequence, the four-door saloon coachwork was built by Park Ward but the lines were the responsibility of the Chassis Division's versatile Ivan Evernden. The similarity of the finished product to the 1946 Mark VI 'Standard Steel' saloon is immediately apparent.

The Division was also engaged in the creation of an even more radical project in the form of a Continental version of the Mark V Bentley, named the Corniche and also intended for production in the 1940 model year. Regarded by the Division as its most important car, its origins were rooted in a tuned and lightened 1938 4¼-litre Bentley created for the Greek racing driver Nicky Embiricos and fitted with a streamlined coupé body designed in France by Georges Paulin and built there by Pourtout. Radically, the traditional Bentley radiator was replaced by a more aerodynamically efficient cowl.

The Paulin Bentley was discussed at board level because Harvey-Bailey and Robotham believed there were corporate lessons to be learnt from this car – although there was a directorial reluctance to adopt the radical front end treatment.

Despite these reservations, Harvey-Bailey took the concept one stage further and the result, in February 1939, was an experimental Bentley Mark V chassis fitted with a Pourtout-styled four-door saloon body built by Vanvooren in Paris and in which Ivan Evernden also had a hand. Unfortunately during testing in France in August it was involved in an accident, at which point the body was removed and the chassis was returned to Derby. The outbreak of war put an end to the project although the concept of an aerodynamic Bentley coupé was revived in 1952 with the arrival of the Evernden-styled R-type Continental.

With Rolls-Royce engaged in the

The Rolls-Royce Wraith, introduced for the 1939 season, began to reflect this new thinking and its welded chassis frame, lacking the customary rivets, reflected a more cost-conscious environment. A scaled-down version of the Phantom III's independent front suspension was employed and the 4.6-litre straight-six engine was a development of that used in its 25/30hp predecessor.

The arrival of the Wraith underlined the fact that the 4¼-litre Bentley was a fine car but one which, alas, was beginning to suffer from bearing problems if driven hard for long distances. It also lacked independent front suspension and was starting to look decidedly dated.

Its intended successor was the Chassis Division's first complete project, and was to have been launched as the Mark V Bentley at the 1939 Paris and London motor shows. These events were however cancelled because of the outbreak of

war; a batch of 18 chassis numbers had already been allocated, though, and 11 cars were completed in 1939/40 before the war interrupted the programme. Nevertheless, the Mark V represents the starting point of what was to emerge in 1946 as the Rolls-Royce Silver Wraith and Bentley Mark VI, lines that were to endure, respectively, until 1959 and 1955.

A new chassis frame, with a substantial central cruciform – rivets were back! – reflected the fitment of independent front suspension, PIII-related but much simplified. The wheelbase of 10ft 4in (3.15m), was 2in (5.1cm) shorter than its predecessor, whilst the engine was mounted further forward in the frame, thus creating more interior room. The six-cylinder overhead-valve 4.2-litre engine was essentially the same as that used in the Wraith, although it differed in having big-end bearings made of AC9, a new alloy developed at Derby.

production of the Merlin, Vulture and Peregrine aero engines, chassis production ceased at Derby in 1940, never to be revived there. In 1939 Ernest Hives accordingly disbanded the two-year-old Chassis Division. What was left of the department was taken over by Roy Robotham, who housed the depleted engineering team – headed by Ivan Evernden, now chief designer – in the bleak surroundings of what had been the Clan iron foundry, a disused factory located just to the north of the village of Milford, near Belper and about five miles (8km) from Derby. Robotham himself was soon seconded to tank design and did not return to

Derbyshire until August 1943.

In the meantime work had been proceeding on the chassis of the post-war Rolls-Royce and Bentley family. This would be based, in effect, on the Mark V Bentley frame but with power from the new rationalised 4.2-litre six-cylinder engine.

Now Robotham had to address the overriding problem of bodywork. "It was clear that not only would coachbuilt bodies made in the pre-war manner be of doubtful quality, but they would also be prohibitively expensive", he later recalled.[2] He also recognised that there would be a shortage of skilled craftsmen to undertake the work.

The Phantom III was the last Rolls-Royce to be designed regardless of cost. This limousine is by Thrupp & Maberly and, finished in maroon, it was displayed by Rolls-Royce on its stand at the 1938 Motor Show. In all, T&M bodied 34 Phantom IIIs. (LAT)

The B-series engines

The post-war range of Bentleys and Rolls-Royces was powered by the six-cylinder F-head overhead-inlet/side-exhaust engine that was one of the rationalised units designed in 1938. It remained in use until the 1959 arrival of the V8 unit.

Although an experimental 4¼-litre overhead-camshaft 'six', dating from 1934, had been built and tested in 1937, this was dispensed with because of worries about the camshaft drive, thereby leaving the way clear for the IoE design. Unlike Rolls-Royce's earlier six-cylinder engines, which possessed separate aluminium crankcases and cast-iron cylinder blocks, the new family used integrated cast-iron blocks with the extra weight offset to some extent by an aluminium cylinder head. The distinctive overhead-inlet/side-exhaust configuration was adopted because, as the smaller line of six-cylinder engines evolved from 1922 onwards, so the narrow bridge in the cylinder head between the inlet and exhaust valves became progressively thinner as the diameter of the valves increased over the years. The arrival of the F-head unit and the resulting presence of a single overhead valve immediately eliminated the problem.

In mid-1938 the decision was made to proceed with these six-cylinder, eight-cylinder and four-cylinder units. The need for their creation was underlined by the fact that there was no significant relationship between the Phantom V12 and the 'sixes' used by the Wraith and the Bentley 4¼-litre.

The new engines were accorded the B-series name and were therefore titled B40, B60 and B80. They shared the same 3.5in x 4.5in (88.9mm x 114.3mm) bore and stroke, which produced capacities of 2,838cc, 4,257cc and 5,675cc, with power outputs, respectively, of 82bhp at 3,500rpm, 126bhp at 3,750rpm, and 164bhp at 3,750rpm. Cost considerations, the *raison d'être* of their creation, resulted in their sharing the same pistons, connecting rods, main bearings and big-end bearings, valves and valve gear, oil pump, and various other parts. Only 23 components were peculiar to each engine.

The first B60 was used in experimental Wraith 29-G-V1 from January 1939, and in its Bentley 9-B-V contemporary.

The B80 'eight' was similarly used in 30-G-V11 from April 1939 and in May of that year it was mounted in an experimental Mark V chassis. Such was its performance that it was nicknamed 'Scalded Cat' because, as Robotham recalled, "it behaved not unlike a feline on whose tail boiling water had been poured." The B80 made its public debut in the 1949 Dennis fire engine and the following year in the limited-production Rolls-Royce Phantom IV, but it never appeared in a production Bentley.

The 2.8-litre four-cylinder version was not used in any Rolls-Royce car. However, military versions of the B40, B60 and B80 were developed for the Army's post-war programme to standardise engines across its fighting vehicles, and the 'four' was used in the 4wd Austin Champ. The 'six' was most notably used in the Daimler Ferret scout car and the Humber one-ton truck, and the straight-eight in the Alvis Saladin armoured car, the Saracen APV and the amphibious Stalwart.

Robotham began to think the unthinkable: Rolls-Royce/Bentley would have to compromise the bespoke nature of its products, epitomised by the quality of its handmade coachwork, and share a commonised pressed steel body, just as other car makers did. This meant that, for the first time in its history, Rolls-Royce would be responsible for the manufacture of a complete motor car, as opposed to merely the chassis.

A dialogue Robotham established with the Cowley-based Pressed Steel Company in January 1944 revealed that the tooling costs for such a body would amount to at least £250,000. To make the equation work, it would be necessary for the company to sell 5000 bodies of the same design.

Although this flew in the face of the Rolls-Royce ethos, Robotham believed that "we had no alternative but to buy these tools or go out of the automobile business." He also made no secret of the fact that he hoped the expenditure might force the firm to produce 10,000 cars a year. In the event the highest annual output figure attained by Rolls-Royce was 3,347 cars built in 1978.

Robotham was able to convince the equally pragmatic Ernest Hives of the need for a Pressed Steel body and the tools were ordered, although the board, chaired by Arthur Sidgreaves, was more sceptical. However, Robotham responded that if they were delayed, Rolls-Royce would lose its place in Pressed Steel's bulging order book, thereby curtailing the start of post-war car production by a good year at least.

Faced with this *fait accompli*, the directors reluctantly agreed and as a result Rolls-Royce launched its post-war programme in the spring of 1946. However, as will emerge, tradition over-rode truism and it was only the Bentley that was initially offered with standardised bodywork. The Rolls-Royce line, by contrast, still benefited from hand-crafted coachwork in the pre-war manner, much to the delight of its equally conservative customers.

[1] *Hives, The Quiet Tiger* by Alec Harvey-Bailey
[2] *Silver Ghosts and Silver Dawn* by William Robotham

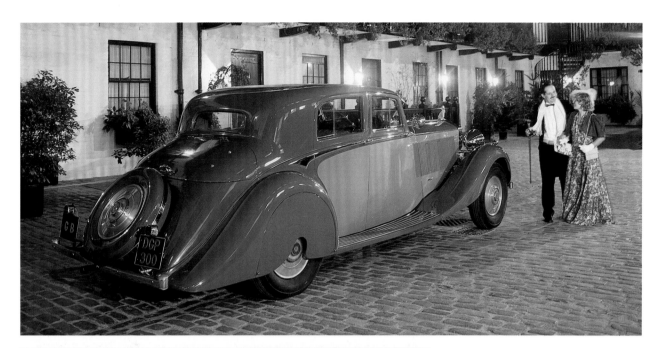

Above: This Phantom III is a 1936 model with sports saloon coachwork again by Thrupp & Maberly. It was built for Count Haugwitz Reventlow, father of Scarab race-car creator Lance Reventlow and future husband of Woolworth's heiress Barbara Hutton. (LAT)

Below: Precursor to the post-war Mark VI Bentley, this Mark V with in-house Park Ward body was completed in April 1940 and used during the war by Arthur Sidgreaves, Rolls-Royce's managing director. It is shown here in 1942 whilst on loan to *The Motor*'s, technical editor Laurence Pomeroy. (LAT)

Above: The Wraith of 1938 was the first Rolls-Royce to feel the effects of a more realistic approach to car design. This is a 1937 experimental Park Ward Special Saloon, as featured in the model's sales catalogue. (Rolls-Royce)

The Silver Wraith, Silver Dawn and *Bentley Mark VI*

The Silver Wraith is a deceptive model. Outwardly it resembles a Rolls-Royce in the pre-war idiom, being a magnificently appointed and refined car that was only available with bespoke coachwork.

But beneath the body is a chassis and engine that were the products of the rationalisation programme begun in 1937. It was intended to banish what managing director Arthur Sidgreaves had condemned as "the Phantom III mentality," the PIII being the last Rolls-Royce to have been designed regardless of cost.

The Silver Wraith was announced to the press in April 1946, with its Bentley Mark VI stablemate, complete with standardised Pressed Steel saloon body, being unveiled the following month. The Bentley was destined to be built in far greater numbers than the Rolls-Royce, with no fewer than 7,521 examples of the model and its R-type successor being manufactured until production ceased in 1955. This amounted to 85 per cent of Crewe's output.

Both cars were closely mechanically related but their wheelbases did vary: at 10ft 7in (3.22m), the Rolls-Royce's was 7in (18cm) greater than the Mark VI's. The difference had been introduced so that the Silver Wraith frame could accommodate limousine coachwork.

Under the bonnet, which was noticeably devoid of louvres, was the 4.2-litre IoE six-cylinder engine that had been running experimentally before the war and which was making its first public appearance in a Rolls-Royce product. In most essentials it was identical to the unit that powered the Bentley, although the Silver Wraith was fitted with a different camshaft and a single dual-choke downdraught Stromberg carburettor instead of the Mark VI's traditional twin SUs.

Whilst the engine shared the same 89mm x 114mm internal dimensions and 4,257cc capacity of the pre-war Wraith, there the resemblance ended: the F-head design represented a

Bespoke and off-the-peg: Rolls-Royce's stand at the 1954 Motor Show with a Park Ward Touring Saloon in the foreground and an H. J. Mulliner Touring Limousine behind, both on Silver Wraith chassis. In the left background is a left-hand-drive Silver Dawn with a Silver Wraith Hooper Seven-Passenger Limousine behind. (Rolls-Royce)

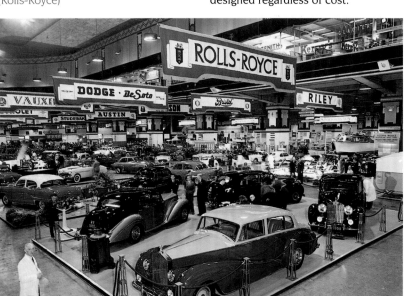

departure from the make's familiar overhead valves, even though it had featured on Henry's Royce's original 10hp car of 1904. In the interests of refinement the side-mounted camshaft was driven by a resin-bonded fabric gear wheel. Tappet adjustment was no longer a significant servicing requirement – which was just as well, because the

exhaust units, set low in the block, were barely accessible.

In a bid to reduce cylinder wear, the upper 2¼in (57mm) of the bores were plated with 0.0015in (0.038mm) of chrome. Lower down, the nitrided crankshaft, balanced and counterweighted, was machined all over. A thing of beauty in its own right, it ran in seven Vandervell lead-

Above: Rolls-Royces and Bentleys against the drab background of post-war London in July 1946 for the Society of Motor Manufacturers and Traders' parade to celebrate the British motor industry's 50th anniversary. Left to right: Silver Wraith with H. J. Mulliner sedanca de ville body and a Hooper Touring Limousine alongside a brace of Mark VI Bentleys. (Author's collection)

Right: The third prototype Silver Wraith, a Hooper Touring Limousine, chassis WTA2, delivered in September 1946, with at the wheel Roger Cra'ster, a long-serving Rolls-Royce employee; alongside is the company's 1905 10hp car. The location is the Blake Street entrance of the original Royce and Company factory at Hulme, Manchester that was demolished in 1965. The first Royce engine was run in 1903 in the stable yard that was behind the wide door on the right. (Rolls-Royce)

Factory and foundry

As will have been apparent, the design and development of the Silver Wraith and Bentley Mark VI fell into two distinct phases and locations. From 1937 until the outbreak of the Second World War in 1939, the work was undertaken at Rolls-Royce's Derby factory. From thereon it continued in the less salubrious surroundings of the Clan Foundry, which housed the experimental department until its transfer to Crewe in April 1951.

Work on the development of the range continued throughout the war. In 1945 the Pressed Steel Company was commissioned to body experimental Rolls-Royce and Bentley chassis with unified four-door saloon bodywork on the lines of a full-sized wooden model produced

at the Foundry. These cars were respectively designated Ascot I and Ascot II and the former had a square-cornered scuttle and bonnet to follow the angular lines of the Rolls-Royce radiator whilst Ascot II, which was completed first, in March 1946, was identifiable by its more rounded contours to accommodate the Bentley radiator. In the event the company decided only to introduce the Bentley version, although Ascot I, which took to the road in July 1947, emerged two years later as the Rolls-Royce Silver Dawn.

The policy of simultaneously launching near-identical Rolls-Royce and Bentley models was not wholly implemented until 1955, when the Rolls-Royce Silver Cloud and Bentley S-series shared the same bodywork.

bronze indium bearings. As well as the customary torsional vibration damper, the crankshaft incorporated RR's familiar spring drive to counter camshaft rattles. At its opposite end the flywheel featured a spring centre intended to dampen down undesirable crankshaft oscillations. The steel connecting rods were similarly externally-machined and, as on all Rolls-Royce engines since 1919, the floating gudgeon pins were force lubricated via a drilled oilway in each rod. A by-pass oil filter was employed.

Outwardly apparent, and less in the Rolls-Royce tradition, the dynamo and water pump broke with previous practice by being belt-driven rather than gear-driven. Henry Royce would not have approved!

The engine developed 122bhp at 3,750rpm. Contrary to current popular opinion, Rolls-Royce made no secret of this figure, which appeared throughout the motoring press. The company did not become really coy about the horsepower of its power units until the arrival of the straight-six's 4.9-litre derivative in 1955.

In an era when the traditional

radiator was fast disappearing, Rolls-Royce's famous offering, surmounted by the equally famous Spirit of Ecstasy mascot – now in a kneeling position (see box) – proudly proclaimed the Silver Wraith's pedigree. With the Second World War having ended a little under a year before the car's announcement, *The Autocar* struck an appropriately patriotic note when it spoke of the radiator becoming "a hallmark of our national pride". The chromium-plated vertical shutters, controlled by a thermostat located in the header tank, also followed past precedent.

The company had used a unit-construction engine and gearbox since the 20hp model's arrival in 1922. The Silver Wraith was no exception in this regard and the four-speed 'box, with synchromesh on second, third and top gears, was traditionally actuated by a right-hand gearchange with a visible gate. By contrast, the fitment of a proprietary Borg & Beck clutch, in place of a corporate unit, reflected more enlightened cost-conscious times.

Drive to the live rear axle was, in the

Rolls-Royce Silver Wraith
(swb 4.2-litre)
1946–1951

ENGINE:

Six cylinders in line, iron block, alloy head

Bore x stroke	89mm x 114mm
Capacity	4,257cc
Valve actuation	Inlet-pushrod, exhaust-side
Compression ratio	6.4:1
Carburettor	Single Stromberg
Power	122 bhp at 3,750rpm

TRANSMISSION:

Rear-wheel drive. Four-speed, with synchromesh on second, third and top gears. Optional automatic with fluid coupling from October 1952

Final drive ratio: 3.727:1

SUSPENSION:

Front: Independent, wishbone and coil spring with cross-coupled hydraulic dampers.

Rear: Live axle with half-elliptic springs

STEERING:

Cam and roller

Turns lock-to-lock: 3.5

BRAKES:

Front: hydraulic drum

Rear: mechanical drum

Mechanical servo assistance

WHEELS/TYRES:

Steel disc wheels

6.50in x 17in

BODYWORK:

Coachbuilt: aluminium panels on wooden or alloy frame. Separate chassis.

Saloon, saloon with division, limousine, limousine with division, sedanca de ville, drophead coupé, fixed-head coupé, cabriolet, landaulette

DIMENSIONS:

Length*	17ft 7in (5.36m)
Wheelbase	10ft 7in (3.22m)
Track - front	4ft 10in (1.47m)
- rear	5ft 0in (1.52m)
Width*	6ft 1in (1.55m)
Height*	5ft 11in (1.80m)

* Dependent on type of body fitted (H. J. Mulliner sedanca de ville quoted)

WEIGHT:

Typical body   42.1cwt (4,705 kg)

PERFORMANCE:

(Source: *The Autocar*)

Max speed not measured [over 80mph (127kph)]

0–50 mph (0–80kph)	17.2sec
0–60 mph (0–100kph)	24sec
0–70 mph (0–112kph)	37.4sec

PRICE INCLUDING TAX WHEN NEW:

Chassis £1,835

Touring limousine (Hooper) £4,409

Seven-seater limousine (H. J. Mulliner) £3,961

NUMBER BUILT:

Chassis: 1,247 (4.2 and 4.5-litre)

Rolls-Royce Silver Wraith (swb 4½-litre)
1951–1953

As 4.2-litre except:

ENGINE:

Bore x stroke	92mm x 114mm
Capacity	4,566cc
Carburettors	Zenith
Power	Not disclosed

Rolls-Royce Silver Wraith (Long wheelbase)
1951–1955

As 4½-litre except:

DIMENSIONS:

Track - rear	5ft 4in (1.52m)
Wheelbase	11ft 1in (3.37m)

WEIGHT:

Typical body	46cwt (2,336kg)

Rolls-Royce Silver Wraith
1955–1959

ENGINE: As Silver Cloud I

TRANSMISSION:

Automatic transmission standard from October 1955

STEERING:

Power assisted steering optional from October 1956

PRICE INCLUDING TAX WHEN NEW:

Mulliner Seven-seater limousine £6,760

NUMBER BUILT:

639 all types

Bentley Mark VI
1946–1952

As Rolls-Royce Silver Wraith (swb) except:

ENGINE:

Carburettor	Twin SU HD4

From May 1951 4½-litre engine, as Silver Wraith except:

Carburettors	Twin SU H6

WHEELS/TYRES:

6.50in x 16

BODYWORK:

Four-door saloon by Pressed Steel.

Separate chassis

DIMENSIONS:

Length	15ft 11½in (4.86m)
Wheelbase	10ft 0 in (3.04m)
Track - front	4ft 8½in (1.43m)
- rear	4ft 10in (1.47m)
Width	5ft 9in (1.75m)
Height	5ft 4½in (1.63 m)

WEIGHT:

35.3cwt (1,793 kg)

PERFORMANCE:

(Source: The Autocar)

Max speed	92mph (148kph)
0–50mph (0–80kph)	12.5sec
0–60mph (0–100kph)	17.5sec
0–70mph (0–112kph)	25.8sec

PRICE INCLUDING TAX WHEN NEW:

Chassis £1,785, Steel saloon £2,997

NUMBER BUILT:

Chassis

5,201 (4.2-litre and 4½-litre)

Bentley R-type
1952–1955

As Mark V1 except:

DIMENSIONS:

Length	16ft 8in (5.08m)
Width	5ft 10in (1.77m)

WEIGHT:

24.1cwt (1,228 kg)

PERFORMANCE:

(Source: *The Autocar*)

Max speed	100mph (160kph)
0–50mph (0–80kph)	10.0sec
0–60mph (0–100kph)	13.8sec
0–70mph (0–112kph)	19.1sec

PRICE INCLUDING TAX WHEN NEW: £4,392

NUMBER BUILT: 2,320

Bentley Continental (R-type)
1952–1954

As R-type except:

ENGINE:

Compression ratio:	7.25:1
Carburettors	Twin SU H8

TRANSMISSION:

Final drive ratio:	3.077:1

BODYWORK:

Coachbuilt, aluminium panels on aluminium frame. Separate chassis.

Fixed-head coupé

DIMENSIONS:

Width	5ft 11½in (1.81m)
Height	5ft 3in (1.57m)

WEIGHT:

33.5cwt (1,701kg)

PERFORMANCE: (Source: *The Autocar*)

Max speed	115.4mph (185.7kph)
0–50mph (0–80kph)	10.5sec
0–60mph (0–100kph)	13.5sec
0–70mph (0–112kph)	6.3sec

PRICE INCLUDING TAX WHEN NEW:

Coupé £7,608

NUMBER BUILT: 207

Bentley Continental (R-type)
1954–55

As 4.2-litre except:

ENGINE:

Bore and stroke	95.25mm x 114.3mm
Capacity	4,887cc
Compression ratio	6.6:1

TRANSMISSION:

Optional four-speed automatic with fluid coupling

interests of smooth running, via a divided propeller shaft.

The box-section chassis, complete with a substantial central riveted cruciform, was in effect inherited from the short-lived Mark V Bentley of 1939, and its Packard-inspired coil-and-wishbone independent front suspension sprang from the same source. The rear suspension used conventional leaf springs, and steering was by cam and roller.

Like so much on the car, the brakes represented a combination of the idiosyncratic and the conventional. The Silver Wraith has the distinction of being the first Rolls-Royce to be fitted with hydraulic brakes, but these were confined to the front wheels. However, whilst the fluid delivery was

by Lockheed it was used in conjunction with Girling shoe actuation, to obtain the best attributes of both systems.

The rear drums continued to be mechanically actuated and both sets of brakes were ably assisted by the mechanical servo driven off the right-hand side of the gearbox that had featured on all Rolls-Royces since 1925 and was derived from an Hispano-Suiza design. The steel disc wheels were of 17in diameter, which contrasted with the Bentley's smaller, 16in rims.

These mechanicals were in essence to serve the Silver Wraith throughout its 11-year production life, but they only represented a part of the whole. This is because each car, like every

Rolls-Royce built since the marque's 1904 creation, differed one from the other in being the recipient of a magnificent hand-crafted body. Less desirably, this pushed the weight of the typical Silver Wraith saloon up to beyond two tons (2,032kg). The activities of the almost exclusively London-based principal coachbuilders who bodied the Silver Wraith are chronicled in Chapter Five.

The model was announced with a range of factory-approved coachwork. In chassis form the Silver Wraith cost

A Hooper sedanca de ville body on Silver Wraith chassis ALW47, delivered in August 1953 to Armenian businessman Nubar Gulbenkian. (LAT)

A Park Ward bodied Silver Wraith at the Rolls-Royce Enthusiasts' Club's rally held at Englefield House, Berkshire in 1974. (LAT)

£1,835 including Purchase Tax – that radiator ensuring it commanded £50 more than the Bentley – and the Park Ward Sports Saloon was listed at £3,802 including PT and a seven-seater Limousine at £3,961 including tax. H. J. Mulliner's sedanca de ville, a pre-war anachronism with division and front opening roof, cost £4,409. Hooper, the *crème de la crème* of this coachbuilding elite, provided its Touring Limousine for the same £4,409, a tidy sum which in 1946 would have bought no fewer than four and a half 3½-litre Jaguars!

This was opulence in the pre-war manner, but a more sober note was struck by the Mark VI Bentley 'Standard Steel saloon', which cost £2,997 on its announcement. Ivan Evernden's four-door four-light body had, in the words of T*he Autocar*, "a clean-cut style of its own, graceful and characteristic". Inside, 'there is about the interior trim that atmosphere of good taste and luxury which is not easy to produce'. There was "hardly a screw head to be seen", the magazine approvingly observed. The leather upholstery and walnut veneer were indeed worthy of a coachbuilt car, but then the interior was the work of corporate styling engineer John Blatchley, late of Gurney Nutting.

The Mark VI was the right car at the right time. And it also chimed perfectly with the political climate. Clement Attlee's Labour government had been elected in 1945 and, whilst pledged to creditable objectives of full employment and the introduction of a welfare state, it possessed a rather spartan outlook as far as luxuries were concerned. Rolls-Royce was well aware of this prejudice and I can do not better than to quote Alec Harvey-Bailey, who was head of technical services at Derby at the time, to provide invaluable perspective which places the Mark VI firmly in a corporate context.

"The Labour government, steeped in austerity and ration books, was actively anti-Rolls-Royce motor cars," he wrote[1]. "The somewhat understated Mark VI steel saloon, with a radiator few recognised, enabled customers to enjoy high standards of motoring without receiving the official opprobrium that had gone with a Rolls-Royce."

The Bentley could also be specified with bespoke bodies but, in the event, the overwhelming majority, no less

Choosing Crewe

Rolls-Royce and Bentley motor cars have been built at Crewe, Cheshire, since 1946 – and that because of the Second World War. It was on 9 July 1938 that work began at Pym's Lane on the construction of a plant so that Rolls-Royce could expand the production of its legendary Merlin aero engine which was already being built at Derby.

Crewe was far from being the first choice. Shrewsbury, Worcester and Stafford were all suggested by the company in addition to the 60-acre (24 hectares) site at Crewe, but that location was favoured by the influential Air Council for the erection of this latest Shadow Factory.

The government-initiated and government-funded Shadow Factory scheme dated from 1936. It recognised that war with Germany was inevitable and there would be an urgent need for new factories to allow for the expansion of aero-engine production. In the words of Air Chief Marshall Hugh Dowding, the resulting new facilities were so called because the "aim is to create a second image of the original."

The Crewe plant which 'shadowed' Derby, designed by architect W. G. Phillips, was built on the site of Merrill's Farm, which had hitherto grown potatoes and possessed a dairy herd. The first engine, a Merlin II, was completed on 20 May 1940 and dispatched on 10 June, the month before the Battle of Britain began. By the time that production, which peaked in 1943, had ceased in 1945, a total of 28,488 Merlins and its Griffon successor had been completed, which was only some 3,700 fewer than Derby managed.

Hives was determined that, as the largest plant, Derby should be wholly devoted to aero-engine production. The rest, as they say, is history. Crewe therefore became the home of the Motor Car Division, established in 1946, and Rolls-Royces and Bentleys have been produced there ever since.

But a new chapter in the factory's story will open on 1 January 2003 when Rolls-Royce leaves the plant, and Bentley moves centre stage – the Silver Seraph series ceasing production in 2002.

Ironically, the factory is now owned by Volkswagen, an enterprise that was originally created to build a German 'people's car' initiated up by Adolf Hitler, the man whose expansionist ambitions lead to the construction of Crewe in the first place...

Unlike Derby, which only produced Rolls-Royces in chassis form, Crewe built complete cars. Here the wooden door fillets are being fitted to a Silver Cloud. (Rolls-Royce)

Imperial shadows: an original colour photograph of a late Silver Wraith. This H. J. Mulliner limousine was delivered in July 1958 to Tunku Abdul Rahman, prime minister of the Malaya Federation, established in the previous year. (Rolls-Royce)

The standard Pressed Steel 4.2-litre Mark VI saloon. Pictured in post-war Waterloo, this particular car was road-tested by *The Autocar* in April 1950 and attained a speed of 86mph (138kph). (Author's collection)

than 80 per cent of the total, were fitted with the standardised saloon body.

A Mark VI chassis was the first product of the newly-introduced Motor Car Division, and was completed on 12 February 1946. Its Silver Wraith equivalent followed two days later. The first Pressed Steel Bentley saloon was delivered on 21

September, and just two Silver Wraiths, both with Hooper bodies, were finished during 1946, so start-up was a fairly protracted affair. One of these two Wraiths, a Touring Limousine (chassis WTA2), was completed in September and used by Rolls-Royce for display purposes. The second – and the first car to go to a private owner – was a limousine for HRH the Princess Royal, who took delivery in December. This was at a time when the King and Queen remained firmly wedded to Daimler, maintaining a royal commitment that dated back to 1902. But, as set down in Chapter 3, by 1960 the monarchy would have switched its patronage from Coventry to Crewe.

Wraith deliveries did not begin in earnest until 1947, and if there was such a thing as a 'standard' Silver Wraith, this accolade would go to Mulliner's four-door, four-light Touring

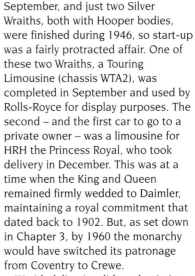

A 1951 'for export only' Silver Dawn in its original 4.2-litre guise at Hampton Court, a favourite corporate backdrop. The Dawn was fitted with a 4.5-litre engine from the 1952 season. (Rolls-Royce/LAT)

A 1951 Bentley Mark VI appropriately pictured against the stately home of Attinghall, near Shrewsbury. (LAT)

Limousine, an updated version of the coachwork used on WTA2, and of which a total of 309 were to be produced. Also popular, with 110 examples built, was the sedanca de ville from the same coachbuilder. Mulliner also contributed 86 commodious six-light Limousines on the Wraith chassis.

In-house Park Ward was to build 276 saloon bodies and 13 drophead coupés. Gurney Nutting had made a speciality of that style in pre-war days, but produced just 11 dropheads from 1948 until its closure in 1950. The company had been owned since 1945 by Rolls-Royce distributor Jack Barclay, a business that in 1937 had

acquired James Young of Bromley, Kent, which was itself to be responsible for 189 Silver Wraith saloons as well as 167 limousines. Freestone & Webb, meanwhile, produced 51 saloon bodies until its end came in 1958, whilst Hooper, Mulliner and Park Ward all made Landaulette bodies in penny numbers.

In 1949 The Autocar road-tested an H. J. Mulliner sedanca de ville Silver Wraith and whilst it did not subject it to the indignity of a measured top speed, inferred this was between 80mph and 90mph (128kph to 144kph). But "the charm, the appeal, the true practical worth of this car is not that it has the highest performance," wrote the magazine, "but...the way in which it behaves and handles and its day-in, day-out consistency".

The Wraith's Mark VI stablemate was also praised for its flexibility. "In brief, a superlative form of road travel is provided from very little above walking pace in top gear without snatch to a genuine speed well exceeding 90mph (144 kph)". The Bentley was comfortable, quiet, and "can be handled with the greatest of ease despite its size". It was, the testers concluded, "a wonderful combination of town carriage and mile-eater on the open road".

When Rolls-Royce began car production in 1946 the British government, faced with a country bankrupted by war, compelled its car makers to export their products to gain valuable foreign currency, in particular dollars, for the exchequer. In consequence many manufacturers dispatched as much as 80 per cent of their output overseas.

The Spirit of Ecstasy

The Silver Wraith was enhanced by the presence of the famous and well-established Spirit of Ecstasy mascot which is as identifiable with the marque as the classically-inspired radiator it surmounts. However, from 1946 until 1955 the cars were fitted with a variation of the original design in the form of a kneeling lady that had been available as an option since 1934.

Spirit of Ecstasy, the best-known motoring mascot in the world. This is the so-called 'kneeling lady' used on the Silver Wraith. (LAT)

Although known as the Spirit of Ecstasy, the beautiful Art Nouveau statuette of a standing lady by Charles Sykes was described as 'The Spirit of Speed' in the March 1911 agreement between the artist and Rolls-Royce. The model was Eleanor Thornton, who was secretary to Sykes and was the mistress of pioneer motorist and keen Rolls-Royce owner Lord Montagu of Beaulieu – father of the current Lord Montagu. Available as an option, at a cost of four guineas (£4.20), on the Silver Ghost from 1911, the mascot was standardised after the war and appeared on the 20hp from its 1922 introduction.

Unusually, Sykes, not the company, was responsible for the production of the mascot. First made of white metal and then bronze, he finally settled on a predominantly copper mix, to which were added small quantities of zinc and tin. Initially the figure was nickel-plated but from the early thirties it was chromed over a nickel base.

With the more aerodynamically-aware climate of that decade, Rolls-Royce commissioned from Sykes a second mascot with a lower frontal area. The corporate conveyance of 26 January 1934 refers to "the figure of a women kneeling with draperies flowing". Sykes continued to produce the mascot until 1948, his 73rd year, when its manufacture was taken over by Rolls-Royce, who took the opportunity of changing the metal to stainless steel. These mascots carried, as before, the artist's signature although the practice was discontinued in 1950, the year Sykes died.

The 'kneeling lady' used by Rolls-Royce after the war was fitted to the Silver Wraith, the long-wheelbase version on the D-series cars which ceased production in 1955 and on the Silver Dawn and the A-series and B-series Phantom IVs. However, the 'kneeling lady' was revived in the 1980s and fitted to those cars destined for Arab customers.

With the arrival in 1955 of the Silver Cloud, Rolls-Royce reverted to the original standing lady mascot – which became retractable with the 1980 arrival of the Silver Spirit. Further to this, her dimensions were reduced by some 20 per cent on Spirits built from the 1996 model year. The mascot that began life in 1911 a proud 7in (18cm) high, now measures 3½in (9cm), precisely half the original size.

The layout of the Mark VI's instrument panel differed from that used on its Rolls-Royce Silver Wraith contemporary. (LAT)

Dear departed

While the Silver Wraith was bought by Rolls-Royce's traditional well-to-do customers, it was also in demand by undertakers. Of these, the Scottish Co-operative Wholesale Society bought no fewer than 27 chassis between 1949 and 1952, to be bodied as hearses. This branch of the CWS had set up a Motor Body and Cartwright department in the early thirties and the Rolls-Royces were bodied at premises in the Rutherglen district of Glasgow and in the city of Perth. The company also purchased ten Park Ward Limousines that were used as following cars. However, in

In addition to the Scottish CWS, such coachbuilders as Alpe & Saunders, Dottridge Brothers and William Denby built hearse bodies on the Silver Wraith chassis. This rare four-door example of 1948 is by Woodall Nicholson, one of two 'Wraiths it bodied. (Paul Harris, Classic Hearse Register)

due course the Rolls-Royces were discontinued and replaced by Armstrong Siddeleys. One Silver Wraith CWS hearse survives in the Museum of Scottish Transport in Glasgow while another can be seen on display at the National Museum of Funeral History in America.

However, Crewe was an exception in this regard: Rolls-Royces were only produced in chassis form and its market was, in any event, a limited one. In consequence only 585 Silver Wraiths, some 30 per cent of the total, were sent abroad. Interestingly, the export figure for the related standard-bodied Bentley Mark VI was even lower: as the make was not widely known outside Europe, only 927 cars, or a mere 18 per cent of production, went overseas.

In the first instance those Rolls-Royces built for export were essentially similar to those sold on the home market. Such sales began in 1947 and the first example of Mulliner's Touring Limousine was one of a batch of Rolls-Royces and Bentleys that were shipped to America on the 'Mauretania' in October of that year.

It was not until 1949 that left-hand-drive cars began to leave Crewe. Repositioning the steering gear caused a particular problem for the company because it rendered the cars' distinctive right-hand gearchange inoperable. The replacement was a not wholly satisfactory steering-column-mounted gearlever curiously positioned to be operated by the driver's left hand.

The first Mark VI to be so equipped was delivered in March 1949, and the Silver Wraith followed three months later. This car, an example of Mulliner's increasingly popular Touring Limousine, was in the hands of its American customer in June.

Of the overseas markets, the US was destined to be the most popular destination, with 165 Silver Wraiths imported, followed, unexpectedly, by France, which took 55 cars – although many of these found their way to the wealthy denizens of the Riviera. Next came the traditional British Empire outlets of Australia, taking 44 cars, and Canada, which received 35 in all.

Interior of a Mark VI, showing the individual front seats and the right-hand gearchange. (LAT)

The Mark VI's rear compartment with the picnic tables down. Also note the footrests. The ash trays built into each of the armrests are a sign of the times. (LAT)

The Silver Dawn became available on the home market in October 1953. The enlarged boot, shared with the Bentley R-type, is shown to advantage. (LAT)

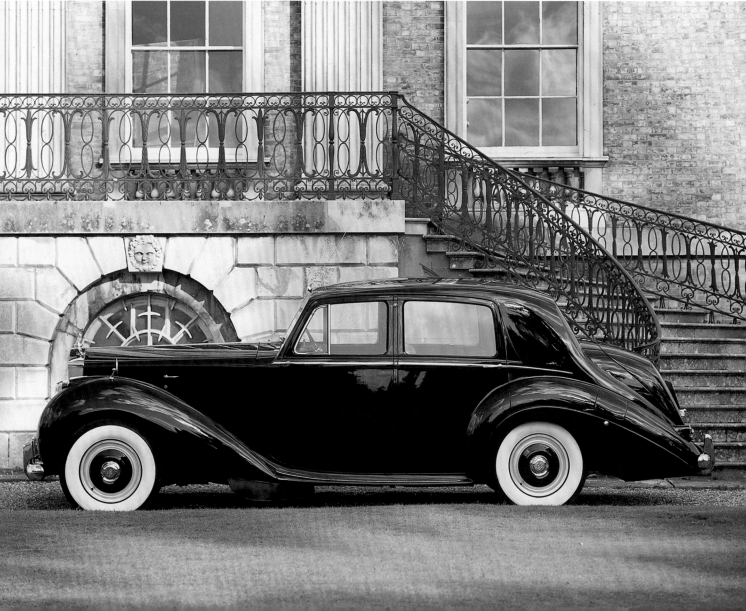

What's in a name? (i) The Wraith

Up until the 1925 arrival of what was named the 'New Phantom', Rolls-Royces were known, the short-lived V8-powered Legalimit of 1905/06 excepted, by the RAC horsepower rating of their engines. The first instance of the Wraith name being used on a Rolls-Royce was a Silver Ghost, chassis 1101, built in 1911 and used by the company for trials. Wraith was subsequently used in 1938/39 as a model name for the short-lived successor to the 25/30hp. When the Rationalised Range of Bentleys and Rolls-Royces was conceived in 1938, the Silver Wraith name was applied to the largest model. This was a limousine on a 11ft 1in (3.38m) wheelbase, to be available with both six-cylinder and eight-cylinder engines. In 1939 the 'eight' was renamed the Silver Phantom, which left the 'six' as the Silver Wraith – the name with which it entered production in 1946.

The 4.5-litre IoE six-cylinder engine of a 1953 Silver Dawn. (LAT)

These were relatively small numbers and in mid-1949 Rolls-Royce introduced a model that was aimed specifically at export markets. The Silver Dawn, the company stressed, was a car for the owner-driver and was accordingly based on the standard-bodied Bentley Mark VI. It had existed in experimental form since 1946 and in consequence was the first Rolls-Royce to be fitted with quantity-produced bodywork. Appropriately it was introduced at the International World's Fair staged in Toronto, Canada.

Selling for $14,000, the equivalent of £3,500, this was a significant £2,813 less than the Silver Wraith Touring Limousine, which by then retailed at £6,313. This escalating price was not, it should be noted,

Rolls-Royce's doing but reflected the fact that in 1948 a government the company regarded as vindictive had doubled purchase tax to a swingeing 66⅔ per cent on those cars costing over £1,000. This penalty was rescinded by Labour chancellor Sir Stafford Cripps in his 1950 budget but was promptly reintroduced in 1951 and thereafter dropped to a 25 per cent low in 1962.

Some 60 per cent of Dawns – 462 cars, in total – were sent overseas. Although the chassis could be acquired for bodying by specialist coachbuilders, only 64 were so enhanced, drophead coupé bodies being a popular choice. Park Ward produced 27 and H. J. Mulliner two, whilst Hooper, James Young and Freestone & Webb respectively made

12, 11 and six saloons on Silver Dawn chassis.

Mechanically all the cars from Crewe remained essentially faithful to the 1946 specification but it was found that the plated bores only lasted for some 40,000 miles (approximately 64,000km), at which point the chrome started to break down. In 1948 the practice was discontinued and the plating was replaced by the fitment of 2¼in-deep Bricrome inserts.

A more radical change was introduced in mid-1951, when the engine's capacity was enlarged by upping the bore to 92mm to produce a displacement of 4,566cc.

A 1954 R-type Bentley with its distinctive larger boot, in company with the related Silver Dawn of 1953. (LAT)

Simultaneously the crankshaft webs were thickened, and a full-flow oil filter introduced. The latter modification was effected because although the B60 engine had in the main proved to be remarkably reliable, there had been instances of big-end failure, attributable to the original by-pass oil system which only functioned satisfactorily if the car was regularly serviced. The arrival of the new engine was soon followed by the replacement of the Stromberg carburettor with a Zenith unit.

A more significant departure, peculiar to the Silver Wraith, occurred in 1951, and was destined to change the character of the car. The wheelbase was extended by 6in (15cm) to 11ft 1in (3.38m), and the result was a rather grander offering as the increased chassis length lent itself more to limousine bodywork. Weight rose and performance fell, but this was of no great import, as the Rolls-Royce was invariably chauffeur-driven. The first example was delivered in January 1952 and, for a time, both versions were produced; but manufacture of the shorter-wheelbase chassis ceased later in the year, although deliveries continued into 1953 and 1954.

In the meantime the spirit of the pre-war Bentley was being rekindled with the announcement, in February 1952, of the Continental coupé with its impressive factory-designed but Mulliner-built body. Its lighter weight, greater aerodynamic efficiency and higher rear axle ratio produced a top speed of 115mph (185kph) which made the Continental the fastest four-seater car in the world. Initially all cars were exported and the model did not become available on the home market until the end of 1952. The price was an eyebrow-raising £7,608.

The Bentley saloon line underwent revision for the 1953 model year with the arrival of the R-type, which was instantly identifiable by its larger boot. Unlike the original, the lid now hinged at the top and the car was 7½in (19cm) longer than its predecessor – which required some changes to the rear suspension. Inside, the pre-war inheritances of a hand throttle and choke control gave

Driving the Bentley Mark VI

The first impression on entering a Mark VI or R-Type is how old-fashioned it seems. The narrow cockpit with its dashboard set under the wooden screen rail is real pre-war stuff, as is the large three-spoke wheel with its central controls for mixture, hand throttle and adjustment of the dampers. Perhaps surprisingly, you sit lower than on later cars, and in a slightly more reclined position.

The interior is in delightfully simple good taste – and is even more low-key in early cars with their plain rather than fluted leather. Quick-release front window mechanisms – one firm movement of the long lever and they shoot up or down – are a pleasant feature, as are the adjustable armrests on the front doors. The rear compartment, with its substantial rear-quarter panels, is intimate but not cramped: although the seat is relatively narrow, there's plenty of legroom, to the point where footrests are provided. Veneer picnic tables that cantilever smoothly out from the seat backs are another nice touch.

The right-hand gearchange, the short lever tucked away to the side of the driver's seat, is likely to be a novelty. When the gearbox oil is cold, the idea doesn't seem too clever. The lever is very firm in its gate, making it impossible to stir it around until you

find the gear you are seeking, and locating neutral can as a result be difficult. But once the oil has warmed you begin to appreciate what a delightful change it is. There's a long throw into first, which you can sometimes miss until you learn to take your time; the same applies for the change to second, which should not be rushed. Once you have the measure of the 'box, you'll find the synchromesh good and that the shift has a delicious well-oiled feeling of mechanical accuracy far removed from the dumbed-down rubberiness of many a modern car's anaesthetised change mechanism: you really do feel as if you are sliding finely machined cogs along precision-engineered shafts.

This beguiling gearchange is matched to a soft, well-cushioned clutch of average weighting and to a braking system fully up to the demands likely to be made of it. Pedal travel is quite long, with an initially quite gentle response, but firmer braking brings the servo into play quite sharply, to the point where you can stand the car on its nose with an injudicious right foot.

As for the steering, this is neither too light nor too heavy, and has a fluid action and satisfactory precision. The suspension is firmer

than on later cars, but not to the point of harshness, and roll is reasonably well checked, so the car doesn't feel a liability on twisty country roads.

Relative to say a V8-powered S2, the straight-six seems somewhat obtrusive – it's in no way harsh, but you're always aware of its burbly beat. In comparison to an ordinary saloon of the day such as a Morris Oxford or Ford Consul, the Bentley is deliciously refined, and that's probably a fairer perspective. In any case, you're not exactly short-changed by the generously-dimensioned IoE power unit: creamy, torquey performance keeps you comfortably up with today's traffic and makes cruising at the legal limit relaxingly unstrained, and marred only by the wind noise characteristic of a car of this era.

Overall, the Bentley feels surprisingly sporty, with very real get-up-and-go – a character later models were to lose. Situating it in the classic-car spectrum, you could say that it combines the classily restrained good taste and quality of a Rover P4 with a generous dollop of extra performance, the whole wrapped in a package exquisitely executed but somewhat pre-war in flavour.

way to an automatic choke.

Ever with an eye to refinement, in the 1953 model year the Motor Car Division began to offer the General Motors four-speed Hydra-Matic automatic transmission across the range. The unit had to be modified to accommodate the gearbox-driven mechanical servo and there was a manual override actuated by a stubby lever mounted on the right of the steering column. Power was transferred from the engine via a fluid flywheel. The company thus became the first British motor manufacturer to offer an automatic gearbox. It was,

however, only specified on export chassis, cars for the home market not being so equipped until the 1954 season – by which time Rolls-Royce was manufacturing the 'box itself rather than buying it in from GM. The following year Hydra-Matic was standardised on most Crewe products.

The year 1955 saw the arrival of the Rolls-Royce Silver Cloud, complete with standardised bodywork shared with the companion S-series Bentley and powered by a 4.9-litre version of the B60. At this point the Silver Dawn was discontinued, but the Silver Wraith was fitted with the enlarged

The delightful dashboard of the R-type Continental. (LAT)

The R-type Continental with its magnificent H. J. Mulliner coupé body. Initially only available for export, this car was delivered to its UK owner in July 1953. (LAT)

As the fastest four-seater of its day, this rear view of an R-type Continental was a familiar sight on the world's highways in the 1950s. (LAT)

H. J. Mulliner bodied all but 15 R-type Continental chassis so those enhanced by other coachbuilders are rare. The drophead coupé (left), is one of four built; with its fixed head equivalent, there were just two, both by Park Ward. The BOAC aircraft is a Canadair Argonaut, appropriately powered by four Rolls-Royce Merlin engines. (Rolls-Royce)

Buying Hints

1. All these cars are powered by Rolls-Royce's B60 engine which was designed to run for 100,000 miles (160,000km) without attention. In consequence, it tends to be very reliable. Having said that, pre-1948 units did suffer from piston trouble caused by chrome plating the tops of the bores, a process that was discontinued at chassis WCB30. The original by-pass oil filter wasn't really up to the job and bearing failures did occasionally occur, so the arrival of a full-flow oil filter with the 4½-litre engine of 1951 resulted in a rather better power unit. Fortunately the Bentley Mark VI, R-type and Silver Wraith are all fitted with an oil-pressure gauge and an acceptable pressure is 20 to 25psi (hot) at 30mph (50kph). You must be prepared for a relatively high oil consumption from the IoE 'six'. About 200 miles (300km) per pint is average. A further sign of wear is piston slap when cold, this distinctive noise fading as the engine warms up.

2. Overheating is not uncommon – not least as the alloy head is prone to silting up. A blocked radiator could also be to blame, and the cause may not be old age. It can be the result of iron oxide detaching itself from the cylinder block and being conveyed to the radiator core, thereby blocking the waterways. If this has happened, the only answer is a replacement or rebuilt radiator. Rolls-Royce cured the problem by reversing the polarity of the dynamo!

3. The right-hand gearchange is a delight to use – although the same cannot be said for the steering-column gearshift of the left-hand-drive export cars. Like the engine, the gearbox shouldn't present any major problems. However, one shortcoming is that the distance pieces in the layshaft tend to disintegrate. Run the car until the oil is warm. Then select bottom gear. Using a small throttle opening, hold the lever and if you experience any kickback you know that trouble is in the offing. The 'box has a traditionally noisy bottom gear, and in addition the teeth tend to chip if changes into first have been ham-fisted; although the clicking noise – or clattering if the wear is really bad – may be a distraction, it is not particularly serious. You can put any unacceptable transmission vibration down to a worn centre propeller shaft bearing. The substantial rear axle, by contrast, should provide thousands of miles of trouble-free motoring; an oil leak at the front felt seal is the only ailment you're likely to encounter.

4. The fact that the Silver Wraith is fitted with a Bijur automatic chassis lubrication system doesn't mean that it is still working! A good check is to pump the pedal and see if there are drips of oil at all four corners of the car. If previous drivers have not been in the habit of depressing the appropriate pedal every 100 miles (160km) the device's circulatory system is likely to have become blocked. This is the most common cause of wear in the independent front suspension, the top and bottom wishbone pins and king pins being the most likely suspect points. The semi-elliptic leaf-spring rear suspension is trouble-free, although again a blocked Bijur system could have provoked excessive wear in the threaded shackles. Additionally, with the cars weighing over two tons (2,032kg) the springs are likely to have settled.

5. Conversely, clutch judder may well be the result of over-use of the Bijur system, with excess oil vapour having reached the friction plates. Slipping the clutch will burn off the excess.

6. The hydro-mechanical brakes should not present any particular problems but if they are sluggish in operation (or judder) the chances are that the oil seal that prevents the gearbox lubricant reaching the servo linings has failed. You can confirm this by taking a car for a run and then peering underneath for any tell-tail signs of dripping lubricant.

7. If the engine begins to falter under harsh acceleration, the most likely cause is the failure of one of the two SU fuel pumps.

8. The substantial chassis frame should not give trouble – at one place it is no less than 7in (18cm) deep. But it is prone to corrosion at the point where it begins to rise over the rear

engine and was destined to survive, whilst selling at a much reduced rate, for a further three years. Power steering was introduced early in 1956, when the Silver Cloud and the S-series received it.

Production of the Silver Wraith finally ceased in 1958, although cars continued to be bodied into 1959. For the record the last chassis, LHLW 52, was delivered to Mulliner in October 1958 and this Touring Limousine was completed in February 1959. However, the Ghanaian embassy in Bonn did not receive its Hooper Limousine, HLW40, until August – which really did mark the end of the line for these long-lived cars.

In all, 1886 Silver Wraith chassis, 1,247 short-wheelbase and 639 long-wheelbase, had been built since 1946. These were bodied by 31 coachbuilders worldwide but of this total, five companies were responsible axle. Whilst you're examining the car's underside, check the state of the exhaust system. Replacements are expensive.

9. With their all-steel body, the Mark VI, R-type and Silver Dawn are far more susceptible to deterioration than the coachbuilt Silver Wraith. The first all-important points to check are the rear body mounts directly above the rear axle. You may have to remove the back wheels to inspect them but it's worth the effort because the mounts have been known to rust completely away. If they have, make an excuse and leave: repairing the damage will probably cost you more than the price of the car. Rust also attacks the nearby inner body skin around the rear wheelarches, the lower edges of the door, the bottoms of the centre pillars (which support both doors), and the sills; a particularly vulnerable point is the forward section of the sill where it joins the scuttle, and you should be warned that repair could be expensive if the adjoining structure is also rotten. Additionally the front wings are prone to corrode around the sidelights. These were originally leaded in place, and you shoud be on the lookout here for signs of bubbling and/or filler. At the rear of the car, rust attacks the spare wheel well, and the cover for the spare wheel locker beneath the boot floor. It can also affect the adjoining base of the bootlid although this only applies to the Mark VI, as the R-type's lid is made of aluminium. If the car you are examining is fitted with rear wheel

spats, these are also a prime candidate for the rust bug.

10. The sliding roof is a nice feature but it's also another place for water to enter. Therefore check inside the car for signs of a discoloured roof lining in the immediate vicinity of the recess. Drainage of water from the roof channels is looked after by tubing that incorporates rubber elbows at roof level. These can perish and allow water to run down the door pillars and settle on the scuttle: check for corrosion on the scuttle, just ahead of the door handles.

11. Re-trimming one of these cars in leather is hugely expensive, so don't be tempted by a car with a poor interior. Refurbishing the woodwork is also likely to be costly. Finally, if detailed authenticity is important, check that the under-dash toolkit is complete: replacing missing items doesn't come cheaply.

12. If you are contemplating a Silver Dawn, which shares the same body as its Bentley contemporary, first check that you are examining a Rolls-Royce and not a Mark VI or its R-type successor that has been so converted by grafting on an RR radiator in place of the original. Your first port of call is therefore the car's chassis number: you'll find the chassis plate under the bonnet on the right-hand side of the engine bulkhead. The Dawn had an 'S' prefix, or 'L' in the case of the left-hand-drive car, whilst

a Bentley used 'B' as a prefix. If you're still not satisfied, then you'll also find the chassis number stamped on the frame just ahead of the steering box.

13. The condition of the coachbuilt body fitted to the Silver Wraith should be a key consideration of your purchase. That means not only the state of the metal panelling but, also, and above all, that of the interior. Retrimming is an extremely costly business and however well the work is executed, something is always lost in the process. So pay particular attention to the state of the leather upholstery and, if it is in poor condition, and the coachwork is not particularly sought-after, then move on to another example. But if the interior is presentable, then turn your attention to the bodywork. This, in all probability, will be made of aluminium which has the advantage of not rusting although it does corrode and crack. Of much greater concern is the state of the framework that supports it. By 1950 such coachbuilders as Hooper and H. J. Mulliner had adopted alloy for their bodyframes and in 1954 Park Ward made the switch from steel to alloy. Freestone & Webb and James Young tended to use a combination of alloy and traditional ash. The latter is susceptible to deterioration and the state of the doors, in particular how easily they shut, or if they have dropped and need to be lifted into place, is probably the best indication of what problems, if any, lie beneath.

for 1804 bodies, or 95 per cent of the whole. H. J. Mulliner led the field with 518, followed by Park Ward (480), Hooper (469), James Young (217) and Freestone & Webb (120).

The demise of the Silver Wraith spelt the end of a great British coachbuilding tradition, although the

Silver Cloud could be fitted with bespoke bodies and all examples of the Wraith's low-volume Phantom V successor had coachbuilt bodies.

But by 1959 Hooper and Freestone & Webb had ceased their activities and that year H. J. Mulliner joined Park Ward as Rolls-Royce's second in-

house coachbuilder. Only James Young remained in business: it survived for a further eight years, thanks to Rolls-Royce contracts, before it too closed its doors, at the end of 1967.

[1] *Hives' Turbulent Barons*, by Alec Harvey-Bailey

The Silver Cloud
and Bentley
S-series

The talents of corporate stylist John Blatchley are shown to good effect in this contemporary colour photograph of a Rolls-Royce Silver Cloud, introduced in 1955. (Rolls-Royce)

The integration of the Rolls-Royce and Bentley marques, foreshadowed by the Silver Dawn/Mark VI, was completed in 1955 with the arrival of the Silver Cloud and its S-series Bentley equivalent. Sharing the same Pressed Steel four-door saloon body, the new cars retained, like their predecessors, a separate chassis. This permitted the continued production of coachbuilt bodies although these were built in diminishing numbers throughout the ten-year manufacturing life of the two sister cars.

If the Silver Cloud did anything, it was to restate the Rolls-Royce theme of a well-appointed luxury saloon. But whilst most of Crewe's production up until its arrival had carried the Bentley name, the scales tipped in favour of the Silver Lady from 1959 onwards. There were, in fact, more retrospectively titled S1 versions of the new model than the equivalent Cloud but with the arrival of the V8-engined cars, the balance swung back to Rolls-Royce. This marked the beginnings of a dilution in the Bentley character that – incredibly – led to the marque's near extinction.

Apart from the B-series six-cylinder

In its original form, the Silver Cloud was powered by an enlarged 4.9-litre version of the B-series six-cylinder engine. This is the car used in the 1958 *The Autocar* road test. (Author's collection)

IoE engine, which only survived until 1959, the cars were completely new. Work on the project had begun in earnest in 1950 under the direction of Harry Grylls, who in the following year replaced William Robotham as chief engineer of Rolls-Royce's Motor Car Division.

In concept these new models perpetuated the theme begun in 1946 with the Pressed Steel Mark VI Bentley. A tangible starting point came with the construction, in 1951, of an experimental Bentley saloon that was accorded the Siam coding.

Next, in October 1952, came Bentley 20-B, with a body designed by John Blatchley which closely resembled the finished product. It was the first commission he undertook when the corporate styling department moved in 1951 from the Clan Foundry to Crewe, and it also

The Silver Cloud's driving compartment with its map table extended and handbook displayed. This is a 1957 car. (LAT)

marked his appointment as Rolls-Royce's chief styling engineer. Blatchley was clearly inspired in his work by H. J. Mulliner's peacock-blue Mark VI sports saloon exhibited on the Bentley stand at the 1950 Motor Show.

Mechanically the experimental 20-B was also closely related to the final design in that it was built on a new box-section – as opposed to channel-section – chassis. Power came from an as-yet-unannounced 4,887cc version of the B60 engine.

A second experimental Bentley, 21-B, followed in 1953 and later in the same year the 22-B coding was finally allocated to a Rolls-Royce version. There were a further three vehicles all with Park Ward bodies, although the production versions, as the then-current Bentley R-type saloon, were to be manufactured in volume by Pressed Steel at its Cowley factory.

The new cars were announced in April 1955, with the Silver Cloud selling for £4,796 whilst the S-series Bentley, at £4,669, was £127 cheaper. Outwardly similar apart from their radiators and hub caps, their respective chassis prices of £2,555 and £2,465 were listed as an indication that the cars would still be available for the fitment of bespoke bodies.

Outwardly Blatchley's design was wholly in keeping with Rolls-Royce's restrained understated image and, accordingly, it looked a little dated – which is not surprising, considering that it had been conceived four years previously.

The body was principally constructed of 20-gauge steel although to save weight the doors, bonnet and bootlid were variously made of 16-gauge or 18-gauge aluminium, and the front doors were now forward-hinged rather than old-fashionedly rear-hinged. With an overall length of 17ft 8in (5.38m) and a height of 5ft 4in (1.63m) high, it was 11in (27.9cm) longer and 2in (50mm) lower than the R-type.

The body was secured to the chassis by 12 rubber-mounted bolts.

Shadwell Harry Grylls 1909-1983

As chief engineer of Rolls-Royce's Motor Car Division between the years 1951 and 1968, Harry Grylls (Gry) had overall responsibility for the Silver Cloud and Silver Shadow, arguably the most significant models of the company's post-war years.

After education at Rugby and Trinity College, Cambridge, where he read mechanical engineering and ran a trio of Aston Martins, the Cornish-born Grylls joined Rolls-Royce and its Experimental Department in 1930. He remained there for nine years and was also able to see Henry Royce at work at West Wittering.

But there was clearly no love lost

Power in the land: chief engineer Harry Grylls, the man with responsibility for the Silver Cloud line and its Silver Shadow successor. (Rolls-Royce)

between him and his boss from 1937, W. A. (Roy) Robotham. Tellingly, in Grylls's famous 1963 Institution of Mechanical Engineers paper, *The History of a Dimension*, describing the evolution of the rationalised B-series engines, there is no mention of Robotham's key role. But Robotham got his revenge. You will look in vain for Grylls' name in his readable, though not wholly accurate, autobiography *Silver Ghosts and Silver Dawn*, published in 1970!

On the outbreak of war in 1939, Harry Grylls became personal assistant to general works manager Ernest Hives, although during the final months of hostilities he was involved with the planning of the post-war range of cars. It was 1949 before he moved to Crewe as technical production engineer, and he became chief engineer in 1951. Subsequently, in February 1968, he became the Division's technical director. Although regarded as aloof and cynical by some colleagues, he remained totally dedicated to the pursuit of excellence, as laid down by Henry Royce.

Following retirement in his 60th year in 1969, Harry Grylls continued for a time as a consultant, while during his leisure hours he enjoyed music, restoring sundials and, characteristically, studying the aerodynamics of boomerangs. He died on 17 October 1983 at the age of 74.

The box-section frame was some 50 per cent stronger than its predecessor and similarly featured a central cruciform. With a wheelbase of 10ft 3in (3.12m), it was 3in (7.6cm) longer. Coil-and-wishbone independent front suspension was retained but the design used a wholly new semi-trailing configuration to increase wheel movement; steering was by cam-and-roller. At the rear traditional leaf springs were still used, with the

addition of a Z-shaped anti-roll bar to reduce spring wind-up. The 15in disc wheels were 1in smaller than those fitted to the R-type and the drum brakes were accordingly of smaller diameter but had wider linings. The familiar mechanical servo continued, boosting the same front-hydraulic and rear-mechanical braking.

Under the bonnet, the 4,887cc capacity of the F-head 'six' had been achieved by increasing the bore from

Rolls-Royce Silver Cloud I
1955-1959

ENGINE:
Six cylinders in line, iron block, alloy head

Bore x stroke	95.2mm x 114.3mm
Capacity	4,887cc
Valve actuation	Pushrod
Compression ratio	8:1
Carburettors	Twin SU HD6
Power	Not disclosed

TRANSMISSION:
Rear-wheel drive
Four-speed automatic with fluid coupling

Final drive ratio	3.42:1

SUSPENSION:
Front: Independent, wishbone and coil spring
Rear: Live axle with half elliptic springs

STEERING:
Cam and roller, optionally power assisted from
March 1956. Turns lock-to-lock: 5

BRAKES:
Front: Hydraulic drum
Rear: Mechanical drum
Mechanical servo assistance

WHEELS/TYRES:
Steel disc wheels 8.20/15

BODYWORK:
Four-door steel and aluminium saloon by
Pressed Steel. Separate chassis.

DIMENSIONS:

Length	17ft 8in (5.38m)
Wheelbase	10ft 3in (3.12m)
Track – front	4ft 10in (1.47m)
– rear	5ft 0in (1.52m)
Width	6ft 2¾in (1.90m)
Height	5ft 4in (1.62m)

WEIGHT:
37.7cwt (1,917 kg)

PERFORMANCE:
(Source: *The Autocar*)

Max speed	106mph (170kph)
0-50mph (0-80kph)	9.4 sec
0-60mph (0-100kph)	13.0sec
0-70mph (0-112kph)	18.4sec

PRICE INCLUDING TAX WHEN NEW:
£4,796

NUMBER BUILT:
Silver Cloud I: 2,231
Bentley S1: 3,107

Rolls-Royce Silver Cloud I (Long wheelbase)
1957-1959

As Silver Cloud I except:

Wheelbase	10ft 7in (3.22m)
Overall length	17ft 10in (5.43m)

PRICE INCLUDING TAX WHEN NEW:
£6,894

NUMBER BUILT:
Silver Cloud: 121
Bentley S1: 35

Rolls-Royce Silver Cloud II
1959-1962

As Silver Cloud I except:

ENGINE:
V8 alloy block, alloy heads

Bore x stroke	104.4mm x 91.44mm
Capacity	6,230 cc
Valve actuation	Pushrod
Compression ratio	8:1
Carburettors	Twin SU HD6
Power	Not disclosed

STEERING:
Power-assisted cam-and-roller

PERFORMANCE:
(Source: *The Autocar*)
Max speed

113mph (181kph)	
0-50mph (0-80kph)	8.3sec
0-60mph (0-100kph)	11.5sec
0-70mph (0-112kph)	15.5sec

PRICE INCLUDING TAX WHEN NEW: £5,802

NUMBER BUILT:
Silver Cloud II: 2,417
Bentley S2: 1,932

Rolls-Royce Silver Cloud III
1962-1966

As Silver Cloud I except

PERFORMANCE:
(Source: *Autocar*)

Maximum speed	115mph (185kph)
0-50mph (0-80kph)	7.7sec
0-60mph (0-100kph)	0.8sec
0-70mph (0-112kph)	14.2sec

PRICE INCLUDING TAX WHEN NEW: £6,277

NUMBER BUILT:
Silver Cloud III: 2,044
Bentley S3: 1,318

Rolls-Royce Silver Cloud II/III (Long wheelbase)
1959-1964

As Silver Cloud I long wheelbase except V8
engine, as fitted to Cloud II and III

NUMBER BUILT:
Silver Cloud II: 299
Bentley S2: 57
Silver Cloud III: 253
Bentley S3: 32

92mm to 95mm, the enlarged unit having powered the Bentley Continental coupé from July 1954. The new cylinder head had six ports rather than four, improved breathing via twin SU carburettors – hitherto a well-established Bentley preserve – and in consequence enjoyed more power. This was 'undisclosed' but what was now designated the B61 engine in reality developed about 150bhp.

Below stairs the seven-bearing crankshaft now featured four balance weights rather than the established six. These were integral with the crankshaft rather than being separately attached to it, this new configuration saving both manufacturing time and money.

Automatic transmission had been an optional fitment on the Silver Wraith since October 1952, and the Derby-built Hydra-Matic four speed 'box was standardised on the Silver Cloud. With no manual option, the long-running right-hand gearchange thus became a thing of the past. However, it continued to be offered on the Bentley until 1957.

Despite the fact that the bodies were now mass-produced by Pressed Steel, the interior echoed that of a coachbuilt car in that there was walnut veneer and the finest quality leather in abundance, everything being in simple but exquisite good taste.

John Polwhele Blatchley, born 1913

John Blatchley became Rolls-Royce's chief styling engineer in 1951, the same year as Harry Grylls was appointed chief engineer. He accordingly had overall responsibility for the lines of the Silver Cloud and Silver Shadow and, unquestionably, was the most talented Rolls-Royce stylist of the post-war years.

After education at Great Chesterfield College, Essex, Blatchley, having developed an early fascination for motor cars and their styling, failed his exams for Jesus College, Cambridge. Instead he attended the Chelsea School of Mechanical Engineering and then the School of Motor Bodybuilding at the Regent Street Polytechnic. In 1935 he applied for a job with Gurney Nutting, where his talents were recognised by its chief designer, the great A. F. McNeil, who became his mentor. But on McNeil's departure in 1937 for James Young, Blatchley became chief designer at the age of 23.

With the outbreak of war he moved to Rolls-Royce's Aero Division headquarters at Hucknall, Nottinghamshire, and spent much of the war designing aircraft cowlings. Hearing of the company's post-war plans, he applied for a transfer to the Motor Car Division and in 1946 he joined the Clan Foundry experimental department as a styling engineer.

Although the Bentley Mark VI saloon, designed by Ivan Evernden, was well advanced, Blatchley was concerned by its lack of elegance and detail sophistication and used his experience at Gurney Nutting to refine some exterior details. He was also responsible for the Bentley's 'coachbuilt' interior.

When the department moved, in 1951, to Crewe, Blatchley was appointed chief styling engineer and became 'JPB' in corporate parlance. His first task was to address the lack of luggage accommodation on the Mark VI and the outcome, in 1952, was the bigger-booted R-type. He went on to be responsible for the acclaimed lines of the Silver Cloud and Silver Shadow. But in the wake of the increasing volume of safety regulations that were impinging on his work, in March 1969 he took early retirement at the age of 55.

In truth there was little to choose between the Cloud's weight of 37.7cwt (1,917kg) and 105mph (169kph) top speed and the vital statistics of the R-type Bentley. However, acceleration was marginally better, with 60mph arriving in 13 seconds, which was some 0.8 of a second quicker. Less happily, petrol consumption was in the region of 10–15mpg, which contrasted with the 12–16mpg of its predecessor.

The Cloud and S-series were available with bespoke coachwork, and in the case of the Rolls-Royce this accounted for some nine per cent of the entire line. Hooper enclosed and touring limousines were offered from 1956, with touring limousines also being available from Park Ward and H. J. Mulliner – the latter firm being responsible for almost all the drophead coupé versions of the Cloud. The Bentley could similarly be ordered with special coachwork and the options included a James Young two-door saloon and, briefly, four-door closed coachwork from Freestone & Webb.

Those owners who had craved refined performance could opt for the Bentley Continental coupé. Enhanced with a high-compression – 7.25:1 – version of the straight-six engine, it was perpetuated for 1956 in S-type guise and was distinguished from its R-type predecessor by a higher waistline and the absence of rear wheel spats. Produced in limited numbers, it survived until 1959 but, significantly, was not replaced. Thirty-two years were to pass before the company once again offered a high-performance Bentley coupé.

Two further R-type Continental body styles had been introduced for the 1955 season – a four-seater sports saloon and a drophead, both by Park Ward – and these were continued on the 'S' chassis. For 1957 the Continental's engine compression ratio was again raised, to 8:1, the inlet valves were increased in diameter and the twin SUs were upped in size from 1¼in to 2in.

Rolls-Royce had decreed that only two-door bodies were to be fitted to the Continental chassis, but it was forced to relent when for 1958 H. J. Mulliner produced a handsome and distinctive four-door saloon. Priced at £8,033, some £2,490 more than the factory's standard offering, it was given the Flying Spur name and was also produced by Park Ward, Hooper and James Young. Available also on the Silver Cloud chassis, these Continentals were essentially identical to the mainstream models, with the exception of a higher rear axle ratio and slightly slimmer tyres. Fuel consumption was thus a little better.

The impending demise of the bespoke Silver Wraith saw the 1958 arrival of lengthened versions of the 'S' and Cloud. This was achieved by adding 4in (10cm) to the wheelbase, which permitted the fitment of extended coachwork with the obligatory electrically-operated interior division. Bodies for both marques were invariably by James Young, Hooper (albeit briefly) and, in the case of the Cloud, by H. J. Mulliner. There were also some extended versions of the standard Pressed Steel line. But the extra weight meant a falling off in performance, so from the summer of 1957 a higher-compression 8:1 engine, which developed 180bhp at 4,000rpm, was introduced to all models.

The elongated side window identifies this long-wheelbase version of the Silver Cloud introduced in 1957. (LAT)

The picnic tables, here on a Cloud I, that have been a feature of the Rolls-Royce family since the Bentley Mark VI. (LAT)

The long-wheelbase cars were destined to survive until 1964. By then most were bodied by James Young, one of the few remaining practitioners of a craft in terminal decline, a state of affairs that had come to a head in the late fifties and was an inevitable consequence of Crewe becoming increasingly wedded to Pressed Steel bodywork.

As set down in Chapter 4, the outcome was that in 1959 Rolls-Royce purchased H. J. Mulliner and in 1961 merged it with its other in-house coachbuilder to create H. J. Mulliner, Park Ward Ltd, based at the latter's Willesden premises.

As far as the Silver Cloud and 'S' lines were concerned, it was not long before they belatedly began to benefit from refinements which reflected the increasing popularity of the cars in America. In March 1956 power-assisted steering became an optional fitment on export models, and this was extended to the home market from the 1957 model year. A Chrysler air-conditioning system simultaneously became available on those cars destined for overseas customers.

It was to be the 1960 season before the range benefited from a new engine: announced in September 1959, it would still be in production at the time of writing, some 41 years later. Work on the unit had begun in earnest in 1951 and was assigned to a

Jack Phillips 1913–1995

Arthur John 'Jack' William Phillips, was responsible for the design of the alloy V8 engine introduced in the Silver Cloud/S-series in 1959, was a self-made man in the very best sense of the phrase, and displayed a diligence and capacity for hard work that was worthy of Henry Royce himself. It says much for the quality of his design that at the time of writing, the Phillips engine, albeit much revised, remains in production in the Rolls-Royce Corniche, the Bentley Continental and the Bentley Red Label, no less than 41 years later.

Born at Darley Abbey, Derby, Jack Phillips left the local Church of England school in 1927 at the age of 14 with no academic qualifications, other than harbouring a burning desire to work for Rolls-Royce. He joined local electric engineers Newton Brothers, making nuts and bolts but never lost sight of his ambition and was a regular visitor to Rolls-Royce's employment office. His

diligence paid off and in 1928 he was taken on as a trade apprentice – but not before he had left Newton, because the company would not accept anyone who already had a job.

Eventually, in 1932, he joined the experimental department and, determined to obtain technical qualifications, he spent the next seven years educating himself. The first two were spent attending evening classes so he could qualify for a mechanical engineering degree. Next came a five-year part-time course at Derby University, for which he was one of the first recruits to be given day release by the company, and there were also three or four nights a week of study-work.

When Rolls-Royce formed its armaments division in 1938, he was appointed leading designer under Dr S. M. Vaile. He became a mentor to Phillips, and the greatest influence on his life. With the ending of the war Jack Phillips rejoined the experimental

department at the Clan Foundry and in 1950 he arrived at Crewe.

In his later years he fiercely challenged the assertion that the V8 was of General Motors origin. In 1995 he wrote* that it was "hurtful to those of my team, all of whom were... without doubt the most skilled engineers in the country when the V8 was designed and developed at Crewe."

Despite this achievement, Phillips was most proud of the military K-series multi-fuel six-cylinder horizontally-opposed two-stroke engine on the Diesel cycle of the mid-sixties. Because of its application, it would run on anything from "hair oil to petrol", he said.

Jack Phillips retired from Rolls-Royce in 1973, moved to Norwich and died on 29 December 1995 at the age of 82.

*Rolls-Royce Enthusiasts' Club Bulletin, issue 209

Above: The Silver Cloud drophead coupé was essentially a much modified saloon. Most were built by H. J. Mulliner, later H. J. Mulliner, Park Ward. This is the Silver Cloud I version. (LAT)

Right: A Bentley S-type Continental for 1957 with two-door sports saloon body by Park Ward. (Rolls-Royce/LAT)

Previous page: Delivered in October 1958 to Mrs E. C. Snagge, this two-door saloon on a Bentley Continental S1 chassis was by James Young. (LAT)

team headed by Jack Phillips (see box).

The company had arrived at the configuration after deciding not to employ the existing B80 straight-eight then powering the Phantom IV. This would have resulted in an unnecessarily long car at a time when ease of parking was becoming a significant requirement for British customers – and when, simultaneously, the increasingly important American buyer was demanding more interior space.

The compact 90° V8 reconciled these two marketing considerations even though such a configuration had been rarely employed by British motor manufacturers. Such engines were, however, universally popular on the other side of the Atlantic. The company's long experience of alloy cylinder blocks with wet cylinder liners reached back to the V12 Phantom III of 1936–39 and to the Merlin aero engine. The combination offered a weight advantage over cast-iron and, in consequence, the

RR into BMC equals Princess R

Announced in August 1964, the British Motor Corporation's Vanden Plas Princess 4-litre R with its Rolls-Royce engine reflected poorly on both participants. Based on BMC's Farina-styled Vanden Plas 3-litre saloon, the six-cylinder BMC C-series engine was replaced by the Rolls-Royce F60 unit. But unlike the cast-iron B60 'six' used in the Bentley Mark VI, Silver Wraith and Silver Cloud I/S1, the over-square 95mm x 91mm 3.9-litre IoE engine was an all-aluminium dry-liner unit. Developed for Crewe's stillborn Burma, a

The Vanden Plas Princess 4-litre R unhappily combined Pininfarina styling with BMC manufacture and Rolls-Royce power. (LAT)

smaller, potentially higher-volume unitary construction Bentley, it produced a claimed 175bhp at 4,800rpm. Automatic Borg-Warner transmission, power steering and brakes completed the package.

In practice the Rolls-Royce engine, designated FB60 in BMC form, was found to be unduly noisy, which was always a problem with aluminium units, and the steering was surprisingly heavy, while build quality, the responsibility of the Vanden Plas factory in Kingsbury, North London, left much to be desired.

Although BMC had optimistically spoken of producing 200 Princess Rs a week, by 1967 the figure was nearer to 200 a year. When the car was withdrawn early in 1968, just

6,555 examples had been completed. The 4-litre R was the only one of several proposed Rolls/BMC projects to see the light of day: behind the scenes Rolls-Royce, in collaboration with BMC, had been working on a Bentley version of the car, coded Java, and it went on to explore the idea of Rolls-Royce and Bentley versions of BMC's unsuccessful 3-litre saloon, as eventually announced in 1967. No doubt fortunately, nothing concrete came of these thoughts.

BMC also contemplated using the FB60 unit in a sports car nicknamed Fireball XL-5. Work on the Hydrolastic-suspended two seater began in 1963 and a twin-overhead-camshaft version of the Rolls-Royce 'six' was completed in 1966 for possible use in the car. But the project was killed by BMC's merger that year with Jaguar, as it would have clashed with the superlative E-type. It was, in any event, a flawed, unhappy concept, unloved by all those associated with it.

The FB60 was also considered as a possible replacement for the corporate C-series 'six' in the ageing Austin-Healey 3000 and in 1967 a trio of experimental roadsters were so-engined. Its presence, in what could have been the 4000, required the body to be widened by six inches (152mm). But, once again, and perhaps fortuitously, the Jaguar alliance claimed another victim.

complete unit weighed some 10lb (4.5kg) less than the B61 'six' it replaced, albeit at the cost of a rise in noise levels. It should be made clear that Crewe's V8 was not, contrary to subsequent popular myth, a General Motors design, or a pale copy of a GM engine, although the engineering team would undoubtedly have been failing in its duty if it had not studied existing V8s which, invariably, were of American origin.

The result was an over-square engine of 104mm bore and 91mm stroke, the shortness of the stroke not only permitting higher revs but also preventing the unit from being excessively wide – an inviolate parameter being its fitment under the Cloud/S-series bonnet. It was for this reason that a potentially more powerful experimental 5.3-litre version of 1957, with hemispherical cylinder heads and inclined valves in

the manner of Chrysler's famous 'Hemi' V8, was not proceeded with, as it would have resulted in a much wider car.

At the engine's heart was a five-bearing counterbalanced crankshaft with side-by-side connecting rods and with oil contained within – horrors of horrors – a pressed-steel rather than cast-aluminium sump. The centrally-mounted camshaft was gear-driven, chains having never been on Crewe's

An S1 long-wheelbase chassis of 1959 graced with a drophead coupé body by James Young. (Rolls-Royce/LAT)

Rolls-Royce chose the Bentley stand at the 1959 Motor Show to unveil its new Continental S2 Park Ward drophead coupé with its distinctive continuous wing line, the work of freelance Norwegian designer Vilhelm Koren. (LAT)

agenda, and activated the overhead valves, positioned 28° to the vertical, via Chrysler self-adjusting hydraulic tappets. The identical cylinder heads were, like the block, made of aluminium alloy. Purpose-designed 1½in twin SU carburettors were mid-mounted diagonally across the engine. Less conveniently, the sparking plugs were located underneath the exhaust manifolds, which meant that a plug change on the right-hand cylinder bank necessitated the removal of the adjoining front wheel to gain access to a detachable plate introduced into the engine bay...

By contrast, the belt-driven dynamo was conveniently positioned at the very top of the engine and the front of the V8 was dominated by no fewer than four belts which, variously, drove the water and hydraulic pumps, the power steering, and – if fitted – the air

A 1964 Silver Cloud III two-door saloon by Mulliner, Park Ward. Electric windows and air-conditioning were available at extra cost. (Rolls-Royce/LAT)

A late Silver Cloud III Mulliner Park Ward drophead coupé with its distinctive twin headlamp treatment. (LAT)

conditioning compressor.

Although Rolls-Royce maintained that the horsepower developed by the 6,230cc V8 was 'adequate', the technical editor of *The Autocar*, Harry Mundy, who knew a thing or two about engines, estimated it to be around 200bhp.

With the arrival of the V8, the Pressed Steel saloons became the Silver Cloud II and Bentley S2 although, externally, there was

nothing to indicate the change of power unit. Even the exhaust pipe did not provide a giveaway because it retained a single outlet. However, inside the cars there were improvements made to the heating and ventilation, and power assisted steering was standardised.

As for performance, there could be little doubt that there was a new engine beneath the centrally hinged bonnet. Top speed was now nudging

the 115mph (185kph) mark and the 2.4 ton (2,438kg) cars would cruise happily at 90mph (145kph).

But when *The Autocar* came to evaluate the Cloud II, it commented adversely on the V8. The road-tester was moved to point out that "when the engine reached its normal running temperature, its idling was neither completely smooth or silent" – which suggested imperfect carburation. The writer was also disturbed to report

Above: The interior of the SC III, more modern in flavour than that of the standard saloon, it has an instrument binnacle not dissimilar to that on the 'Graber' Alvises of the time. (LAT)

Left: A contemporary colour photograph of an H. J. Mulliner S-type Continental. Although outwardly resembling its R-type predecessor, it is identifiable by the swage line that was extended to the rear wings. (Rolls-Royce)

Below: The distinctive ignition master switch that was fitted to Bentleys and Rolls-Royces of this period.

that the Cloud had a tendency to run hot in traffic and, occasionally, to stall. This was not what one expected of a Rolls-Royce.

In addition to the mainstream saloons, there was a choice of no fewer than five Bentley Continental bodies and of these the most memorable was a new in-house Park Ward drophead coupé with a distinctive straight-through wing line. It was the work of freelance Norwegian stylist Vilhelm Koren, who was working under contact to the Crewe styling department. H. J. Mulliner also contributed a hardtop body derived from its elegant but now ageing fastback coupé, and in addition a four-door Flying Spur saloon, whilst James Young offered two-door and four-door styles.

The V8-powered models had only been in production for two years when in 1961 the Conservative

Driving the six-cylinder Silver Cloud

Although the Cloud marked a step towards modernity for Rolls-Royce, it was still a small step: look inside a Cloud – or an S-series Bentley – and you could still be in the thirties. Extensive and beautifully-finished woodwork includes a dashboard that seems more a piece of furniture than the control centre of a motor car; the pleated seats and simple door trims carry on where the R-type left off in their self-effacing good taste; the wood-inlaid illuminated mirrors in the rear quarters could have come from a Phantom III.

But in its refinement the Cloud range has moved on. The straight-six engine is as smooth and silent as later V8s – a surprise, this – and is matched to an equally silky automatic transmission. The Cloud gathers speed serenely, without any sense of urgency, and settles into a silent 60mph cruise that flatters but to deceive: kick down through the gears and that languid persona is cast aside. The Rolls-Royce snaps through the gears with bite, yet never a hint of raucousness, and pulls sharply up to 80mph.

But this is no gentleman's sports car. The power steering most cars carry has the well-oiled feel of a piece of precision apparatus but its fluidity is not matched by any great accuracy. Add a fair degree of roll, and you soon find out that you are best off not departing from a decorously gentle style of driving. Such an approach will also avoid over-emphasising the suspension's shortcomings: on good surfaces the ride is as comfortable as you'd expect, but poor 'B' roads can provoke sharp reactions from the rear, and even transmit some shocks into the bodywork.

Driven this way, the six-cylinder Cloud and S1 offer a refined and serene motoring experience analogous to that offered by Rovers and Daimlers of the era, but removed to another plane of quality and whisper-smooth refinement. In no way a poor relation to the V8s – despite the seductive nature of these later cars – the 'sixes' offer unflamboyant and deeply classy transport for those who want to cover ground swiftly but without fluster.

A 1964 Bentley S3 saloon with its distinctive twin headlights shared with the Silver Cloud III. The radiator was 1½in (3.8cm) lower than its predecessor. (LAT)

The S3 in appropriately opulent surroundings – but in truth these Bentley and Rolls-Royce models were conceived to be driven by their owners, not chauffeurs. (LAT)

A small but typically well-executed detail on the Silver Cloud III and the S3 is this cubby hole in the front door with its sliding lid. (LAT)

Chancellor of the Exchequer, Selwyn Lloyd, announced in his Budget that the capital allowance on business cars was to be limited to a figure of £2,000. With the Cloud II then selling for £6,093, Rolls-Royce felt particularly vulnerable. This political initiative was perhaps potentially more damaging than the doubling of purchase tax by the previous Labour administration, because that had been implemented in the car-hungry early post-war years when the demand for new cars outstripped supply.

Even less happily, it spawned an association with the British Motor Corporation which led to the RR-engined 3.9 litre Vanden Plas Princess 4-litre R saloon of 1964, sold at a budget-busting £1,995. Powered by what the company termed its FB60 unit, derived from the familiar IoE sixes, it proved to be an ill-conceived, poorly-executed and slow-selling model (see box). It had also been overtaken by events: in his 1963 budget Selwyn's Lloyd's successor, Reginald Maudling, had repealed the £2,000 ceiling.

Its removal provided some relief to Ray Dorey, who had managed Rolls-

Royce's Motor Car Division since 1951. But he was also concerned about the somewhat qualified reception that had been accorded the V8-powered models. Also aware that quality control at Crewe was not all it should be, it was at his insistence that a third series of cars arrived for the 1963 season, to address these criticisms.

The most obvious external difference between the Silver Cloud III and S3 and their predecessors was a switch to fashionable twin headlamps, thereby answering complaints that the original lights had not been sufficiently powerful. At the same time the cars took on a more modern appearance, as the new lamps were matched to radiators reduced in height by some 1½in (3.8cm).

Less outwardly apparent, though even more important, was the work undertaken to improve the V8's refinement, noise levels, power and performance. In consequence, the engine's compression ratio was upped from 8:1 to 9:1, whilst the original 1½in SUs were replaced by 2in units. The result of these ministrations was a 15 per cent improvement in power, and slightly

Driving the V8-powered cars

Inserting the V8 in the Cloud/S-series gives the car a whole new colouring. At low speeds the car whispers along, the engine so inaudible you'd never divine its configuration. As a carriage for purring through town few vehicles could be more beguiling. But thump down on the accelerator and a refined bellow tells you this is most definitely a V8: as the car surges forward you realise what a dual nature the eight-pot Rolls-Royce – or Bentley – possesses. But don't imagine that the power unit is all grumbly star-spangled grunt when you let it loose. The engine is the other side of the V8 coin from big-displacement American units: silky smoothness is the dominant characteristic – we're talking later cars here – and accelerating up to 70–80mph is achieved without this serene power unit breaking sweat.

The automatic gearbox is largely in character: it shifts smoothly but not totally seamlessly, in a fashion that is delicately sporting rather than luxuriously languorous. The steering-column selector, with its large chrome detent knob, feels decidedly dated, though, and still has the reverse position doubling as the 'Park' function.

The V8 is at its most engaging in the Continentals. Sitting high in the supportive bucket seats of an S2 Flying Spur, the big old-fashioned wheel set low and quite close to you, you're already receiving discreetly sporting messages – amplified by the sweep of the dashboard as it curves round to blend with the door cappings, and by the evocatively pre-war set of white-on-black dials with their charming reverse-sweep needles.

You can forgive the bump-thump from the relatively crude suspension, and the squirming of the cross-ply tyres when worked hard; you can forgive, too, the slight vagueness of the low-geared power steering at the straight-ahead position – it is, after all, nicely weighted at all times, unlike that on the first series of Shadows. The gentlemanly disdain with which the Bentley sweeps past lesser transportation is reward enough, and is matched by braking fully in harmony: the pedal has a meatily firm action that immediately reassures, even if ultimate stopping does require a good lean.

With its exquisite coachbuilt feel – typified by such details as the beautiful hand-crafted window frames and the fine woodwork – the Continental offers bespoke sporting-tinged luxury motoring that is uniquely seductive. After enjoying say a Graber Alvis, where else could a lady or gentleman of taste – and means, let it be said – turn for his or her transportation?

Above: A 1965 Bentley S3 Flying Spur at speed. After the S3, the marque would go into a steep decline until the 1980s. (LAT) Right: The same Flying Spur from the rear. (LAT)

Opposite: The twin headlamps introduced on the Silver Cloud III/S3 appeared simultaneously for 1963 on the coachbuilt variants. This Flying Spur body on a Continental S3 chassis is by James Young. (Rolls-Royce/LAT)

Buying Hints

1. The six-cylinder engines are immensely durable and have been known to last for 300,000 miles (500,000km) although they will have been probably fitted with three sets of replacement pistons and bearings by this time! But as with the Mark VI/Wraith units, they do have a thirst for oil of around 200 miles miles per pint (600km/litre). Fortunately all models are fitted with an oil-pressure gauge and when the engine is hot the needle should be in the white area of the dial, sitting near the centre when the engine is revved. If it fails to reach this sector, it invariably means low oil pressure which can result in a broken connecting rod or worse. Blue exhaust smoke, meanwhile, indicates worn valve guides and seals.

2. Should the engine sound rather fluffy when running, the problem may be caused by the clearances of the side exhaust valves having closed up. They're rather inaccessible, but the correct gap is 0.012in (0.30mm). Another possibility is that the ignition may have been incorrectly adjusted. The distributor contains two sets of points to ensure reliable running at high speeds. It's also worth noting that the higher-compression 8:1 'sixes' are rather fussier performers than the earlier versions.

3. As far as the V8 engine is concerned, the post-1962 Silver Cloud III/S3 unit is a considerable improvement on the original. Having said that, both are extremely reliable and will exceed 100,000 miles (160,000km) without major overhaul. Noisy tappets, these being hydraulic units, will signify that the oil has not been changed at regular intervals and may be an indication that servicing was not undertaken as regularly as it might have been; replacing a full set of 16 tappets will not be cheap. As with the 'six', the V8 does consume oil, at the same rate of some 200 miles per pint.

4. Beware of coolant leaks at the heater matrix – especially on the V8 cars, where there are two matrices awkwardly positioned behind the offside front wheelarch, making replacement a time-consuming and thus costly exercise.

5. The automatic gearbox should not present any major problems, but during your test driving listen for slipping gear bands and a reluctance for the 'box to change up: sluggish or snatchy changes from second to third are a bad sign. If either shortcoming manifests itself, look elsewhere: repairs are expensive. The gearbox has a dipstick accessible from inside

the car, and after the oil level has settled following your test run, a check of the fluid is a good idea. A low level is a cause for concern, but the real giveaway of transmission trouble is dirty oil and a burnt or rancid smell, indicating that the internal bands are slipping.

6. Most of these cars are fitted with power steering. You can easily confirm whether this is the case by raising the bonnet and checking the number of drive belts on the engine. On cars with power steering, there should be three – two for the dynamo, one for the steering pump; otherwise there'll be a single belt, which indicates that the steering is unassisted. When you come to drive the car, check whether it feels extremely light or very heavy, both extremes suggesting that all is not well with the assistance system. Excessive play at the wheel could be wear or perishing of the 'double star' joint between the steering column and the steering box. Finally, fluid leaks at the ram and at the drop-arm seals towards the rear of the wheelarches are not unusual.

7. Like the Mark VI/Wraith, the independent front suspension on the SC1 is kept lubricated by a Bijur automatic lubrication system. It is necessary to top the reservoir

---

improved fuel consumption. In addition the crankshaft was nitride-hardened and the piston gudgeon pins enlarged and offset.

Inside the car the original bench-type front seat was replaced by individual ones although the earlier design remained available as an option. To increase rear legroom, an extra 2in (5cm) was found by the expedient of moving the rear cushion back by that amount and it was more upright in consequence.

The modest changes to the engine resulted in an increase in top speed to 117mph (188kph) and an improvement in 0–60mph (0–100kph) acceleration to the tune of 0.6 seconds. In consequence the final series of this Rolls-Royce and Bentley family is, unquestionably, the best.

Mechanically there was little difference between these models and the fast-diminishing Bentley Continental range, which by then was distinguished merely by narrower-

section tyres. Since 1962 the Continental had been bereft of its Mulliner two-door body, although the Flying Spur survived until the end. The Koren-styled drophead coupés now incorporated angled 'Chinese Eye' twin headlamps and the body style was extended to the Cloud III and also made available in fixed-head coupé form. But with just 312 examples of the S3 Continental sold, 119 fewer than with the S2, the Bentley was beginning to wither on Rolls-Royce's up every 5000 miles (8000km) but the chances are that the small bore pipes have become clogged. If this has occurred, it will be the most likely cause of wear in the front suspension. An easy way to detect this is to rock the car. If the suspension creaks you're in trouble. At the rear check for broken spring leaves, and inspect all the lever-arm dampers for leaks.

8. The servo-assisted hydro-mechanical brakes shouldn't present any major problems. A lack of response can be caused by a build-up of dust in the drums, and the wheel cylinders are prone to seize – which may indicate that the car has been laid up for some time. As with earlier cars, sluggishness and juddering of the brakes may be a servo problem, caused by the failure of the gearbox oil seal.

9. Unlike the coachbuilt Silver Wraith, the overwhelming majority of Silver Clouds/S-series Bentleys are fitted with standardised steel bodies – albeit with doors, bonnet and bootlid of aluminium. The steel parts are therefore susceptible to rust. Beginning with the front wings, the vulnerable areas are the arches, where you'll find within a bracing strut that must be properly secured, while the section directly adjoining the doors is

particularly prone to rust. Look for tell-tail bubbles or signs of body filler indicating past problems, not just at these points but also – at least on single-headlamp cars – around the sidelight pods. Moving further down the car, check the sills – including the vertical face of the inner sills – and the bottoms of the rear wings. Wings are often repaired by putting in new half-wings, up to the swage line, so watch for poor repairs at these points.

10. You really need to put the car on a ramp to examine the chassis, aided by an inspection lamp to scrutinise suspect areas. The box-section frame is particularly robust, but it is vulnerable to corrosion at its extremities. This usually begins around the battery box, which is located at rear of the offside chassis member, and can spread to its opposite number as well as creeping forwards. In truth you'd be well advised to closely examine the entire frame behind the central cruciform. Less commonly, the top of the chassis can rust where it sweeps over the rear axle. Finally, the body mounts can deteriorate: these constitute another important check point. A good starting point is to inspect the nearside front mount visible at the rear of the nearside front wheelarch.

11. Most Clouds and S-series cars are fitted with electric windows and whilst the front ones probably have plenty of use, the rear ones may not have have been similarly exercised. In consequence they can seize up, so check whether this is the case.

12. The rear overriders rot through at the bottom.

13. Again, beware of Bentleys disguised as Rolls-Royces. Winged 'B' motifs on the instruments are an obvious giveaway, as is a 'B' prefix on the vehicle identity plate. Remember that the number on the plate should tally with the number stamped on the chassis rail near the starter motor.

14. The convertibles command higher prices than the saloons; they suffer the same mechanical and coachwork problems. As for the Koren-styled Mulliner Park Ward Bentley Continentals, and SCIII Rolls-Royces, with their distinctive 'straight through' wing line, these suffer from a peculiar body corrosion problem. This is caused by the rear of the car being made of steel whilst the doors and front section is aluminium. The result can be severe bi-metallic corrosion where the two metals meet. You have been warned!

outwardly opulent vine.

When the entire range ceased production in 1966, a total of 14,913 cars – 7,548 Bentleys and 7,365 Rolls-Royces – had been completed. Of these, the Silver Cloud II was the most popular model of both lines, with 2,417 built. Customers had clearly indicated their approval of standardised, rather than bespoke, bodywork.

But these cars, despite latter-day improvements, were becoming increasingly dated in appearance and

mechanical specification.

Competitors, in particular Mercedes-Benz, had switched to unitary body construction, all-independent suspension, and disc brakes. Nearer to home the considerably cheaper Jaguar Mark X of 1961 boasted all these features and even the Morris 1100, which was Britain's most popular car, was fitted with front discs.

Although Rolls-Royce was still a profitable company, the £6.9 million

surplus it achieved in 1965 came exclusively from aero-engine sales. That year the loss making Motor Car Division suffered a record £919,000 deficit, which was mostly caused by the cost of introducing the Cloud/S-series replacement. Announced in October 1965, it was eagerly awaited by potential customers, motoring pundits, and – one assumes – company shareholders. For Crewe the Silver Shadow had not come a moment too soon.

The Phantom IV, Phantom V *and Phantom* VI

In the early post-war years Crewe was preoccupied with the development of its medium-sized Bentley and Rolls-Royce models and although it could have revived the pre-war Phantom line it chose not to do so. The feeling amongst the Motor Car Division's senior management was that such a model would have been out of keeping with the political climate espoused by the Labour government of the day and the austerity being experienced at that time by the British public.

However, external factors, not least the enthusiasm of the Duke of Edinburgh, husband of the future Queen, resulted in the concept being reactivated in 1950. Even then the resulting low-volume Phantom IV was only available to royalty and heads of state, the general public not being able to buy such a large, formal Rolls-Royce until the arrival of the Phantom V in 1959. Its Phantom VI successor of 1968 proved to be the last of the line

Limited edition: Princess Elizabeth's 1950 Phantom IV limousine by H. J. Mulliner, and the first of the line. A second spare wheel was carried on the nearside. (LAT)

and the final example, seemingly a relic of a lost age, was completed in 1992.

As already recounted, the Phantom III had ceased production in 1939 but plans were put in hand to maintain its top-drawer bloodline even if experimental department head William Robotham has since confirmed that the corporate motivation was for prestige rather than profit. Happy days!

The PIII's planned replacement in the Rationalised Range of cars was to be named the Silver Phantom and was

A Royal exception

The first Phantom IV of 1950, built for Princess Elizabeth and the Duke of Edinburgh, bears a unique mascot. In place of the customary Spirit of Ecstasy, it has a silver statuette of St George and the Dragon. When this was first suggested to Rolls-Royce, it feared that the proposed design might break in use. This corporate apprehension was confirmed by testing the figure on a bump rig and it was accordingly reworked so that the dragon's head and tongue, together with the Saint's lance, provided support for the mass of horse and rider.

to be based on a chassis with a wheelbase of 12ft 1in (3.68m), a significant 6in (15cm) greater than the Silver Wraith's frame.

The Phantom IIII had been powered by a complex V12 engine and there was no question of pursuing that particular route. It will be recalled that when the rationalised B-series engine family had been conceived in 1938, there was an eight-cylinder version with the B80 designation.

An experimental car was duly designed to accommodate this 5.6-litre power unit and it was completed in 1939. Officially known as 30-G-VII but informally as Big Bertha, the 12ft 1in chassis was fitted with a commodious Park Ward limousine body and it duly lapped Brooklands at a respectable 91mph (146kph). During a subsequent Continental trip it acquired the name Bertha which was later evolved into Big Bertha.

Run throughout the war, its body was at some stage removed and replaced with bus coachwork. By the end of hostilities it had covered some 160,000 miles (260,000km), thus underlining the reliability of the straight-eight engine. Having been re-engined, Bertha went on to cover no less than 289,000 miles (465,000km) in all before being scrapped in 1953.

Although Big Bertha was the first of five experimental straight-eights, the aforementioned 'Scalded Cat', a Bentley version using the standard

Queen Elizabeth's second Phantom IV, the Hooper-bodied landaulette of 1954, can still be seen in the Royal Mews at Buckingham Palace. The blue light above the windscreen indicates royal ownership. (LAT)

Mark V chassis, was even more exciting. Able to exceed 100mph (160kph), this 1939 car was the following year dispatched to Canada, along with another Rolls-Royce version, for safe keeping during the war. Both were returned to Britain in 1944.

Initially run by William Robotham, it was subsequently loaned to a number of VIPs, including the motoring pioneer Lord Brabazon of Tara and Air Marshal Alec Coryton. Even more significantly, it was also driven by Prince Philip, the Duke of Edinburgh, who clearly relished the Cat's sparkling performance and only reluctantly returned it to Rolls-Royce.

But the company did not wish to reactivate its large car line in a Britain where wartime rationing still endured, even though the Silver Wraith's 10ft 7in (3.23m) chassis was not large enough to accommodate formal limousine coachwork. All the same, Robotham and chief designer Ivan Evernden continued quietly to pursue the idea, to the extent of having a second experimental 'Scalded Cat' built in 1948.

Despite considerable interest also

A 1961 Phantom V with Park Ward's customary Seven-Passenger limousine coachwork. In 1962 *The Motor* attained 101.2mph (162kph) over the flying mile in this car. (LAT)

The Phantom V's driving compartment. The dashboard was similar to that used on its Silver Cloud contemporary, with the loudspeaker for the HMV Radiomobile set directly below the instruments. (LAT)

being shown by potential foreign customers, with the Spanish dictator, General Franco, placing an order in 1948, Frederick Llewellyn Smith, general manager of the Motor Car Division, would not sanction the project and his decision was backed by chief engineer designate Harry Grylls.

However, in 1947 the Duke of Edinburgh had married Princess Elizabeth, and she would one day become Queen. At this time the royal family had a long-term commitment to Daimler and the Royal Mews had, in that very year, taken delivery of two Hooper-bodied Daimler Straight-Eight landaulettes. A third followed in 1949.

But the Duke was all too ready to disregard past protocol and he made a formal request to Rolls-Royce for a state car based on the experimental straight-eight he had so enjoyed driving, even though it was not a catalogued model. It was clearly a request that Crewe could not afford to ignore.

So the Duke of Edinburgh's will

Phantom IV
1950–1956

ENGINE:
Eight cylinders in line, iron block, alloy head

Bore x stroke	88.8mm x 114mm
Capacity	5,675cc
Valve actuation	Inlet-pushrod, exhaust-side
Compression ratio	6.4:1
Carburettors	Stromberg
Power	164bhp at 3,750rpm

TRANSMISSION:
Rear-wheel drive
Four-speed, with synchromesh on second, third and top gears
Automatic with fluid coupling from 1954
Final drive ratio: 4.25:1

SUSPENSION:
Front: Independent, wishbone and coil spring
Rear: Live axle with half-elliptic springs

STEERING:
Cam and roller
Turns lock-to-lock: 3.5

BRAKES:
Front: hydraulic drum
Rear: mechanical drum
Mechanical servo assistance

WHEELS/TYRES:
Steel disc wheels
7 x 17in

BODYWORK:
Coachbuilt: aluminum panels on wooden or alloy frame. Separate chassis frame.
Limousine, saloon, sedanca de ville, drophead coupé, landaulette, cabriolet

DIMENSIONS:

Length	18ft 11in (5.76m)
Wheelbase	12ft 1in (3.68m)
Track – front	4ft 10½in (1.48m)
– rear	5ft 3in (1.60m)
Width	6ft 5in (1.95m)
Height	6ft 2in (1.88m)

Data refers to 1950 H. J. Mulliner limousine for HRH Princess Elizabeth

WEIGHT:
Chassis 29.4 cwt (1,496kg)

PERFORMANCE:
Not road tested by any motoring magazine
Max speed (approx) 100mph (160kph)

PRICE INCLUDING TAX WHEN NEW:
Not publicised; only available to royalty and heads of state

NUMBER BUILT:
18 including Park Ward pick-up retained by the works

Phantom V
1959–1968

ENGINE:
V8 alloy block, alloy heads

Bore x stroke	104.4mm x 91.44mm
Capacity	6,230 cc
Valve actuation	Pushrod
Compression ratio	8:1
Carburettors	Twin SU HD6
Power	Not disclosed

TRANSMISSION:
Rear-wheel drive
Four-speed, automatic with fluid coupling
Final drive ratio: 3.89:1

SUSPENSION:
Front: Independent, wishbone and coil spring
Rear: Live axle with half-elliptic springs

STEERING:
Power-assisted cam-and-roller

BRAKES:
Front: hydraulic drum
Rear: mechanical drum
Mechanical servo assistance

WHEELS/TYRES:
Steel disc wheels
8.90 x 15in

BODYWORK:
Coachbuilt, aluminium panels on steel frame. Separate chassis frame.
Four-door limousine, landaulette

DIMENSIONS:

Length	19ft 10in (6.04m)
Wheelbase	12ft 1½ in (3.69m)
Track – front	5ft 1¼ in (1.55m)
– rear	5ft 4in (1.62m)
Width	6ft 7in (2.00m)
Height	5ft 9in (1.75m)

WEIGHT:
54.8cwt (2,781 kg)

PERFORMANCE:
(Source: *The Motor*)

Max speed	101.2mph (162kph)
0–50mph (0–80kph)	9.7sec
0–60mph (0–100kph)	13.8sec
0–70mph (0–112kph)	19.3sec

PRICE INCLUDING TAX WHEN NEW: £9,694

NUMBER BUILT: 516

Phantom VI
1968–1992

As Phantom V, except from October 1978:

ENGINE:
V8 alloy block, alloy heads

Bore x stroke	104.1mm x 99.1mm
Capacity	6,750cc
Valve actuation	Pushrod
Compression ratio	8:1
Carburettor	Twin SU H1F7
Power	Not disclosed

TRANSMISSION:
Three-speed automatic with torque converter

BRAKES:
Dual-circuit powered braking system to existing drums

WHEELS:
Steel disc wheels
8.90 x 15in

WEIGHT:
53.5cwt (2,721kg)

PRICE INCLUDING PURCHASE TAX WHEN NEW:
£12,843 (1968) to £25,916 (1975). To special order from 1976, price on request

NUMBER BUILT:
374

---

prevailed and the order was duly placed with London-based Rolls-Royce retailer The Car Mart. The royal connections of its managing director, Colonel Ronald Maude, reached back to the twenties when he had supplied the Princess's father, the Duke of York, with a succession of Bean cars.

The outcome was the arrival, in 1950, of what was to prove to be the first Phantom IV, the car being delivered to the royal couple in July of that year. Although it was a rather more docile vehicle than the agile 'Scalded Cat', even so it can be assumed that if pressed this was a 100mph (160kph) car.

Delivered to H. J. Mulliner in July 1949, at a time when Hooper was the preferred royal coachbuilder, the chassis had Big Bertha's 12ft 1in wheelbase rather than Scalded Cat's shorter frame. The massive green limousine coachwork, over 6ft (1.83m) tall, endowed the car with an overall length approaching 19ft (5.79m).

The V's commodious interior with one occasional seat opened. The front seats were upholstered in leather and the rear ones in West of England cloth. The carpeting was, of course, by Wilton and electric windows and a travelling rug were available at extra cost. (LAT)

The cocktail cabinet opened. A nice touch was the felt pad designed to hold the glasses in place when the car was in motion. (LAT)

The elegant coachwork with its large windows and well-lit interior was specifically designed for state occasions and permitted the occupants to be clearly seen by the public and for the royal couple to return the compliment. This was aided by the fitment of a transparent roof panel in the rear that could be obscured by a motor-driven blind. A strip light also supplemented the four interior lamps.

The driver's seat was tailored to accommodate the Duke of Edinburgh's lanky frame, should he wish to take the wheel, and there was the usual electrically-operated interior division. Controls for the heating system – there being no fewer than three heaters – and for the division, electric windows and blinds were positioned within the outer armrests in the rear compartment.

The use on this first Phantom of separate headlamps further added to its rather dated though nonetheless dignified appearance. One reflector was designed to be extinguished and the other to dip, in the old-fashioned dip-and-switch manner, but there was a changeover switch so that if the Phantom were being driven abroad its lighting could be tailored to the rules of that country. Externally, there could be little doubt of this car's ownership because there was a roof-mounted blue police identification light with a socket behind for a flag or a plaque bearing the royal coat of arms.

Powered by essentially the same 5,675cc straight-eight engine used in the 'Scalded Cat', as a rationalised unit it shared its 88mm x 114mm dimensions and IoE configuration with the six-cylinder Rolls-Royce and Bentley engines although an outward difference was the fitment of separate four-cylinder exhaust manifolds; the crankshaft, meanwhile, ran in nine bearings. Breathing through a single downdraft Stromberg carburettor, the B80 produced a publicly-declared 164bhp at 3,750rpm.

The Phantom IV's chassis, in essence, followed that of the six-cylinder cars, with a central cruciform and coil-and-wishbone independent front suspension. Brakes were

The 'missing' Phantom IV

As is well known, 18 Phantom IV chassis were produced but only 17 cars were completed. Whatever happened to the missing one? With such a project it was important that the company undertook development work and a certain amount was carried out on the first chassis, 4-AF-2, that was delivered to Princess Elizabeth in 1950. This testing was continued and extended on the second chassis, number 4-AF-4, which was fitted with a smart truck body by Park Ward. Subsequently powered by an enlarged 6.5-litre engine with automatic transmission, it was operated by Crewe's Transport Department, and was ideal for the swift movement of light loads. Its 90mph (150kph) top speed meant that a number of Rolls-Royce drivers were booked for exceeding the speed limit, which was then pegged at 30mph (50kph) for commercial vehicles. Unfortunately 4-AF-4 was dismantled in January 1964 after it had covered a considerable mileage.

James Young was also responsible for this Phantom V Touring Limousine, the Bromley company having adopted a Hooper-style rear quarterlight from the 1966 season. (Rolls-Royce/LAT)

A Phantom V sedanca de ville by James Young completed in 1960. The electrically operated partition has been lowered. (Rolls-Royce/LAT)

similarly of the hydro-mechanical type, aided by Rolls-Royce's trusted gearbox-driven servo.

When *The Autocar* exclusively revealed details of this car in its 7 July 1950 issue, it concluded its account thus: "it is possible to hope that Rolls-Royce may be encouraged to embark on the production of further examples of this superb chassis. It must be said, however, that no other orders are being accepted".

This chimed with company policy of the day although in the event Rolls-Royce relented; all the same, it maintained the Phantom IV's low-key profile and only accepted orders from heads of state and other members of the British royal family. Between February 1951 and October 1956, a further 17 Phantom IVs were completed, including one with a pick-up body which was retained by the company for test purposes (see box). Of these 17 cars, no fewer than 13 were sold abroad.

The next Phantom IV to be completed went to the Shah of Persia and represented a supreme exercise in self-indulgence in that, as an H. J. Mulliner cabriolet, it was only fitted

with two doors, despite its huge 12ft 1in wheelbase. As for the Shah's near neighbour, the ruler of Kuwait, he took delivery, in July 1951, of a Mulliner saloon, the first of no fewer than four Phantom IVs he was to own. The same month Rolls-Royce's chairman Lord Hives began using a Hooper-bodied limousine although this car was subsequently bought by the Duchess of Kent. The Duke of Gloucester's Phantom IV was by the same coachbuilder even if his car outwardly resembled Princess Elizabeth's Mulliner-bodied vehicle.

Of the four Phantom IVs delivered in 1952, no fewer than three went to the Spanish dictator, General Franco, a mere four years after he had placed his order! Prudently, the Mulliner-bodied cars – two limousines and a cabriolet – had armour-plated rear compartments.

Arguably the finest of the Phantom IVs was the Aga Khan's magnificent Hooper-bodied sedanca de ville. Oil-rich Middle Eastern potentates did indeed have a taste for this most

Fantastic Phantom – the Frua convertible

At 24ft (6.43m) from bumper to bumper it must be one of the longest Rolls-Royces ever made. The car is based on a 1982 Phantom VI chassis bought from Jack Barclay Ltd by property developer Buchanan Michaelson, who commissioned David Ogle to design a body for it, to be built in Italy by Frua. But soon after its arrival there he passed it on to the noted American Rolls-Royce collector James Leake, who worked with Frua for some four years on the design of a new body, which it still retains.

Partially completed, it was returned to England as a bare metal shell and stored in London, before being acquired by a UK-domiciled Swedish enthusiast who commissioned classic car specialist David Royle of Staindrop, County Durham, to complete the project. Beginning late in 1989, the work took three years, and Royle Cars took a stand on the owner's behalf at the 1993 Geneva Motor Show in the hope that the Phantom would attract bids of around £2.1 million. But with the recession still biting, it failed to sell and subsequently passed through the hands of Rolls-Royce and Bentley specialists Frank Dale and Stepsons.

Intended for state occasions, hence the removable flag posts, and being 7ft (2.13m) wide, it can comfortably accommodate seven occupants. Ingeniously the body can take on no fewer than five configurations. The hood and front targa top in place result in an apparently conventional limousine but when the rear hood is lowered the Rolls-Royce becomes a state landaulette. Remove the targa front and the Phantom takes on the role of a sedanca de ville; dispense with both the targa front and the hood and you have a state cabriolet. Finally, an open tourer can be created by lowering the side windows, central division and centre door pillars...

The Frua Phantom VI in state landaulette mode. (LAT)

With targa top, hood and division in place, the Frua Phantom appeared outwardly a limousine . (LAT)

Royle Cars was responsible for this magnificent interior. The fine walnut veneers were imported from America and incorporated floral marquetry made in Sweden. A television and cocktail cabinet were obligatory fitments and the Wilton carpets, replete with the Rolls-Royce monogram, were specially woven. (LAT)

The Phantom VI, introduced for the 1969 season, was outwardly almost identical to the Phantom V although the bonnet was slightly shorter. (Rolls-Royce)

The Phantom VI's dashboard was new, and related to that of the Silver Shadow introduced in 1965. (LAT)

exclusive of Rolls-Royces, their reputed 10mpg (28 litres/100km) thirst clearly being of little concern. The next chassis went, in May 1952, to Prince Talal of Saudi Arabia and his was the only Phantom IV not to be bodied by an English coachbuilder, it being graced with an all-weather convertible body by Franay of Paris. Ingeniously, the individual seat squabs, apart from the driver's, were designed to move forward and swivel to aid exit from the car. The hydraulic plumbing necessary to effect this action was, reportedly, a nightmare. This was the last of the so-called A-series chassis, the B-series taking over before giving way to the C-series designation for the last three cars built in 1955–56.

Moving on to 1953, that year King Faisal of Iraq took delivery of a Hooper limousine whilst his son, the Prince Regent, had a similar offering. Also in 1953 HRH Princess Elizabeth became HM Queen Elizabeth II, and her 1950 Phantom IV was uprated as a state car and repainted in the royal colours of claret and black. In May of 1953 she bought her second Phantom IV although this time the coachwork was, as tradition demanded, by Hooper; a landaulette body was chosen because of its folding rear roof. The car differed from its predecessors in being fitted with the four-speed Hydra-Matic gearbox. This was thereafter standardised, and the auto 'box was retro-fitted to the Queen's original Phantom IV and to the Duke of Kent's car.

In the longer term the Queen's purchase was a clear endorsement of Rolls-Royce as the preferred royal marque; the Daimler landaulette ordered by her father in 1949 was destined to be the last of the line. In 1954 it was taken over by HM Queen Elizabeth the Queen Mother.

The ruler of Kuwait was clearly pleased with his H. J. Mulliner saloon because he ordered a further three Phantoms, all bodied, like his 1951 example, by the same coachbuilder. They were a limousine and a pair of four-light and six-light saloons. The completion, in October 1956, of a Hooper limousine as the Shah of Persia's second Phantom IV marked the end of the line; it bore a strong similarity to King Faisal's cars of 1954.

There was to be a three-year hiatus between the delivery of the Shah's car and the announcement, in September

Above: The substantial Phantom VI boot contained the second air-conditioning unit for the rear passengers. (LAT)

Below: A 1973 Phantom VI landaulette by Mulliner Park Ward. Ordered by a lady owner at a cost of £33,000, she hired a chauffeur, took it to Cannes for the season, and then sold it with just 3,000 miles (4,827km) on the clock. (LAT)

The interior of the same landaulette, with the walnut veneer TV cabinet on the left. Instead of being upholstered in leather, unusually the seats were finished in Dralon. The controls in the rear armrests are for the heater and air conditioning. (LAT)

1959, of its Phantom V successor. Work had begun late in 1957 when two experimental chassis, bearing Park Ward and Hooper limousine coachwork, were tested at home and on the roads of the Continent.

The first production car, a James Young limousine, was displayed at the 1959 Paris Motor Show. Unlike the Phantom IV, it was available to the general public and in this sense it became the first new Phantom to be listed for 20 years. Powered by the 6.2-litre V8 engine simultaneously introduced in the Silver Cloud II and Bentley S2, it had the same 12ft 1in wheelbase as its predecessor although the new Cloud-related frame possessed rather more rear overhang.

This, coupled with an engine considerably shorter than the intrusive straight-eight, meant that it could accommodate the generous rear passenger compartment and large boot that had not been feasible on the Phantom IV. To cope with this necessarily heavy coachwork, an additional box-section crossmember was introduced behind the central cruciform that also housed the bearing for the two-piece propshaft.

The mechanicals also bore a close resemblance to those of the Silver

Cloud II although the pressed-steel front suspension wishbones were replaced by stronger forged items and the Bijur chassis lubrication system was discontinued. Power steering also followed precedent and the servo-assisted hydro-mechanical drum brakes were essentially the same. Air-conditioning was an optional extra at a cost of £275.

Available as a chassis at £3,130, the Phantom V was offered with a standard bespoke body in the form of a capacious Park Ward limousine which retailed at £8,904 – over £3,000 more than the long-wheelbase Silver Cloud II saloon. Two occasional seats were available in the rear compartment, which also contained a cocktail cabinet, the dashboard and door fittings were in figured French walnut, and upholstery was either leather or West of England cloth.

In all, 60 per cent of Phantom Vs were to be bodied by what became in-house Mulliner Park Ward, although of this 307 total, 156 predated the 1961 merger of the two businesses. By contrast, H. J. Mulliner built just nine bodies: eight limousines and one saloon.

Park Ward's design 980, the work of John Blatchley, was in fact to survive, with modifications, for the next 33 years, it being carried through to the subsequent Phantom VI. The only significant outward change of the Phantom V era was the arrival, in October 1962, of twin headlamps, as on the Silver Cloud III and S3 Bentley.

However, the vote for the most supremely elegant coachwork on the Phantom V goes to James Young, whose graceful limousine was a fine tribute to the talents of its designer Albert McNeil. This coachwork received its just reward, as Young's output of Phantom Vs was second only to Mulliner, Park Ward, the Bromley company being responsible for 196 bodies. The balance came from Hooper, which closed its doors at the end of 1959 after bodying one chassis for its valedictory stand at that year's London Motor Show.

Three chassis were allocated to Henri Chapron in Paris, but only two were delivered, one being bodied to a Hooper design ordered after that company had ceased its coachbuilding activities. Woodall Nicholson, meanwhile, was responsible for the single Phantom V hearse.

The overwhelming majority of bodies were limousines although James Young produced ten sedanca de villes. There were also nine open Phantom Vs, of which six were Rolls-Royce's Park Ward State Landaulette, announced in October 1965. This featured an hydraulically-operated folding roof whilst the rear seat could be electrically activated to raise it some 3½ in (9cm) higher than the norm.

Measuring 19ft 10in (6.05m) bumper-to-bumper and turning the scales at 2¾ tons (2,794kg), the new Phantom was a natural choice for heads of state and in February 1960 the Queen added a Phantom V to her two Phantom IVs. Based on the familiar 980 design, it was higher than the usual limousine and had a perspex rear section to the roof that was a development of the transparent

The Phantom VI presented to Queen Elizabeth in 1978 had a lofty body of Edwardian proportions. It differed mechanically in being fitted with the 6.7-litre V8 introduced to the Silver Shadow in 1970, and a three-speed transmission. (LAT)

The driving compartment of the car opposite. In outline the Phantom VI's instrument panel had changed little since its arrival in 1968 but it had been extended to include a central console. (LAT)

panel introduced on the 1950 car and could be concealed by a folding aluminium cover stored in the boot when not in use. Produced under the Canberra II coding, the car was perversely followed in February 1961 by Canberra I, which was modified to permit it to be loaded aboard the royal yacht 'Britannia'.

Queen Elizabeth the Queen Mother, meanwhile, preferred the more traditional landaulette and her Phantom V, delivered in February 1962, was one of the last bodies produced by Park Ward before its merger with H. J. Mulliner.

Other distinguished customers were King Hassan of Morocco and the presidents of Portugal, Singapore and Pakistan. The car was also a firm favourite with the diplomatic service and Phantom Vs were to be found at British embassies as diverse as those of Moscow, Caracas and The Hague.

Such customers were unlikely to be interested in out-and-out performance. But they would doubtless have been reassured to know that a Phantom V could attain 101.2mph (162.8kph), reach 60mph (100kph) in 13.8 seconds, and return 12.7mpg (22 litres/100km) – these figures being obtained by The Motor in its 1962 road test.

The magazine could only enthuse about the quality of "the mobile drawing room", with it scoring strongly on the three counts of "ventilation, warmth and silence" deemed the three prerequisites of first-class travel. On the debit side were a non-adjustable front passenger seat, a 48ft (14.60m) turning circle and drum brakes that still relied on a mechanical servo rather than discs assisted by a vacuum servo. The testers also mourned the passing of the smooth manual Rolls-Royce gearbox, which had been replaced by the sometimes

jerky fluid-flywheel-driven automatic.

By the time that the last Phantom V, a Mulliner, Park Ward limousine, was delivered in June 1968 to the government of Malawi, formerly the British protectorate of Nyasaland, a total of 516 had been completed. This was considerable endorsement of the concept, and the Phantom V was destined to be the most popular member of Rolls-Royce's post-war large car family.

Its Phantom VI successor unveiled in October 1968 was, in essence, a V by another name; a price of £12,843 made it arguably the most expensive catalogued car in the world. Interestingly the chassis cards relating to the first few examples refer to them as 'Phantom V', which indicates that the change of name was essentially cosmetic and very much a last minute decision. This is further underlined by the fact that a Phantom V was displayed on Rolls-Royce's 1968 Motor Show stand which was held in the same month as its successor was announced!

As the Cloud/S-series line had been replaced in 1965 by the unitary-construction Silver Shadow, what was to prove to be the ultimate expression of the Phantom line was also the last

Rolls-Royce motor car to feature a separate chassis frame.

The Mulliner Park Ward Seven-Passenger Enclosed Limousine, as it was officially called, outwardly closely resembled the Phantom V, apart from a slightly shorter bonnet to permit the introduction of the air intake for the air conditioning unit. Mechanically as its predecessor, the Phantom VI retained the drum brakes and attendant mechanical servo that had disappeared from the mainstream models when the last of the Silver Cloud III and S3 Bentleys had ceased production in 1966. The V8 engine did, however, benefit from the redesigned cylinder heads introduced on the Silver Shadow three years before.

The limousine now had the virtue of offering full air-conditioning in both the front and rear compartments, each with independent controls. The forward unit was similar to that used on the Silver Shadow, as was the redesigned dashboard, whilst the rear compartment was serviced by a separate unit in the boot. Rear passengers sat on a seat upholstered in a new twill-type material although leather was retained for the front seats.

The overwhelming majority of Phantom VIs were limousines, but

there was a handful of State Landaulettes and at least one convertible version was produced. The Italian Frua concern also took delivery of two left-hand-drive Phantom VI chassis, of which one was extravagantly fitted with a drophead coupé body.

The Phantom VI was now the responsibility of Mulliner Park Ward but unlike its two-door Corniche and Camargue contemporaries also produced at MPW's North London premises, the big, slow-selling Phantom was invariably the last to receive any across-the-range mechanical updates. The exception was when legislative changes were involved, and in 1972 the model was brought into line with American safety regulations so that it could continue to be sold in the United States.

But demand for what was to prove to be the last of the Phantom line was slowing dramatically. Production had been running at around 30 cars a year between 1968 and 1972, during which time 132 examples were produced. The nine years of the so-called 'safety' specification Phantoms of the 1972–80 era saw numbers drop dramatically and from 1976 the car

was only available to special order. The inflationary climate of the seventies had seen the limousine more than double in price, from £13,123 in 1968 to £25,916 in May 1975, which was itself some £5,800 more than the previous year's listing.

The model had been production for ten years before any major modifications were made to its mechanical specifications and the resulting 'GM400 Package' was first applied to a car presented in March 1978 to the Queen. It had been commissioned in 1976 by the Society of Motor Manufacturers and Traders as the motor industry's gift to celebrate her silver jubilee; it was some 4in (10cm) higher than the norm and had the by-now well-established perspex rear roof section.

The most significant change heralded by the royal car was the replacement of the 6.2-litre V8 with the 6.7-litre unit used in the Silver Shadow since July 1970. As the factory designation suggests, at the same time the old-style four-speed Hydra-Matic gearbox, which had been discontinued on the Shadow in 1968, was replaced by the more modern three-speed GM400 Turbo Hydramatic. This meant the end of

A left-hand-drive Phantom VI landaulette for a Swiss customer. (LAT)

the long-running mechanical servo and its replacement by the Shadow's high-pressure dual-circuit hydraulic system – although the archaic drum brakes were retained.

This royal Phantom VI was the first of 34 cars that were built up until 1980 when the model was incorporated into the Silver Spirit's VIN (Vehicle Identification Number) series. A mere 33 Phantoms were built thereafter, which is the equivalent of about three cars being delivered each year. Unsurprisingly, when fuel injection arrived for the 1987 season, it was not extended to the Phantom which retained its carburettors.

The model was not destined to survive the recession-hit early nineties, and accordingly the last Phantom VI was completed in January 1992 for that great Rolls-Royce collector, the Sultan of Brunei; the chassis, tellingly, dated from 1990. This made a total of 374 cars built in 23 years. A line that was almost as old as the company, and that had begun with the Silver Ghost in 1906, was no more.

The
Coachbuilt cars

For the first 50 or so years of its existence, Rolls-Royce's fortunes were inexorably linked to the coachbuilders who complemented its chassis with coachwork of an elegance and quality that justifiably became world-famous. But as will have been apparent, the company's decision in 1944 to switch to Pressed Steel shells spelt, in the longer term, the end for the bespoke body and thus of the already ailing British coachbuilding tradition.

In terms of sheer volume, it was a decline that had begun in the mid-twenties. This was at a time when all cars were fitted with coachbuilt bodies, that is to say they were based on a wooden framework – usually of ash, although spruce was used on cheaper models – that was then skilfully clad with hand-formed panels of steel, at the lower end of the market, or aluminium on more expensive makes.

But the arrival of machine-made mass-produced pressings from the late 1920s onwards spelt the effective end of the hand-crafted, bespoke body, although its presence was maintained in the upper reaches of the market, as exemplified by the

A contemporary photograph of Park Ward's fixed-head coupé body on the Bentley Mark VI chassis, introduced at the 1950 motor show. Subsequently extended to the R-type, it was also available on the Rolls-Royce Silver Dawn until 1955. (Rolls-Royce)

Coachbuilt bodies were, by the nature of their construction, hand-crafted. This wooden frame being created for a Rolls-Royce dates from the 1920s. By the post-war years the wood had almost invariably been replaced by steel or aluminium alloy. (Rolls-Royce)

The customer is always right! Hooper was responsible for this unconventional 1947 two-tone bronze Silver Wraith for Nubar Gulbenkian. The front wings were wide enough to permit the wheels to turn and the rear roof panel was retractable. (LAT)

Rolls-Royce and Bentley makes.

In 1926 no fewer than 63 coachbuilders displayed their elegant wares at London's motor show, but by 1938 that figure had dropped by over half to a mere 25 businesses. This was the year in which Rolls-Royce introduced the Wraith, its last model to be appear before the outbreak of the Second World War. The Wraith's chassis were variously bodied by a total of 17 British coachbuilders and of these the most significant were

Park Ward, which headed the field with 170 cars, followed by Hooper (72), H. J. Mulliner (62) and Thrupp & Maberly (42).

All of these companies survived the war, although Thrupp & Maberly discontinued its bespoke coachbuilding activities to concentrate on so-called 'special bodies' for its Rootes parent. As will emerge, its place was very effectively filled by James Young, which did not close its coachbuilding department

until 1967, much later than its contemporaries.

By the time that the Silver Wraith was discontinued, its chassis had received some 20 different British bodies in a league table headed by H. J. Mulliner with 518 cars and Park Ward in second place with 480, followed by Hooper (469), James Young (217) and Freestone & Webb (120).

Of these five businesses, all, with the exception of Freestone & Webb,

Freestone & Webb's 1953 Silver Wraith Saloon Limousine, design number 3092. (Author's collection)

were owned by corporate parents, with Hooper being allied to BSA and thus Daimler, James Young to Rolls-Royce and Bentley distributor Jack Barclay, whilst John Croall was a similar Edinburgh-based business and the proprietor, until 1959, of the H. J. Mulliner company.

All of these coachbuilders, bar two, had graduated to motor cars after many years of producing horse-drawn carriages and Hooper stood at the apex of this world. Established in 1807 as Adams and Hooper in London's Haymarket, Hooper (Coachbuilders) Ltd dates from March 1896, the year which effectively marks the birth of the British motor industry. Prestigious showrooms were established at 54 St James's Street, in the heart of clubland, and a works was opened at 77 King's Road, Chelsea, this being enlarged in 1911 and remaining in use until 1947.

Hooper built its first Rolls-Royce body in 1908, the same year in which

a second factory was occupied at The Ring, Blackfriars Road. Hooper and Rolls-Royce were natural allies in pre-First World War days, although at that time Barker was the Derby company's preferred coachbuilder. For most of the inter-war years Hooper operated under the chairmanship of Lieut-Col E. W. Hamilton and demand for its bodies remained strong. Whilst other companies experienced the chill wind of a changing world in the following decade, in 1933 this Rolls-Royce of coachbuilders built a third works at Western Avenue, Acton, which was the largest facility of its type in London. With Hooper's purchase, in 1938, of Barker, its one-time rival, it had no fewer than four factories, with additional premises at Elveden Road, Willesden, used until 1959, and another in Dukes Road, Acton.

Whilst Hooper was responsible for bodying many Rolls-Royce chassis, it was more closely associated with Daimler and its lofty, magnificently executed Daimler limousines were essential wear for the British royal family. It was in 1940, and maybe prompted by Rolls-Royce's purchase of Park Ward, that Hooper was

acquired by BSA, Daimler's parent company.

This did not prevent it from continuing to body Rolls-Royce chassis, with its coachwork being designed by Hooper's outstanding stylist Osmond Rivers, who had joined the company in 1911, and became its managing director in the post-war years. He continued to weave his magic on Rolls-Royce's behalf, but his most extravagant works were reserved for the famous Docker Daimlers of the 1951–55 period.

Hooper moved with the times, and in 1950 Rivers introduced extruded alloy frames, but as the decade progressed the company became all too aware that its orders from Rolls-Royce were dropping dramatically, from 40 bodies delivered in 1956, to 26 in the following year, to just 19 in 1958. In January 1959, a year which would yield just 14 sales to Rolls-Royce, Hooper was confidentially informed that the successor to the Silver Cloud/S-series would employ unitary construction.

At one point Hooper contemplated taking over its great rival, H. J. Mulliner, but it could not afford

The Silver Dawn drophead coupé, as
produced by Park Ward between 1950
and 1954. (Rolls-Royce)

the proffered price. HJM, for its part,
was in a similar predicament but, as
will emerge, the lines of
communication it enjoyed with Rolls-
Royce were far stronger. Hooper
suffered in this regard by being
corporately allied to Daimler, the
long-time if now tarnished rival to
'The Best Car in the World'.

The logjam was broken by Mulliner

approaching Rolls-Royce to ask it to
take the business over; this it duly
did, early in July 1959. For its part,
Hooper built its last bodies in
October and formally closed its doors
in November. The Park Royal factory
was vacated on 31 December, but in
1960 a service and repair service was
opened at Kilburn for those cars fitted
with Hooper coachwork.

This Park Ward drophead coupé body,
design 555, on a Silver Dawn chassis,
was finished in pale ivory with green
hood and matching upholstery. It was
bought by Mrs H. Lenaghan and
displayed on the company's stand at
the 1953 motor show. (LAT)

Silver Dawn hatchback: this 1954 car was converted to Harold Radford Countryman specification, combining the carrying capacity of an estate car with the comfort of an elaborately-equipped saloon. The folded dust flap could be extended to form a picnic table. (LAT)

From 1946 until mid-1947, when the government closed the loophole, what were known as utility cars, or shooting brakes, were exempt from purchase tax because they were classed as commercial vehicles. However, the style persisted; this Silver Wraith by Freestone & Webb was delivered in September 1950 to F. C. Tetley. (Author's collection)

After 154 years Hooper was no more. But Rolls-Royce already owned Park Ward and its 1959 acquisition of Mulliner led, in 1961, to the creation of a company styled as 'H. J. Mulliner, Park Ward Ltd', located at Park Ward's Willesden works.

It had been in 1919 that William MacDonald Park and Charles Ward, who had both been employed at the North London depot of the French Sizaire-Berwick company, opened their coachbuilding company at 473 High Road, Willesden. The premises had previously been the by-then-redundant stables of the London General Omnibus Company. Park was the coachbuilder, having worked for Argyll and Lacre, but Charlie Ward was

a mechanical engineer and he became managing director. He had graduated from the Regent Street Polytechnic and trained with the South Metropolitan Gas Company and Fiat Motors, before becoming works manager at Sizaire-Berwick.

Park Ward & Company Ltd, as it was originally called, built its first Rolls-Royce body in 1920 and its association with Derby was further

Aburnson (Coachbuilders) of Lancing, Sussex, was responsible for this rather less assured utility body on a 1949 Bentley Mark VI chassis. The interior had an appropriate 'walnut finish'. (LAT)

This foursome coupé with electrically-operated windows on the Bentley chassis is by James Young. Probably the first Mark VI to receive bespoke coachwork, it was completed in September 1946. (LAT)

underpinned when in 1922 it became involved in an ultimately aborted scheme to produce standardised coachwork on the 20hp chassis, this being an impressive endorsement of the credentials of a still-young company.

Park Ward's flexibility and readiness to adopt new procedures were a factor in Rolls-Royce becoming a minority shareholder in the business in 1933. This was in marked contrast to the company's once-favoured coachbuilder, Barker, whose bodies became heavier and more dated in appearance as the decade progressed. In buying into the firm, Rolls-Royce was motivated by the need to secure coachwork supplies for Bentley, which it had just acquired. This was to lead to Park Ward producing more bodies for Derby Bentleys than any other coachbuilder – 1,066 in all, representing 45 per cent of all Rolls-Royce's pre-war Bentleys.

In 1936, attracted by the twin requirements of strength and lightness, Park Ward announced its steel-framed, aluminium-clad body which dispensed with the traditional wooden framework. A further element of standardisation was also introduced that year when it began the manufacture of wings formed on Kirksite dies – low-cost tooling suitable for short production runs.

Despite these initiatives and a steady demand for its bodies, by the late thirties Park Ward was again in financial trouble. It lost £2,658 in the first six months of 1938, and that year Rolls-Royce acquired the remaining shares in the business, at a cost of £82,000, thereby ensuring its survival. Bentley body supply was thus assured and the skilled workforce remained intact. In 1939 the business became a wholly-owned subsidiary and although Charlie Ward still ran it, Park having departed some years previously, Rolls-Royce was represented at director level by Arthur Sidgreaves, Robert Harvey-Bailey and Francis Honeyman.

After the war, following the creation of Rolls-Royce's Crewe-based Motor Car Division, its general manager and director, Dr Frederick Llewellyn Smith,

became Park Ward's chairman although Ward remained as managing director. The company's long-serving chief designer, Jack Pagan, was replaced by his one-time junior draughtsman, Peter Wharton, who had joined the company in 1934 and continued as Park Ward's senior stylist until his retirement in 1979.

By this time all Park Ward's bodies were steel-framed, with wood only being used for the construction of prototypes although it was still used for dashboards and door fillets, which were variously made of such traditional woods as mahogany and burr walnut and Coromandle veneers. Leather was invariably light in colour, in blue or grey. Externally a Park Ward body could be identified by a thin line painted either side of the chromium moulding at its waistline.

But in 1952 what independence Park Ward had enjoyed since 1939 came to an end following a series of meetings between Charlie Ward and Rolls-Royce's Llewellyn Smith and Jack Scott. Its products were compared, side by side, with those of H. J. Mulliner and the outcome was that Park Ward lost its design autonomy. Rolls-Royce wanted a family resemblance between the bodies being designed at Crewe by chief stylist John Blatchley, appointed in 1951, and those produced at Willesden. As a result the corporate styling department assumed responsibility for the exteriors of all Park Ward bodies although Peter Wharton continued to design their interiors. Practically all the company's work at this time was on Rolls-Royce and Bentley chassis but it did undertake commissions for other car makers until 1953.

Blatchley's most enduring design to be executed at Willesden was of course the limousine coachwork for the Phantom V. Introduced in 1959, the basic design survived, with variations, until the 1992 demise of the Phantom VI, a total of 33 years.

Since 1961 Park Ward's name has

been allied to that of H. J. Mulliner, whose origins reach back to 1790. Established in 1900 when Henry Jervis Mulliner acquired the coachbuilding business of Mulliner, London Ltd, it was a member of a coachbuilding dynasty that included Arthur Mulliner in Northampton and Mulliners (Birmingham) Ltd.

H. J. Mulliner & Company's original premises were in the heart of the West End at 28 Brook Street, Mayfair, and its associations with Rolls-Royce dated from 1907 when it built its first body on a Silver Ghost chassis. One of its earliest customers was the Hon Charles Rolls, for whom Mulliner memorably produced a two-seater touring body with space to transport his ballooning equipment.

In 1908 the Mayfair premises were sold to Rolls-Royce and the business moved to its coachbuilding premises, opened in 1906, which were located in the Bedford Park Works in the leafy west London suburb of Chiswick. In the same year of 1908 Mulliner sold his business to John Croall, chairman of the prestigious Edinburgh-based coachbuilding company of John Croall and Sons, which dated from 1897. As with so many of its contemporaries, it had originally built carriages and was appointed royal warrant holder to Queen Victoria in 1847.

Seven years later, in 1915, the Chiswick-based firm became H. J. Mulliner & Co. Ltd, although the company was managed by HJM's

brother-in-law, Frank Piesse, who also became a director of Croall's company. The continuity of management worked well and by the late 1920s H. J. Mulliner was seen as being on a par with the respected Hooper and Barker concerns.

As was the case with Park Ward, Mulliner was receptive to new ideas and innovations and this asset was combined with elegant design and magnificent craftsmanship. In this way it was able to survive the difficult thirties by concentrating its activities on Bentley and Rolls-Royce chassis to the exclusion of most other marques.

In 1944 Piesse was replaced as managing director by the Australian-born Harry Talbot Johnstone, who joined H. J. Mulliner from the Glasgow-based Albion Motors. His son Arthur became general manager in 1948, having undertaken a commercial training course with Rolls-Royce. The talented chief designer, also works director, was Stanley J. Watts, who died in 1956, and he was replaced by ex-Hooper man Herbert Nye.

Relations with Rolls-Royce were good and in 1950 Watts had worked closely with the factory's Ivan Evernden on the coupé body of the famous Bentley Continental which was built at Chiswick between 1952 and 1959. This followed an experimental lightweight Bentley coupé of 1950 in which a light-alloy frame, inspired in part by Touring's

Park Ward bodied this Mark VI chassis. This drophead coupé features an hydraulically operated hood and dates from 1947. (LAT)

Mulliner, Park Ward and Alvis

In 1958, Coventry-based Alvis had all but ceased car production because of the difficulties it was experiencing in finding a contractor to build the bodies for its Graber-styled 3-litre saloon. After an unhappy two-year liaison with coachbuilders Willowbrook of Loughborough, who made bus bodies, in January 1958 Alvis approached Mulliner, Park Ward, then of course owned by Rolls-Royce. It agreed to produce the Alvis bodies at its works in Willesden, North London, at a cost of £750 for the saloon or £800 for the drophead coupé.

Final assembly would also be undertaken there, with the completed cars then being delivered to Alvis's Holyhead Road factory for final testing and dispatch.

The resulting Alvis TD21, at £2,993, was sold for £457 less than its low-volume TC 108G predecessor when it appeared in October 1958. But there were teething problems with jamming doors, poor paint quality and water leaks. Alvis believed its work was playing second fiddle to in-house Rolls-Royce and Bentley contracts but by 1961 the problems had been largely resolved. Mulliner, Park Ward continued to build Alvis bodies until the last of the line, the TF21, ceased production in 1967.

But this was not destined to be the last of Alvis's association with Rolls-Royce. After it discontinued car manufacture, its well-established military vehicle line moved centre stage and, in this context, it was responsible for armour plating versions of the Phantom VI, coded project Alpha and carried out under sub-contract from Mulliner, Park Ward. The first example was delivered in May 1968 to one 'Darius P. Browne' , better known as the Shah of Iran.

The Series II TD21, introduced in February 1962, is regarded as the best of the Alvises built by Park Ward. In the background is a TF21, the last of the line. (LAT)

Superleggera concept, replaced the traditional wood framework.

Mulliner's premises were expanded in 1948 to embrace further facilities at 212 King's Road, Fulham, although these were subsequently disposed of; following the 1961 merger with Park Ward, the Chiswick works was used for body repairs until the late sixties. After the amalgamation, Mulliner Park Ward, as it was rendered from the 1970s, was the principal supplier of bespoke coachwork for Rolls-Royce – although the panels were now aluminium pressings rather than being hand-crafted. As recounted in Chapters 6 and 7, it was not only

responsible for the production of the Phantom and Corniche but also, until 1978, the Camargue and, later, the Silver Spur limousine.

Mulliner, Park Ward continued to manufacture the Corniche but the lease was due to expire on the Willesden premises and these were demolished in 1982. In the previous year of 1981 came a move to the nearby Rolls-Royce service station at Hythe Road, Scrubs Lane, established there in 1939. An adjacent former Triplex Safety Glass factory, vacated in 1971 following the firm's purchase by Pilkington, was also taken over, as were two further

premises in Scrubs Lane.

This was a far from satisfactory solution but the economic recession of the early eighties played havoc with more ambitious plans. In 1983 the service station was relocated to a North Acton site and Mulliner, Park Ward concentrated its activities on both Hythe Road premises. There it remained until the end of 1991, when the department was transferred to Crewe – where the name still lives on, although not as a coachbuilder but as an enhancer of production models.

However, a much slimmed down H. J. Mulliner Coachworks remained at Hythe Road producing Corniche and

Above: This silver-grey Mark VI drophead foursome body is by Park Ward and was upholstered in grey and red. It was one of seven Crewe products, of which three were Bentleys, shipped to America on the *Mauretania* for a 1947 promotional visit. (LAT)

Below: Before the 1953 arrival of the R-type Continental, H. J. Mulliner was responsible for this coupé body, finished in grey with a blue interior, that was displayed on its stand at the 1949 motor show. Note the slimmed-down and daringly canted Bentley radiator. (LAT)

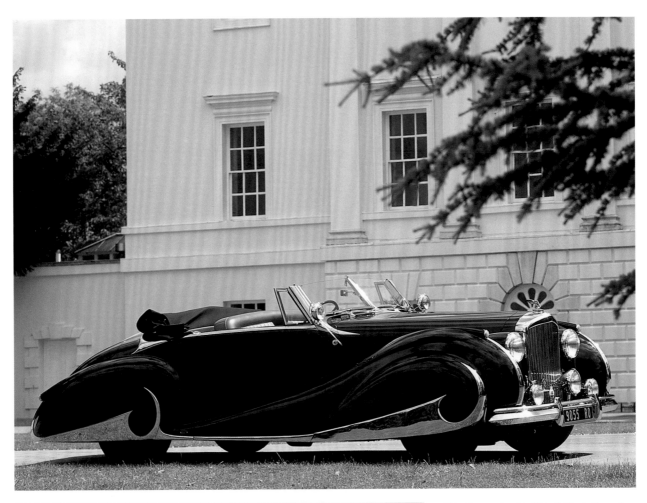

This Franay-bodied Mark VI, delivered in July 1947, was built for F. Gadoi of Boulogne. The divided opening windscreen is a more recent fitment and replaces the original single flat pane. (LAT)

Lady Lilly Hague, wife of former Blackpool councillor Sir Harry Hague, was the first owner of this Mark VI sedanca coupé by Gurney Nutting, completed in January 1949. (LAT)

Although Gurney Nutting is credited with this black and silver sedanca coupé on a Mark VI chassis, it actually appeared on the stand of its James Young associate company at the 1949 motor show. (LAT)

This body on a Mark VI chassis is by Pinin Farina. In all it was responsible for so enhancing five such Bentleys, four coupés and one drophead coupé. (LAT)

Continental convertible bodies-in-white until the impending demise of these models saw that facility's closure in 1994. Then from 1996 the company began to separate the two names, with the Park Ward identity being applied to the top-of-range Rolls-Royce products and the H. J. Mulliner name to its Bentley opposite numbers.

Mulliner and Park Ward were destined to survive as long as they did because of their ownership by a corporate parent, in this instance Rolls-Royce. This similarly applied to James Young, which since 1937 had been owned by Jack Barclay Ltd, Britain's largest Rolls-Royce and Bentley distributor. It had been making bodies for horse-drawn vehicles at

Bromley, Kent, since 1863 and as with so many of its contemporaries it progressed to motor-car coachwork, its first body being built in 1908 on a Wolseley chassis for the town's Member of Parliament.

Paradoxically James Young had not been primarily associated with Rolls-Royce during the inter-war years, being more usually concerned with bodying Talbot, Lagonda and Bentley chassis. Styling was invariably undertaken by works director G. H. Wenham. Then, in December 1937, came the acquisition by former 'Bentley Boy' Jack Barclay. So buttressed, the company continued coachbuilding activities, the war years excepted, at its premises at 37 London Road, for a further 30 years.

This was principally because Barclay had succeeded in luring the talented Albert 'Mac' McNeil, of Gurney Nutting, to join James Young as chief designer, with a seat on the board. Although Gurney Nutting and Company Ltd only bodied 12 Silver Wraith chassis, this prestigious coachbuilder was destined to play a catalytic role in Rolls-Royce affairs. As with Park Ward, it was established in 1919 although J. Gurney Nutting's background was in the related trade of building and joinery. He must have had a flair for spotting talent, because he secured the services of young Albert F. McNeil as his chief designer, fresh from working in the same capacity for the Cunard Motor & Carriage Company. Gurney Nutting

This Pinin Farina body was on an R-type Continental chassis and was commissioned by Rolls-Royce. Work began in November 1953, and it was completed in April 1954 and displayed at that year's Turin Motor Show. (LAT)

A 1953 R-type with H. J. Mulliner saloon body. (LAT)

went on to build its first Rolls-Royce body, on the 20hp chassis, in 1925.

A fire in 1923 at its original premises in Oval Road, Croydon, led to the business moving to fashionable Elystan Street, off King's Road, Chelsea, and in 1930 it moved once again, this time to nearby 1 Lacland Place, Danvers Street, in a works previously occupied by the Elkington Carriage Company. Gurney Nutting was closely associated with the Cricklewood-built Bentley and its total of 360 bodies for these cars was only exceeded by Vanden Plas. Having produced coachwork for the Prince of Wales, in 1931 the firm received the royal warrant, but whilst it continued to body the Derby Bentleys it was overtaken by the likes of Park Ward, Thrupp & Maberly, Vanden Plas, H. J. Mulliner and Hooper.

McNeil's 1937 departure might have spelt the end of the business, but fortunately his 23-year-old replacement proved to be in the same league. Senior draughtsman John Blatchley had joined the firm in 1935 but he was only destined to remain in the job for two years because the Second World War broke out in 1939 and he left for Rolls-Royce's Aero Division.

After the war he joined the company's Motor Car Division and he went on to style the Silver Cloud and Silver Shadow. After the war J. Gurney Nutting fell seriously ill and he appealed to Jack Barclay to buy the business, which he duly did in October 1945, four months before Gurney Nutting's death. But with Blatchley having been retained by Rolls-Royce, Gurney Nutting had no designer, so 'Mac' McNeil found himself undertaking work for both James Young and his old employer. On the demolition of the Lacland Place premises, the Gurney Nutting business moved in 1947 to a works at London Road, Morden, previously occupied by coachbuilders Ranalah. Mostly drophead coupés were produced, and the last of these, Silver Wraith WGC76, for playwright R. C. Sherriff, was completed in July 1950.

Thereafter McNeil lavished his considerable talents on James Young and the resulting bodies on the Silver Wraith, the Silver Cloud/S-series and – above all – the Phantom V, were, it must be said, stylistically superior to those of the in-house Park Ward product, created by his one-time assistant John Blatchley.

As the coachbuilt cars gave way to the Pressed Steel Silver Cloud/S-series line, James Young, along with

Mulliner Park Ward, continued to offer bespoke bodies on these chassis, sold from Jack Barclay Ltd's premises at 18 Berkeley Square.

In common with Park Ward, James Young also replaced the traditional wooden frame with steel for stress-bearing members, retaining seasoned five-to-eight-year-old ash for the stringers; 16swg aluminium was used for the body panels. The firm celebrated its centenary in 1963, at which time it was employing some 120 craftsmen and producing about 50 to 60 bodies a year – of which around 60 per cent were for overseas customers. Even at this date such interior furnishings as door handles and window winders were cast at the works.

The beginning of the end came in 1965 with the arrival of the unitary-construction Silver Shadow/T-series and although James Young displayed two-door versions at that year's London Motor Show these were adaptations of the four-door Pressed Steel shell.

But McNeil died in November 1965, just one month after the beige and black touring limousine he had designed for the Phantom V chassis had won a gold medal for coachwork at the show. The last of these bodies were completed in November 1967, at which point James Young ceased its coachbuilding activities. Like Hooper,

Last burst of glory: a Freestone & Webb body on a Bentley S1 chassis, dating from 1956 but modernised with S3 twin headlamp units. (LAT)

This R-type with Harold Radford Countryman coachwork was run in the 1954 Monte Carlo Rally by Irishmen B. Macartney-Filgate and R. W. Holmes. Setting out from Glasgow, they finished 107th overall. (LAT)

it continued for a time to offer a service facility for those cars graced with its coachwork.

Freestone & Webb had built its last Rolls-Royce body 11 years previously, in 1958. The company's foundation bore some similarities to Park Ward, it having also been established in the inter-war years, and similarly being based in the north London suburb of Willesden. Throughout its history Freestone & Webb occupied the same premises, namely the Unity Works at 101–103 Brentfield Road, Stonebridge Park. V. E. Freestone was chairman and joint managing director and had as his business partner Arthur John Webb, previously manager of H. J. Mulliner's Brook Street premises. Webb had begun his coachbuilding career in Huntingdon, and after his time at Mulliner he had joined the Kingsbury Aviation Company during the First World War. In August 1923 he co-founded Freestone & Webb Ltd, and initially associated the company closely with Bentley, then based at nearby Cricklewood.

With 232 Bentleys bodied by Freestone & Webb, the firm was Bentley's fourth-most-popular coachbuilder, but with the collapse of W. O. Bentley's enterprise, Webb left in 1930 to pursue what was to prove to be the ill-timed revival of Cunard.

An early advocate of the Weymann

fabric body, Freestone & Webb bodied its first Rolls-Royce in 1925 and ten years later introduced, on the 3½-litre Bentley chassis, the so-called 'razor edge' styling with which it was thereafter associated.

It continued to body many Rolls-Royce Silver Wraith chassis in the post-war years at a time when its managing director was Major Williams, who by all accounts had been chief tester for the old Bentley Motors. The designer was Len Hedges, formerly draughtsman at H. J. Mulliner, and his Hooper-inspired two-tone bodies with their strong curvilinear wings were both distinctive and magnificently executed. They concealed what was described as composite frames with central pillars either made of wood or fabricated

from T-section steel – although, in the interests of lightness, these were later replaced by box-section aluminium, which also came to be used for the windscreen pillars.

Arthur Webb died in December 1954 at the age of 73 and the business's independent existence came to an end when it was acquired, in May 1957, by the Swain Group which included Rolls-Royce dealer H. R. Owen and coachbuilders Harold Radford. Freestone & Webb survived for a further year and its last body was a drophead coupé Silver Cloud, delivered in June 1958.

To all intents and purposes the craft of the coachbuilder, which had made a seemingly effortless transition from the horse-drawn to the horseless carriage, was no more.

The Silver Shadow, Silver Wraith II *and Bentley T-series*

Rolls-Royce's legendary Silver Ghost, on which the company's fortunes were built, ceased production in 1925 and it was not until 40 years later, in 1965, that a model of equal corporate significance made its appearance.

With some 32,000 four-door Silver Shadow saloons produced in 15 years, the model was not only the best-selling car since the Ghost: additionally its assured, understated styling concealed unitary body construction, disc brakes and all-independent suspension – technological refinements appearing on a Rolls-Royce product for the first time in the marque's history.

Of even greater significance to the company, the Shadow was, after the first six years of its manufacturing life, a profitable model. Its growing popularity and reliability ensured that the Motor Car Division was in a sufficiently robust shape to weather the financial storm of 1971 when the seemingly impossible happened and Rolls-Royce succumbed to bankruptcy, trading for two years under receivership until it was floated on the stock market.

The period up to the company's

The two most significant models in Rolls-Royce's history: a Silver Shadow with the company's Barker-bodied original Silver Ghost of 1907 that it has owned since 1948. (Rolls-Royce)

Silver Shadow production underway at Crewe. It was the most complex model then produced by Rolls-Royce. (Rolls-Royce)

1980 merger with Vickers saw demand for the Shadow and its derivatives maintained, and in 1978 no fewer than 3,347 cars left Crewe, this being the highest annual production figure of its day and one that has never been bettered. But whilst the Silver Lady's fortunes continued to ride high, the decline of the Bentley name accelerated and the 2,280 T-series cars built between 1965 and 1980 represent a mere seven per cent of the total number of Silver Shadows produced.

Studies for the new model had begun over 11 years before its launch when, in February 1954, chief engineer Harry Grylls and his team began to think in terms of producing a monocoque car, under the Tibet coding, to succeed the Silver Cloud. Once the Cloud was in production, 1958 saw work on the new car began in earnest.

By this time the concept was based around a four-door saloon with a 126in (3.20m) wheelbase, powered by the 6.2-litre V8 which was due to enter production the following year. There were also thoughts about a short-wheelbase Bentley version powered by the 4-litre six-cylinder engine eventually used in the later Vanden Plas Princess 4-litre R. Coded Burma, this project was in due course sidelined.

The first experimental Tibet was completed in August 1958 and incorporated the proportions, if not the detail, of the finished product – it was not until the May 1962 arrival of the Tibet II that styling began to resemble the definitive Silver Shadow.

In 1963 the SY designation replaced the Tibet name, the first experimental car in this series having a hand-built black-painted Crewe-built body and a Bentley radiator. Completed in March 1964, this antedated by only 18 months the unveiling of the production car. The first experimental SY with a Pressed Steel body, meanwhile, was completed in November.

The Silver Shadow and its Bentley T-series equivalent were announced in October 1965, priced respectively at £6,556 and £6,496. This made them some £900 more than the Cloud III/S3 family, but in technical terms the design represented a significant leap forward. It was, in consequence, the most complex model ever offered by Rolls-Royce. A slightly smaller car than its predecessor, the Shadow had a 9ft 11½in (3.04m) wheelbase, 3½in (8.9cm) shorter than that of the Silver Cloud, and was lower, wider and – at 41.6cwt (2,113kg) – about 1.75cwt (762kg) lighter. The boot, all the same, was significantly larger.

The lines of the four-door Pressed Steel saloon body had been magnificently executed by John Blatchley. Bereft of any unnecessary decoration, the design was clearly intended for a long production run – although not the 15 years it eventually lasted. Like its predecessors, much of the bodywork was steel although the doors, bonnet and bootlid were made of aluminium.

Beneath was a steel substructure with the engine and independent rear

The dashboard of the Shadow in its first incarnation: austere and a touch old-fashioned. (Rolls-Royce)

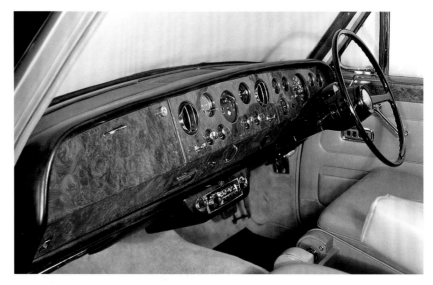

The interior of a 1972 Shadow shows the restrained good taste so typical of these cars. (LAT)

suspension carried on separate box-section subframes. The move to unitary construction also increased the amount of interior space available, the absence of a chassis frame allowing the floor to be lowered by several inches.

The 6.2-litre engine was essentially the same as that used in the Cloud III, although the cylinder heads were redesigned to allow the sparking plugs to be more conveniently repositioned above the exhaust manifolds rather than below them. Some two per cent extra – but still undisclosed – power was claimed. Twin 2in SU HD8 carburettors were carried over, fuel injection, as Mercedes-Benz had been introducing progressively from 1954, clearly still being some way off. As for the transmission, improvements were made to eliminate the jerkiness of the four-speed automatic gearbox, and the casing and some of the internal parts were now of aluminium.

Front suspension was new in concept but followed the familiar wishbone and coil spring layout in conjunction with Girling telescopic shock absorbers. The trailing-arm independent rear also used telescopic dampers, and the entire suspension operated in conjunction with a sophisticated high-pressure hydraulic automatic height-control system.

Encompassing high-pressure actuation of the brakes, this was the most innovative aspect of the Shadow, and used Citroën hydropneumatic technology. It did not, however, provide interconnected suspension in the manner of the French company's DS and the Hydrolastic-suspended Morris 1100. There were in fact two independent systems charged by two camshaft-actuated hydraulic pumps located in the vee of the engine. These in turn fed a pair of spherical accumulators located low on the left-hand side of the engine and pressurised to 2,500psi; these channelled fluid under pressure to levelling rams located directly above the front and rear suspension units. The object was to keep the basic trim of the car constant, regardless of the number of occupants and luggage carried.

The use of such high-pressure

hydraulics meant that the brakes also broke with the past in that the mechanical servo, which had served every Rolls-Royce since 1925, was abandoned. In its place power assistance was contributed by the engine-driven pumps, the forward unit being responsible for just 47 per cent of the front and rear braking, on a 31:16 split. The second hydraulic circuit contributed a further 31 per cent to the front discs and also supplied the height-control circuits.

The complicated footbrake mechanism incorporated distributor valves for the two powered systems together with a conventional master cylinder which applied a proportion of power to the rear brakes. But with noise levels an ever-present consideration, the all-round 11in (279mm) discs, conventionally outboard at the rear, were bound with stainless steel wire to reduce squeal when they were applied. Steering was by Saginaw power-assisted recirculating-ball and the steering wheel broke with tradition in having two spokes instead of the customary three.

Inside the Shadow bristled with ingenuity, leather and walnut, the customary folding rear picnic tables being juxtaposed with electrically-activated eight-position seats and electric windows. The automatic transmission was similarly refined and activated by an electric motor which gave finger-tip control. Air-conditioning was available at £178 extra, whilst inertia-reel seat belts cost a few pence short of £20.

Deliveries began in the spring of 1966, and the Silver Shadow was soon being accorded a warm welcome by road testers. "We have no hesitation in describing it as a worthy successor to the Clouds and Phantoms", wrote *Autocar*, the magazine achieving a top speed of 115mph (185kph) and a 0–60mph figure of 10.8 seconds – about the same as the Silver Cloud III. Refinement was much improved and the brakes were deemed excellent, criticisms being mainly confined to intrusive tyre noise regardless of the road surface. The journal also

Rolls-Royce Silver Shadow I (6.2-litre)
1965-1970

ENGINE:
V8 alloy block and cylinder heads

Bore x stroke	104.1mm x 91.4mm
Capacity	6,230cc
Valve actuation	Pushrod
Compression ratio	9:1
Carburettors	Twin SU HD8
Power	Not disclosed

TRANSMISSION:
Rear-wheel drive
Four-speed automatic with fluid coupling
From July 1968 three-speed automatic with torque converter. Final drive ratio: 3.08:1

SUSPENSION:
Front: Independent, wishbone and coil spring
Rear: Independent trailing arm and coil spring
Automatic hydraulic height control

STEERING:
Power assisted recirculating ball
Turns lock-to-lock: 4.25

BRAKES:
Front: Hydraulic disc
Rear: Hydraulic disc
Power assistance from two engine-driven hydraulic pumps

WHEELS/TYRES:
Steel disc wheels 8.45 x 15in

BODYWORK:
Unitary construction four-door saloon in steel and aluminium by Pressed Steel

DIMENSIONS:

Length	16ft 11½in (5.16m)
Wheelbase	9ft 1½in (3.03m)
Track– front	4ft 9½in (1.46m)
– rear	4ft 9½in (1.46m)
Width	5ft 11in (1.80m)
Height	4ft 11¾in (1.49m)

WEIGHT:
41.6cwt (2,113kg)

PERFORMANCE:
(Source: *Autocar*)

Max speed	115mph (185kph)
0–50mph (0–80kph)	7.8sec
0–60mph (0–100kph)	10.9sec
0–70mph (0–112kph)	14.3sec

PRICE INCLUDING TAX WHEN NEW: £6670

NUMBER BUILT:
Silver Shadow I: 16,717
Bentley T1: 1,703

Rolls-Royce Silver Shadow I (6.7-litre)
1970-1977

As Silver Shadow 6.2-litre except:

ENGINE:
V8, alloy block, alloy heads

Bore x stroke	104.1mm x 99.1mm
Capacity	6,750cc

DIMENSIONS:
Wheelbase* 10ft (3.04m)

PERFORMANCE: (Source: *Autocar*)

Maximum speed	117mph (188kph)
0–50mph (0–80kph)	7.4sec
0–60mph (0–100kph)	10.2sec
0–70mph (112kph)	13.8sec

PRICE INCLUDING TAX WHEN NEW: £9925

*From April 1974

Rolls-Royce Silver Shadow II
1977-1980

As 6.7-litre Silver Shadow I except:

ENGINE:

Carburettor	Twin SU HIF
Compression ratio	8:1

STEERING:
Power-assisted rack-and-pinion

WHEELS/TYRES: 235/70 HR-15

DIMENSIONS:

Length	17ft 0½in (5.19m)

WEIGHT: 40.29cwt (2047kg)

PRICE INCLUDING TAX WHEN NEW: £25,992

NUMBER BUILT: Silver Shadow II: 8425
Bentley T2: 558

Rolls-Royce Silver Shadow (lwb) & Silver Wraith II
1969-1980

As 6.2-litre and 6.7-litre Silver Shadow except:

DIMENSIONS:

Length	17ft 3½in (5.27m)
Wheelbase	10ft 5in (3.17m)

WEIGHT: 44.8cwt (2,272kg)

PRICE INCLUDING TAX WHEN NEW:
With division £10,375; without division £9,708

NUMBER BUILT:
Silver Shadow: 2,776 Bentley T1: 9
Silver Wraith II: 2,135 Bentley T2: 10

Rare indeed: the original two-door Silver Shadow created by James Young. (LAT)

The flight to bankruptcy

It was supremely ironic that Rolls-Royce's bankruptcy of February 1971 was related not to its invariably loss-making Motor Car Division but to the aero-engines which had so profitably dominated its activities since the early 1930s. The company's troubles were rooted in a fixed-price contract it signed in 1968 with the American Lockheed Corporation to supply the RB211 jet engine, the first of a new generation of so called 'big fan' units, to power the wide-bodied TriStar airliner.

Rolls-Royce's brilliant director of engineering, Adrian Lombard, had decreed that the RB211's 25 massive fan blades be made of Hyfil, a type of carbon-fibre which was stronger and lighter than the

traditional titanium. Sadly, he died suddenly in 1967. In practice it was found that Hyfil was susceptible to bird strikes and erosion, so the engine was redesigned with 33 narrower titanium blades, which put its weight up. In addition the predicted 40,600lb (18,416kg) of thrust failed to materialise. It was a tragic vindication of the axiom of Ernest Hives that "if the engineers are wrong we are all wrong".

Development costs soared out of control and in 1970 Rolls-Royce's chairman, the mercurial Sir Denning Pearson, was belatedly replaced by Lord Cole. It was too late, and bankruptcy followed in 1971. Rolls-Royce was nationalised, and did not return to the public sector until 1987 when it was privatised by

Margaret Thatcher's Conservative administration.

In 1970 Rolls-Royce had recalled Dr Stanley Hooker, recently retired former chief engineer of its jet division, who recruited some of his talented grey-haired contemporaries and they redesigned the unit. Hooker's revised RB211-22 ran for the first time on 3 February 1971, the day before the bankruptcy. Sadly, if he had been summoned a year earlier the crisis could have been averted. A more powerful version followed in 1973, Hooker was given a well-deserved knighthood in 1974, and the RB211 received its ultimate endorsement in 1978 when Boeing took the unprecedented decision of choosing it for its 757, in preference to an indigenous jet engine.

Although there was a Bentley version of the Silver Shadow, named the T-series, most customers opted for a Rolls-Royce. In truth the Bentley radiator did not so lend itself to its new reduced dimensions. (Rolls-Royce)

Rear-three quarter view of a T1; the Everflex roof covering and the sunroof are probably later additions. (LAT)

considered that the model's soft ride had been tuned to the demands of American customers. Whilst this was true (see box), the US suspension was even more so! The writer also commented adversely on the slow response of the power-assisted steering, and whilst the air-conditioning worked well enough, it was felt that there were too many controls needed to operate it.

Although the arrival of the unitary construction Silver Shadow effectively spelt the end of coachbuilt variants, James Young unveiled a two-door version at the 1965 London Motor Show. Based on the Pressed Steel four-door body shell, it was

available as a Rolls-Royce (35 made) and a Bentley (15 made) but was discontinued in February 1967 and the Bromley business ceased its coachbuilding activities later that year.

In March 1966 deliveries began of left-hand-drive Shadows, their transmission differing significantly from that of the home-market cars: from the outset they were fitted with a three-speed General Motors GM 400 Hydramatic – as the name was now rendered. This had the merit of being considerably smoother in operation than its predecessor on account of engine power being transmitted by a torque converter rather than employing the by-then dated fluid

Interior of a Bentley T1: the wood-framed mirrors in the rear quarters are a charming feature retained from earlier models. (LAT)

Left: The dashboard of a Silver Shadow, as adapted in 1969 for American safety regulations, with padding much in evidence and a central console. (LAT)

Above: The rear compartment, as modified for US safety regulations in 1969. The picnic tables were dispensed with and recessed door handles introduced. Each door contained an ash tray and cigar lighter. (LAT)

Right: Externally the Silver Shadow I changed remarkably little over the years, although side marker lamps, illuminated with the side lamps, arrived in May 1969 as another US safety requirement. (LAT)

coupling. The auto 'box was bought complete from America – unlike the four-speed automatic, which had been built at Crewe. The four-speeder continued to be fitted to right-hand-drive cars until mid-1968.

March 1966 also saw the arrival of the factory's own two-door saloons, as announced at the Geneva motor show and intended to replace the coachbuilt versions of the Silver Cloud and the Bentley Continental. It was to be a further 18 months before a convertible version of the two-door Shadow made its appearance, at the 1967 Frankfurt Motor Show; it came complete with power-operated hood and sold for £10,511, which was some £3,540 more than the four-door

saloon. These cars are discussed in the next chapter.

A long-wheelbase Shadow, with optional electrically-operated interior division, arrived in May 1969 and was also available in Bentley form – although only nine such cars were completed. The model had been foreshadowed, as it were, by a one-off lwb Silver Shadow of summer 1967, produced for Princess Margaret and her husband Lord Snowdon.

The new model had an extra 4in (10cm) between the wheel centres. The conversion was effected by Mulliner Park Ward but the cars were completed at Crewe. They were instantly recognisable by their black Everflex-covered roof, longer rear side

windows and smaller back window.

A redesigned instrument panel featured a padded dashboard surround and rocker switches, to comply with newly-introduced US safety regulations. This was essential, because the first 90 or so lwb cars were destined for American customers: the first right-hand-drive cars for the British market were not built until 1970.

This dashboard was introduced across the range and was followed in the autumn of 1969 by the ride-height control being deleted from the front suspension. In practice its contribution had been found to be negligible. In November of that year air-conditioning was standardised and

Sir David Arnold Stuart Plastow, born 1932

One of the key players in Rolls-Royce's post war history, David Plastow (DP) was the architect of the company's 18-year alliance with Vickers.

The son of a garage proprietor – "cars have always been in my blood" – Plastow was educated at Culford School, Bury St Edmunds. Unusually for a public-schoolboy of the time, in 1950 he joined Vauxhall on a five-year engineering apprenticeship and he remained at Luton until 1958, by which time he had become a sales engineer.

That year he became Rolls-Royce's North of England representative; he was factory sales manager from 1960 to 1963, and he became marketing director in 1967. In January 1971, at the age of 38, he was made managing director, just weeks before the company's devastating bankruptcy and ensuing receivership.

He continued in this job when Rolls-Royce Motors was formed in 1972. Later, in 1975, Plastow became a non-executive director of Vickers and on that company merging with Rolls-Royce in 1980 he was appointed its chief executive and moved from Crewe to London and its Millbank Tower headquarters. He was knighted in 1986 and became Vickers chairman in the following year, but he left in 1992 to join the Inchcape Group in the same capacity, a position he held until 1995. In 1994 Rolls-Royce appointed Inchcape as its importer and distributor in China: over the previous two years, when it first entered the market, Rolls-Royce had sold a total of 50 new cars there.

Sir David Plastow, the architect of Rolls-Royce's 18-year association with Vickers. (Rolls-Royce)

The long-wheelbase version of the Silver Shadow appeared in May 1969 and is identifiable by its Everflex-covered roof. (LAT)

John Shaw Hollings 1923–1996

John Hollings (Hgs) replaced Harry Grylls as Rolls-Royce's chief engineer in 1968. As such he had overall responsibility for the Silver Shadow II and its Silver Spirit successor.

Educated at Stowe, John Hollings was a Cambridge graduate. He joined Rolls-Royce's aero-engine division at Derby in 1948 as a designer, and did not transfer to the Motor Car Division until 1965. In the interim Lord Hives had recognised his worth and in 1957 Hollings became chief designer of Rolls-Royce and Associates, which produced reactors for nuclear submarines. Later, in 1962, he became manager and chief engineer of the Admiralty's Research and Test Establishment at Dounreay.

He therefore moved to Crewe with a wide experience of Rolls-Royce design in the air and on the water. Hollings first became chief quality engineer, and succeeded Grylls in 1968, also replacing him as engineering director the following year. In his 1981 Henry Royce Memorial Lecture he paid tribute to his team of "senior engineers who had worked on the birth of Silver Shadow [and] remained to continue their good work. These included Fred Murray, MacCraith Fisher, Ron West, Fritz Feller, Jock Knight and many others."

Hollings saw the Silver Spirit/Mulsanne lines into production in 1980 but left in the management purge enacted by Vickers in the autumn of 1983. However, he continued to undertake some consultancy work for the company. He died on 23 July 1996 at the age of 73.

John Hollings, whose Rolls-Royce career before his appointment as chief engineer embraced aero engines and nuclear power. (Rolls-Royce)

Vickers: from rolling mill to Rolls-Royce

Vickers owned Rolls-Royce Motors for the 18 years between 1980 and 1998. Its association with the company was a deep-rooted one – after all, Alcock and Brown's famous 1919 crossing of the Atlantic was undertaken in a Vickers Vimy powered by a pair of Rolls-Royce Eagle engines.

Founded in Sheffield in 1828 as Naylor, Hutchinson and Vickers, this steel-rolling-mill company was from the outset dominated by the last-named company's Edward Vickers. His sons, Tom and Albert, took the business over and in 1867 it emerged as Vickers, Sons and Company. Armaments production began in 1888 and shipbuilding followed in 1897. However, a diversification in 1903 into motor manufacture proved to be calamitous, when it acquired Wolseley Motors which proceeded to consume substantial sums of money until it was sold in 1926 to William Morris.

Its interests were further consolidated in 1927 by an amalgamation with the similarly diverse Armstrong Whitworth, the new company being named Vickers-Armstrong. Vickers had begun to build aircraft in 1911, and this activity was underpinned in 1928 with the acquisition of Supermarine, whose principal asset was its chief designer Reginald Mitchell. It therefore became the manufacturer of the legendary Merlin-engined Spitfire fighter, which first flew in 1936.

But after the war, and with election of a Labour government, Vickers suffered from the nationalisation of its steel business, denationalised in 1954, but once again returned to public ownership in 1967. It was similarly stripped of its shipbuilding and aerospace interests in 1977. It was against this background that, in August 1980, Vickers acquired Rolls-Royce Motors, with its assets of £63.3 million, for £29.5 million in shares. The car company thus joined a diverse business which embraced such products as medical equipment, scientific instruments, lithographic plates, milk-bottling machinery, office equipment and tanks.

an alternator and a stainless steel exhaust system introduced.

Although the 1970 Shadows were outwardly unchanged, in July the V8 received its first capacity increase since its 1959 introduction. With 6,750cc, achieved by increasing the stroke from 91mm to 99mm, the revised power unit was initially fitted to cars destined for export, and was intended to compensate for performance lost by de-toxing equipment and the extra weight that came with it.

The new engine was extended to the two-door saloon and convertible Shadows which in March 1971 emerged as models in their own right, under the Corniche name. These cars and their two-door predecessors are discussed in the next chapter. The launch was, however, overshadowed by an extraordinary event which occurred on 4 February 1971: Rolls-Royce declared itself bankrupt. As the details in the accompanying box indicate, this was unrelated to the Crewe-based Motor Car Division and was a result of the company's mainstream aero-engine activities. The newly elected Conservative government felt it had no alternative, in view of Rolls-Royce's defence commitments, technological prestige and skilled workforce, but to nationalise the business.

This did not include the Motor Car Division, which also encompassed Continental light aero engines and diesels. Renamed Rolls-Royce Motors in March 1971, this continued to so trade for over two years, until May 1973, when it was offered for public flotation.

Management changes followed. Graduate engineer Dr Llewellyn Smith had been the Division's chairman since 1957 and managing director until 1968 when he was replaced by Geoffrey Fawn. Llewellyn Smith had intended to retire early in 1971 but he was overtaken by events and was obliged first to see the business through the trauma of the parental

Two British institutions meet in London's St James's Park. This Silver Shadow dates from 1976 – note the absence of the rectangular air intakes, these being deleted for the 1974 model year, at which stage quartz-halogen fog lamps were standardised. (LAT)

collapse. He was replaced as chairman in late 1971 by merchant banker Ian Fraser.

Just weeks before the events of February 1971, 38-year-old marketing director David Plastow had replaced Fawn as MD and he was destined to play a pivotal affair in the destiny of Rolls-Royce cars for the next 21 years. Significantly, Plastow came from the sales side of the business although he had served an engineering apprenticeship. Nevertheless it was a break with the past. Had not Lord Hives once described Rolls-Royce as "a company of engineers, run by engineers for engineers"? Times were certainly a-changing.

Driving an early Shadow

For many people coming to Rolls-Royce – or Bentley – for the first time, the car on their shopping list is likely to be a Silver Shadow, and quite conceivably an early chrome-bumper car. Perhaps the purchase of the car seems daunting: will it be an intimidating experience driving the car?

Be reassured: the Shadow inspires immediate confidence. You sit pleasantly high and feel at ease straightaway, as you survey the road ahead, the bonnet fully visible and its mascot pointing the way forward. Nor does the car feel unwieldy; indeed, it seems surprisingly narrow for a top-of-range luxury saloon.

If you're used to flashy interiors you may be surprised. The passenger compartment of these cars is manifestly of the highest quality but it is also very plain – from the unpatterned door trims to the undemonstrative flat plank of a dashboard; the latter became less austere on later Shadow I models. Tasteful understatement is the message, enhanced by such old-fashioned but charming details as the chromed twist-switches and the sober white-on-black instrument dials.

Slip off the under-dash T-handle handbrake, engage gear, and the first impression is of the delicate action of the gear selector: electrically-assisted, it clicks with an oiled precision from gear to gear. Slightly thunky as one pulls away, the transmission is blissfully smooth-changing when you're rolling, and kicks down with equal discretion.

Acceleration is indeed deliciously unruffled, snappiness at low speed giving way to lazier mid-range responses. At 40mph you are wafting along in regal refinement; action the throttle and the Shadow will seamlessly gather speed, the V8 spinning like a well-oiled ball-bearing. There's no sudden punch in the back – just a gradual accumulation of forward motion as you haul past slower traffic, your tranquil progress marred only by a degree of wind noise. Braking, too, is a delight. The pedal has just the right length of travel to give a progressive action, and smooth, steady braking will never leave you in trouble. It's an exemplary refining of the Citroën power braking system adapted by Rolls-Royce.

Aggression is not in the Shadow driver's lexicon – above all when we're talking of the early cars. The steering lets you know this before you're a few yards down the road. Light to the point of being over-light, it demands a delicacy of touch in harmony with the slender-rimmed steering wheel. This is not informative steering, and gentle driving, with the wheel being carressed rather than flung about.

The car's chassis behaviour drives this message home – in no uncertain terms, if it's a car with no front anti-roll bar. Even on gentle corners the Shadow keels over and the tyres start howling. You don't need to drive like a hoodlum to discover this: even gently descending a motorway access ramp will have the car rolling like a drunken hippo, and swish-swashing through a roundabout is definitely out of the question. An American used to Cadillacs and the like might well feel at home, and cars with the front anti-roll bar are better, but anyone coming from a Jaguar or a Mercedes should be forewarned; fortunately the highly-regarded Harvey-Bailey suspension kits transform this wayward conduct. Still, at least straight-line stability is good, with no need for constant steering correction, and as a motorway cruiser an early Shadow is a delightfully relaxing proposition.

Additionally, the other side of the coin is that the soft suspension gives a generally very comfortable ride, albeit at the cost of some wallowing from the rear. Undulating road surfaces are tackled better than small imperfections such as potholes, manhole covers are muted out quite effectively, and only a certain amount of bump-thump is transmitted to the cabin. Overall, despite the lack of control, the ride is as cossetting as you'd expect from a Rolls-Royce; the total driving experience is nonetheless compromised, even for those of the most sedate temperament. Don't let this put you off, though: as has been said, a remedy is available.

Silver Shadow production had taken a while to build up and early examples suffered, as the Cloud II had done, from teething problems. Consequently losses had soared to over £1 million in 1966 and 1968's modest £59,000 profit was the exception rather than the rule. Thankfully volumes were increasing and annual production had broken the 2,000 mark for the first time in 1970. Two years later the surplus stood at £4.8 million and in 1974 profits were £3.3 million. This was despite the fact that the world had been thrown into recession by a quadrupling of the oil price.

In the meantime the Silver Shadow continued to receive regular mechanical improvements and in August 1972 compliance was introduced into the front suspension to permit radial-ply tyres to be fitted for better handling and longer tyre life without any noise, vibration and harshness penalties. Ventilated front disc brakes were introduced

The much-improved Silver Shadow II arrived in 1977 and was instantly identifiable by its front airdam and polyurethane-covered front bumper. (LAT)

The Shadow II's dashboard, with an electronic speedometer and a new warning-light panel to the right of the driver. It was essentially carried over to the Silver Spirit of three years later. (LAT)

The Silver Shadow II engine. The SU HIF7 carburettors had improved emission controls and an electric fan, mounted ahead of the radiator, supplemented by a new visco coupled unit. (LAT)

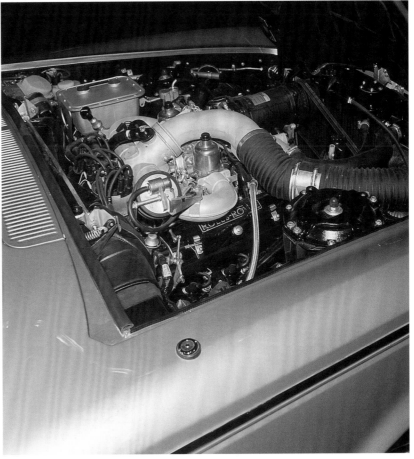

Driving the Shadow II

Proof that the original Shadow was off the pace comes the moment you pull away in a Shadow II. You may not notice much difference in performance despite the 1970 increase in engine size from 6,230cc to 6,750cc, you may be left indifferent by the move from a sweet-changing four-speed gearbox to an equally smooth three-speeder, and you'll still be cosetted by a ride that is distinctly on the soft side.

But the steering in particular is a revelation. It's still light, and the only satisfactory way to conduct the car is by gently carressing that lovely thin-rimmed wheel. Yet the rack-and-pinion mechanism is now so well set-up that although piloting the Shadow remains effortless there is now adequate weight to the steering and a hefty increase in precision.

Inherited from the later radial-shod compliant-suspension Shadow I is a much-improved chassis. Roll is better controlled, so that roundabouts and motorway ramps can be tackled without needing to reduce speed to a level gentle enough to avoid boy-racer tyre-squealing. Gentle pitching over undulating surfaces show that body control is by no means in the Jaguar XJ6 class, but for a big heavy car the Rolls-Royce no longer disgraces itself.

The other virtues are familiar. The performance remains gloriously unruffled, with a slight edge from the extra engine displacement but with, all the same, the impression that the car serenely gathers speed rather than doing anything as undignified as actually accelerating. Braking is well-judged, with excellent progression despite a relatively light pedal action.

The added competence of the Shadow II doesn't change one thing, though: it is a car that doesn't encourage you to drive it in a way unsuited to its genteel character. You don't feel tempted to pick it up by the scruff of its neck, an approach which would be singularly unrewarding. If that's your thing, better stick to a BMW.

---

in June of the following year.

Wider, lower profile steel radials with attendant front suspension changes arrived in April 1974, along with a small ½in (12.7mm) increase in wheelbase to 10ft (3.05m). This change is easily identifiable by the simultaneous arrival of modest flares to the wheelarches to accommodate the new covers. The outcome was better cornering and a reduction in road noise. In 1976, finally, the engine's compression ratio was lowered from 9:1 to 8:1 and OPUS electronic ignition introduced. These changes were intended to improve fuel consumption.

The model had been in production for a little over 11 years, in which time some 2,000 modifications had been effected, when, in February 1977, the Silver Shadow II and Bentley T2 made their appearances. A considerable improvement over the original models, they were seen into production by John Hollings, who in 1968 had replaced Harry Grylls as Rolls-Royce's chief engineer.

Outwardly the new generation of Shadows was identifiable by a front air dam to improve straight-line stability, although this was not fitted to those cars destined for the US where a 55mph (88kph) speed limit was in force. Black polyurethane bumpers, now bereft of overriders, featured in place of traditional chrome blades although those Shadows destined for the US had been so-equipped since the 1974 model year.

Modifications to the engine saw a slight falling off in its still-undisclosed power, thanks to the fitment of SU H1F carburettors to lower emissions levels and improve starting. However, this loss of output was offset by the introduction of a Corniche-style twin-pipe exhaust system which generated less back-pressure than the original. Its fitment was indicated by the presence of twin chromium-plated tailpipes.

More radical was the replacement of the recirculating-ball steering with a more precise power-assisted rack-and-pinion unit. This countered complaints that, despite the fitment of improved, wider tyres and suspension changes, the steering retained a distracting vagueness. Further modifications were simultaneously made to the front suspension to keep the wheels more upright during cornering, the revised geometry removing some of the loading from the tyres.

Passenger comfort was enhanced by the arrival of a full split-level automatic air-conditioning system as introduced to the Camargue in 1975 and extended to the Corniche in the following year. This was coupled to a new much neater dashboard. The revised cars carried the Silver Shadow II name on a plaque mounted on the boot lid. This was the first time the model had been so identified and followed the precedent established on the Corniche six years before.

The Geneva Motor Show of 1977 saw the return of the Silver Wraith name after an 18-year absence, when the long-wheelbase Silver Shadow was so renamed. Benefiting from all the mechanical and cosmetic benefits of the Series II car, the Silver Wraith II was available with or without a separating division, prices being £28,044 for the divided car and £26,886 for the open-plan version. Again, a Bentley version was produced, but only ten examples were built.

The long-wheelbase Silver Shadow was renamed the Silver Wraith II in 1977. (LAT)

A Silver Shadow II from the rear with the model name now displayed on the boot lid. The chromium-plated twin exhaust pipes were another refinement. (LAT)

Demand for the revised Silver Shadow remained strong. In fact no fewer than 8425 examples were built in its four-year 1977–1980 currency – compared with 16,717 Series Is manufactured in the 11 previous years. It was also an indication, if one had been needed, that production had built up very slowly. A total of 32,333 four-door cars – 30,053 Rolls-Royces and 2,280 Bentleys – were completed, with the two-door saloon and convertible and the Corniche and Camargue accounting for a further 4,841 cars up until 1980. This made a grand total of 37,173 and underlines the success of the Shadow line: output would never again attain such levels.

The four-door saloons reached the end of the road in 1980 and in October of that year they were replaced by Silver Spirit. By this time the model was selling for £41,960, some six times the original price. It was, however, a very much better

Colonial Shadows

The Silver Shadow was produced with three types of suspension. Those cars destined for America had relatively soft springing in keeping with other cars sold there. Examples sold on the European market used firmer suspension which gave better handling. There was also an even stiffer variant and, as chief engineer John Hollings later recounted, "we provided it for those countries which were renowned for their ability to damage any normal suspension system. It was known within the factory as 'colonial suspension' and it was only when I innocently mentioned this to one of our of colleagues from Australia that I realised that it was time we gave it a different title!"

Buying Hints

1. The V8 engine fitted in the Silver Shadow should be the least of your problems; all the same, a post-1970 car with the larger 6.7-litre engine is marginally preferable to a car with the original 6.2-litre unit. Unlike the engines fitted to the Silver Cloud and S-series, sparking plug accessibility is acceptable on account of the cylinder heads being redesigned to accommodate the plugs above the exhaust manifolds. Having said that, numbers 3 and 4 on the nearside are particularly inaccessible and the sparking plug threads may have been damaged as a result.

2. Otherwise the engines can easily exceed 100,000 miles (160,000km) without major overhaul. Even then, there's plenty of life left in them and, providing the crankshaft is in good condition, replacing the wet cylinder liners and pistons at 180,000 miles (300,000km) can give the engine a new lease of life. If the engine fails to run smoothly, this may be because someone unknowledgeable has been tinkering with it – these are not power units for weekend DIY enthusiasts; fortunately such problems may well prove straightforward to fix.

3. The GM400 three-speed automatic of later Shadows is a much better gearbox as well as being cheaper to repair than its predecessor. Having said that, both units are relatively trouble-free but after a run have a look underneath for signs of oil leaking from the bellhousing. This indicates that the front pump oil seal is worn and in need of replacement. As with all automatics, slipping gears or a reluctance to change up are signs that all is not well. But in truth, problems experienced with the gearchange are more likely to emanate from the electric motor that selects the gears and it is to be found at the end of the transmission housing.

4. The Shadow's all-independent suspension is relatively trouble-free, although bushes and balljoints do wear. Knocking under braking/acceleration is a sign of badly worn balljoints, and this can be verified by jacking the car up, supporting the bottom arm of the front suspension on an axle stand, and testing for play with a lever. For worn bushes, one test is to stand in a door opening and bounce the car up and down: any knocking or clonking means the bushes are tired. You can also see if the top wishbone bushes are worn by peering down between the chassis rail and the exhaust manifold: if the upper arm is hard against the front of the subframe and there is a large gap at the rear, then the bushes are badly worn.

5. The elaborate self-levelling hydraulics are part of a high-pressure system that also incorporates the braking system. Pressurised at up to 2,500psi, it is susceptible to leaks – as well as to worn-out gas spheres and defective height-correctors. With the engine running, the car should rise up and level itself when passengers get into the rear. On the road, slip the car into neutral, and the back of the car should jack up and go soft, with a knocking sound coming from the height-adjusters as they operate. A sign that all is not well is if a rear passenger hears knocking from the rear under braking: this is likely to signify tired self-levelling.

6. Leaks are another possible ailment. With everything warmed up after a decent run, park the car and leave the engine running. Then move it away and check for puddles of hydraulic fluid on the ground. If you encounter some on the nearside of the engine it will originate from either or both of the accumulators which supply the system. Also check for fluid in the vee of the engine: this could come from a worn 'O' ring within the pump or pumps that charge the accumulators. Evidence of hydraulic fluid at the rear of the car means that the height-control valves are probably leaking.

7. Check that all the warning lights are operating by putting the car in drive and cranking the ignition: all the lights should illuminate. Having verified that the brake-pressure warning light is working, you can check the accumulator spheres for correct functioning. Run the car for four minutes, and then switch off the ignition. Pump the brake pedal twice, and then turn the ignition on: the warning light should not illuminate. Pump the pedal. If it takes 20 or so pumps before the light goes on, then the accumulators are doing their job; three pumps or less before the light goes on and you have problems.

8. Replacing the hydraulic pipes is a nightmare job which takes days of

product than the 1965–76 generation of cars.

In June 1980 news broke that Rolls-Royce Motors' seven years of independence was coming to an end when plans were made public that it was to merge with the Vickers group. David Plastow had been a non-executive director of Vickers since 1975. As the architect of the alliance, he had always believed that, as a small car company, Rolls-Royce's future lay within a large engineering combine. It could thus be insulated, to some extent, from the fluctuations of the global economy.

The merger was formalised in August 1980, and at this point

workshop time; consequently corroded pipes are frequently neglected. When the car is up on a ramp, inspect it therefore for rusted hydraulic lines; conversely, if the pipes look near-new this is a sign somebody has been prepared to spend money on maintaining the car properly. Alas, this is regrettably rare: hydraulic systems are often neglected on low-annual-mileage cars, such as those used for wedding hire. Worse, rotten pipes can be concealed under black-wax rustproofing compound or underseal.

9. The front height-levelling control was only fitted until the 1969 model year which is one very good reason to avoid the first four years of Shadow manufacture. It isn't worth the additional complication and the potential risks of leaks, and indeed most early cars have had the front height-levelling removed.

10. Don't be alarmed if the power-assisted steering feels excessively slack when the engine is not running. This is quite normal and applies to both the original recirculating-ball steering and to the Shadow II's rack-and-pinion system. But, unlike its predecessor, the latter is prone to leakage, so be on the lookout for oil dribbles.

11. Seized brakes can result from problems in the high-pressure hydraulics, so check that all brakes come on and off correctly. Beyond this, the entire system is subject to excessive wear. This not only applies to the pads but also, surprisingly, to the discs, which can deteriorate at a surprising rate.

12. The Silver Shadow's bodywork does not suffer excessively from rust, apart from the extremities of the sills. Like the Cloud family, this is a steel structure although the doors, bonnet and boot lid are made of aluminium. Happily, the all-important floorpan is well covered with a rust-inhibiting black bituminous material, and the hitherto vulnerable front wheelarches are protected with glass-fibre mouldings. All the same, the bottom of the front wing shields can deteriorate, allowing road dirt to get behind, so check for corrosion at the bottom of the front wings. The wheelarches can also rot, so inspect these carefully.

13. While you're contemplating the car's exterior, check for excessive slack in the windscreen wipers. Replacing the wheel boxes is a particularly time-consuming job.

14. The corners of the chrome bumpers on the Shadow I and Bentley T1 can corrode through.

15. A car fitted with a Harvey-Bailey suspension kit, consisting of uprated springs and stiffer anti-roll bars – or the less satisfactory Rolls-Royce kit – will have considerably improved road behaviour.

16. The state of the interior will be readily apparent. Electric windows were fitted from the outset but the early Piper motors and switch gear weren't sufficiently protected from the elements and give trouble. The later rubber encased Lucas units are far more reliable. On the subject of

electrics, be wary of faulty components, as the wiring loom is extraordinarily complicated and an apparently straightforward fault can take a disproportionate amount of time to rectify.

17. Most cars will be fitted with air-conditioning – the split-level system used in the post-1977 Shadow II being far and away the best available. But air-conditioning units tend to suffer a Cinderella existence. If the system doesn't work in the car you are contemplating, the most usual reason is that the refrigerator fluid, which should be changed every year, hasn't been replaced. And when it's left to its own devices it turns to an acid and rots the unit from the inside...

18. There are a lot of tired – and cheap – Shadows on the market. Beware of a £5,000 'cheapie' that might cost £10,000 or more to fix. There's little point in having a £12,000 bill on a car that's only worth £10,000, when with care you could have bought a car where the previous owner has taken the financial rap for bringing it up to top condition.

19. In short, buy as a late and as good a Shadow as you can possibly afford and try to avoid the 1965–70 cars which were still experiencing teething troubles. The larger engine and central door locking both arrived in 1970 which are pluses and these later cars also lack the front height levelling which is an another advantage. Nevertheless, it's the Silver Shadow II of the 1977–80 era which, potentially, represents the best buy.

Plastow became managing director and chief executive of Vickers and Ian Fraser deputy chairman. This followed the abolition of the post of chairman of Rolls-Royce Motors. At Crewe, George Fenn, who in 1976 had

replaced Plastow as managing director, took over as chief executive.

But the world was in the grip of an even more severe recession that had followed the 1979 Iranian revolution and an escalation in oil prices. That

year Rolls-Royce returned a £10.9 million profit and had a new model in the shape of the Silver Spirit. The global economy was moving into uncharted waters: what would the 1980s hold?

The Corniche

The Silver Shadow was not only the most successful Rolls-Royce in the company's history: in 1966 it also spawned a secondary two-door line that was to last an impressive 24 years. Produced under both marque names, although the Rolls-Royce version was by far and away the most popular, the status of these coveted variants was further enhanced in 1971 by the adoption of the Corniche name. The cars proved to be remarkably enduring, as the open version remained in production until 1995, long after the demise of its Silver Shadow parent.

It will be recalled that what had become Mulliner, Park Ward had been responsible, along with James Young, for open and closed versions of the Silver Cloud and Bentley Continental. As recounted in the previous chapter, James Young briefly offered a two-door Shadow-based saloon from 1965 to 1967, but then the company introduced its own versions at the 1966 Geneva Motor Show, these retaining the Silver Shadow and T-series model names.

The two-door cars had been styled

Your carriage awaits... the quality of the Corniche's upholstery and woodwork, undertaken by Mulliner Park Ward, was far superior to that of the Silver Shadow saloon. (LAT)

Starting point 1 for the Corniche: the Silver Shadow two-door saloon introduced at the 1966 Geneva Motor Show, and which remained in production as the Corniche until the Shadow's demise in 1980. (LAT)

Starting point 2: the convertible version of the Silver Shadow that appeared in 1967 was still – as this contemporary colour photograph indicates – identified by the traditional drophead coupé name. (Rolls-Royce)

by John Blatchley's assistant, Bill Allen, and had an upswept wing line inspired by the Silver Cloud. In consequence they differed visually somewhat from the Shadow, with the bonnet the only common panel. Mechanically, there was little change made, apart for the fact that, as the four-door saloons, left-hand-drive examples were fitted with the GM400 three-speed Hydramatic transmission.

The method of building the cars was elaborate, to say the least. The shells were hand-assembled and trimmed at Mulliner, Park Ward and once the body structure was completed, the unpainted shells were transported the 150 miles (240km) to Crewe where the mechanicals were installed. The cars were then returned to Willesden for painting, trimming and finishing. The entire process took

some six months from start to finish.

Eighteen months after the saloon's arrival, the convertible version of the Shadow was unveiled at the September 1967 Frankfurt Motor Show. Allen was not responsible for the conversion, it being engineered by Mulliner Park Ward. Of monocoque construction, and thus having no chassis, the absence of the reinforcing roof meant that

What's in a name? (ii) Corniche

The Corniche is the name given to that part of the French Riviera between the Principality of Monaco and the town of Monte Carlo which has always been a popular resort with the English. Its associations with Rolls-Royce go back to the earliest days of the company when the Hon C. S. Rolls convinced his business partner Henry Royce of the need for an appropriate car for the rich and well-to-do to transfer themselves and their retinues to winter in the area. The result, in 1906, was the fabled Silver Ghost model was to endure until 1925.

As already mentioned, the Corniche name had previously been applied to the experimental Paulin-designed Vanvooren-bodied streamlined Mark V Bentley saloon of 1939. It was revived in 1951 when the name Corniche II was internally allotted to the high-speed Bentley coupé which entered production in 1952 as the R-type Continental. Originally this was a Rolls-Royce name rather than a Bentley one, the famous Phantom II Continental having appeared in 1930.

Announced in September 1967, the Silver Shadow drophead coupé by Mulliner, Park Ward cost, complete with power-operated hood, £10,927, some £3,000 more than the saloon. (LAT)

strengthening members had to be welded on top of the floorpan to increase the body's rigidity. The door apertures were similarly reinforced, with the result that the two-door open car was considerably heavier than the standard four-door saloon!

A nice touch, literally, was the electric windows that stopped half an inch short of their seals and required the application of a secondary button for the glass to complete its travel. This arrangement was adopted to prevent children from trapping their fingers in the glass.

But the extra weight made the

convertible the slowest car in the Silver Shadow line and in 1970 Crewe's engine section began to examine ways of redressing the balance by making improvements to the V8's output. Designated project Gamma, ministrations were made to the valve timing and a big-bore exhaust system was introduced to reduce the power loss.

With this new improved engine in the offing, Rolls-Royce decided to give the two-door saloons and convertibles the Corniche name. By this time the open car was outselling the closed version by the rate of about two to one, with 1938 convertibles sold compared with 1108 two-doors. Perversely, Bentley sales were almost evenly spread between 63 saloons and 65 open cars.

The change was announced on 4 March 1971, a month to the day since the company's celebrated collapse. So just how did the new cars differ from the original two-door models? As if to underline its emergence as a model in its own right, the Rolls-Royce radiator shell was slightly deeper than that used on the Silver Shadow and was daringly raked forward by an almost imperceptible three degrees. New hub caps were introduced for the wheels, with ventilation slots to increase the amount of air reaching the brakes.

The Gamma engine improvements had proved their worth and on British-market cars without the American de-toxing equipment the changes were said to produce a 10 per cent improvement in the still-undisclosed output of the alloy V8. Those Corniches destined for transatlantic customers used the regular Shadow engine.

Inside was a redesigned dashboard, the fitment of a rev-counter providing the model with a sporting feel – this being the first occasion on which a Rolls-Royce had been so equipped. This sporting ambiance was further

There was also a Bentley version of the two-door saloon although it only sold in limited numbers. (LAT)

Rolls-Royce Corniche
1971–1995

ENGINE:
V8, alloy block and cylinder heads
Bore x stroke — 104.1mm x 99.1mm
Capacity — 6,750cc
Valve actuation — Pushrod
Compression ratio — 9.0:1
Carburettors — Twin SU HD8*
Power — Not disclosed
*UK versions fitted with Solex 4A1 from 1977, Bosch K-Jetronic fuel injection from October 1986, MK Motronic fuel injection and management system from October 1989

TRANSMISSION:
Rear-wheel drive
Three-speed, automatic with torque converter
Four-speed from winter 1991/1992
Final drive ratio: 3.08:1

SUSPENSION:
Front: Independent, wishbone and coil spring
Rear: Independent, semi-trailing arms, coil springs. Revised (Spirit-type) from March 1979
Automatic hydraulic height control
Adaptive suspension from 1992 model year

STEERING:
Power-assisted recirculating ball; rack-and-pinion from February 1977
Turns lock-to-lock: 3.5

BRAKES:
Front: hydraulic disc
Rear: hydraulic disc
Power assistance from two engine-driven hydraulic pumps
ABS brakes from 1988 model year

WHEELS/TYRES:
Steel disc wheels
205-15in

BODYWORK:
Coachbuilt aluminium panels on steel frame
Reinforced unitary construction
Two-door convertible, saloon

DIMENSIONS:
Length — 16ft 11½in* (5.16m)
Wheelbase — 9ft 11¾in** (3.04m)
Track – front — 4ft 11½in (1.51m)
     – rear — 4ft 9¾in (1.46m)
Width — 6ft 0in (1.82m)
Height — 4ft 10¾in (1.49m)
* 17ft 0½ in (5.19m) from February 1977
**10ft 0in (3.04m) from April 1974

WEIGHT:
43.0cwt (2,190kg)

PERFORMANCE:
(Source: *Autocar*)
Max speed — 120mph (193kph)
0–50mph (0–80kph) — 6.8sec
0–60mph (0–100kph) — 9.6sec
0–70mph (0–112kph) — 12.7sec

PRICE INCLUDING TAX WHEN NEW:
Convertible — £13,410
Saloon — £12,829

NUMBER BUILT:
Rolls-Royce Corniche: 3,239, of which 1,108 were saloons
Corniche II: 1,234
Corniche III: 452
Corniche IV: 196
Corniche S: 25
Bentley Corniche: 77, of which 63 were saloons
Bentley Continental: 433
Total: 5,146

The saloon version of the Corniche was discontinued in 1981; this is a very early example, carrying a 1971–72 registration. (LAT)

underlined by a wood-rimmed 15in three-spoked steering wheel – although subsequently the saloon wheel was reintroduced and the rev-counter deleted. Another distinguishing feature was a 'Corniche' badge on the offside of the boot lid. The Silver Shadow saloon, by contrast, continued to remain anonymous. On the road the mechanical ministrations proved their worth and the Corniche's top speed of 120mph (193kph) was some 5mph (8kph) faster than its Shadow parent.

All these improvements coincidentally added about 10 per cent to the price of the two-door lines with the saloon selling for £12,829 and the Bentley version for £71 less. As ever, the convertibles were more expensive and cost some £600 more.

At the launch, appropriately in the South of France (see box), Rolls-Royce announced that henceforth special-bodied models would receive any engineering and styling refinements ahead of the saloons. Significantly, this applied to the split-level air-conditioning which was to be introduced on the new Camargue coupé initially built alongside the Corniche at Mulliner Park Ward. This new system was fitted to the two-door cars from January 1976, a good year before its appearance on the Shadow II; new seats and a dished steering wheel also came in at the same time.

It was in 1977 that the Corniche acquired the Shadow II's body refinements and rack-and-pinion steering. US cars were fitted with the new SU HAF carburettors, while those examples for Britain and Europe moved to the four-barrel Solex 4A1 unit being used on the Camargue.

With Rolls-Royce's Silver Spirit waiting in the wings, in March 1979 the Corniche was the unpublicised recipient of its revised independent rear suspension system. The decision had been taken in 1977 to introduce it in this way to gain working experience of the new layout. As the new model moved centre stage from October 1980, the Corniche saloon was discontinued in March 1981, leaving the convertible as the sole survivor of the Shadow series. As the only open car in the Rolls-Royce range it was to prove remarkably enduring.

As described in Chapter Ten, the eighties was the decade of the Bentley revival and one result was the July 1984 renaming of the Bentley version of the Corniche as the Continental. Outwardly the car looked the same but there were colour-keyed bumpers and door mirrors, a new dashboard, improved seats and revised colour schemes. The change was more than justified. Only 77 Bentley Corniches had been produced up until then but by the time that the open Continental was discontinued ten years later, a total of 433 had been completed.

The most significant change for the 1987 model year was the introduction of the fuel injection simultaneously applied to the Silver Spirit. At the

This Corniche benefited from the improvements introduced on the Silver Shadow II but was not officially known as the Corniche II. The headlamp brush cleaners were introduced across the Shadow range during the 1979 model year. (LAT)

Rear view of the convertible with the power-operated hood neatly stowed. The Corniche was the first Rolls-Royce to be identified by a model name on the bootlid. (LAT)

same time the motor for the power-operated hood and its hydraulic pump were repositioned in line with European regulations, and the Flying Lady mascot was made retractable, seven years after this feature had been introduced on the Silver Spirit.

For 1988 the changes were essentially cosmetic, with the arrival of memory-enhanced electrically adjustable seats and an extended central console nonetheless being sufficient for that year's cars to be accorded the Corniche II designation. The principal mechanical change was the fitment of ABS brakes as introduced on the Silver Spirit saloon. Subsequently, in mid-1988, the Continental convertible benefited from the arrival of revised instrumentation, a sport steering wheel and redesigned seats.

Two years later, the 1990 season saw the arrival of the Corniche III with new alloy wheels and, once again, a revised dashboard and improved seats. More significantly, under the bonnet was a new MK Motronic engine-management system.

At this point, in 1989, the world took another financial nose-dive. Rolls-Royce had been relatively unaffected by the first oil price rise but the Corniche line was ageing and the cars now sold for £123,808 apiece, to soar 33 per cent to a

Access to the sumptuously upholstered back seat was good, thanks to the wide doors. (LAT)

Rare indeed: the Bentley T2 Corniche in saloon form. (LAT)

As enduring as the Forth Bridge...The Corniche changed
remarkably little outwardly between its introduction in 1971
and the 1985 season when colour-keyed bumpers arrived.
(LAT)

Below: Although the Corniche IV of 1992 did not look much
different from its predecessors, beneath the surface adaptive
suspension and a four-speed automatic transmission had
been introduced. (Rolls-Royce)

Buying Hints

1. As the Corniche is Shadow-based, the same mechanical check points apply to the Corniche two-door saloons. However, all cars are powered by the 6.7-litre V8.

2. The overwhelming majority of cars are convertibles so the condition of the hood, with a replacement likely to set you back close on £5,000, is particularly important. Whilst the hood mechanism is very robust and not prone to problems, and the material tends not to deteriorate, the stitching does rot. It is best preserved with beeswax.

3. As an open car, the condition of the Corniche's interior is particularly important because retrimming is an expensive business. Having said that, the quality of the trim, and particularly the woodwork used for the dashboard and the door fillets, is far superior to that you'll find in the saloons.

4. The Solex 4A1 carburettor fitted to those Corniches sold on the British market during 1977–86 is a horror. It's fearsomely complex and of a sandwich construction: the securing nuts loosen, the gaskets leak, letting in air, and the result is starting problems. The carb needs to be checked every six months for the above shortcomings.

5. Undue differential noise is a particular problem with most members of the Silver Shadow/Silver Spirit family. The Corniche tends to be an exception in this regard and you shouldn't experience any excessive noise from that quarter.

6. The Corniche saloon benefits from better body rigidity than four-door Shadows, and responds particularly well to the fitment of a Harvey-Bailey handling kit. If an S2/S3 Continental is beyond your reach, an uprated Corniche could prove an interesting and well-priced sporting-tinged alternative.

prohibitive £164,347 in 1992! If Corniche sales were hit by one external factor, the second body blow was a corporate one. Encouraged by the Bentley revival, in 1991 Rolls-Royce announced its new turbocharged Continental R coupé, which would undoubtedly take sales from a model with styling and mechanicals dating back, in essence, to the fifties. Against this background of drastically falling sales, in 1991 news broke that Rolls-Royce was shutting its Mulliner Park Ward facility with a loss of some 500 skilled jobs. It finally closed its doors in 1994, two years after Corniche production had been transferred to Crewe along with the Mulliner Park Ward name.

In truth its presence there made far more economic sense and that year came the Corniche IV which benefited from the latest Silver Spirit updates, of which the most significant was the introduction of the General Motors GM4L80E automatic transmission

The Corniche IV Anniversary model of 1995 was limited to 25 cars and this Swiss registered example was number 19. All were painted the same Ming Blue with a cream hood. (LAT)

The Corniche Anniversary's interior woodwork was also special. A collector's piece! (LAT)

The Bentley revival of the 1980s was extended to the Corniche and from the 1985 season the Bentley version was renamed the Continental, whereupon it promptly gained a new lease of life. (Rolls-Royce)

with four rather than three speeds, as well as adaptive suspension and airbags.

Although the end was in sight, in October 1992 Rolls-Royce announced a 21st anniversary version and 25 cars were finished in Ming Blue with a cream hood. The silver element was present in the wood panels and a silver plaque on the glove compartment lid declared the individuality and significance of this

smart and exclusive model.

Then, in August 1993, the Corniche received the Spirit's much-revised V8 engine, which was some 20 per cent more powerful than its predecessor. Yet the new Azure convertible that appeared in 1995 was not a Rolls-Royce but a Bentley, in effect, an open version of the Continental R.

This spelt the end of the long-running convertible and the final batch of 25 cars, badged the Corniche S, was

completed in the summer of 1995. And that really was the end. In 24 years a total of 5,146 Rolls-Royce Corniche convertibles had been built, along with 1,108 saloons. As already noted, there were 77 Bentley versions.

But five years later, in 2000, the name was revived for a convertible version of the Silver Seraph saloon that had replaced the Silver Spirit in 1998. This latter-day Corniche is described in Chapter 10.

The Camargue

If the Corniche proved to be a remarkably enduring car, the same could not be said of the Camargue coupé of 1975, which at £29,250 was over twice the price of the Silver Shadow. Destined to survive for just 11 years, it was the first modern Rolls-Royce with its body designed by an outside agency, in this case the Italian styling house of Pininfarina.

It was, in truth, a model in the spirit of the Bentley Continental, in that it was intended for the owner-driver. Perversely, though, it was only available in Rolls-Royce form, although one Bentley version was produced. What emerged as the Camargue had begun life as a projected coachbuilt version of the Silver Shadow. It was originally hoped that James Young would be responsible for its body but the

A stylised sketch of the Camargue: the Rolls-Royce radiator was rather more prominent on the finished product. (Rolls-Royce/LAT)

Bromley company's closure of its coachbuilding department in 1967 put paid to that aspect of the plan.

In 1968 Pininfarina displayed at that year's London Motor Show what it described as a 'Bentley Special Coupé'. This four-seater fastback, for businessman James (later Lord) Hanson, possessed distinctive rectangular headlamps which contrasted with the Silver Shadow's twin circular units. The following year Rolls-Royce commissioned Pininfarina to design the top-of-range coupé. The new model was to be similarly based on the Silver Shadow floorpan and, as in the case of all Rolls-Royce styling, the lines were intended to feature the minimum of decoration so the car would enjoy a long manufacturing life. The design was the work of Sergio Pininfarina, son of the founder (see box), and in 1971 work began at Mulliner, Park Ward on the construction of what had been coded the Delta prototype.

This was also the year, it should be

noted, that the open and closed two-door Shadows were given the Corniche name, so did Rolls-Royce really need another two-door car? Managing director David Plastow's response at the launch was that this was what the market wanted...

The first experimental Delta had been completed in July 1972 although the Rolls-Royce radiator was removed in favour of a Bentley one so that the car could be tested on the Continent. Theoretically the model could have entered production in 1973 but in the event it did not appear for a further two years, being finally launched in March 1975. This hiatus was caused by a combination of circumstances, namely the corporate bankruptcy of 1971, the flotation of Rolls-Royce Motors two years later, and a damaging strike at Mulliner, Park Ward which was to build it. Extra time was also needed to perfect the Crewe-conceived air-conditioning system which, in the event, took eight years to develop and was an integral part of

Externally the Camargue changed little over its 10-year life. This is Rolls-Royce's 1975 launch car — the trim on the tops of the doors was later deleted. (LAT)

the model's specification.

Perhaps the most controversial aspect of the car was its styling, especially in comparison with Pininfarina's design for the Fiat 130 coupé of 1971. Whilst the Camargue's rear profile was neat and beautifully proportioned, the front of the car was angular and almost brutal in execution. It incorporated the famous Rolls-Royce radiator which, daringly, was tilted forward in the manner of the Corniche, although this time by 10 degrees. In truth Pininfarina had

wished the radiator to have been rather smaller...

The rectangular lamps of the 1968 Bentley coupé were not perpetuated, but the twinned round headlights were positioned in a clumsy rectangular surround. Energy absorbing bumpers were similar to those already fitted on Silver Shadows destined for the American market from the 1974 model year. All these irreconcilable factors resulted in a far from satisfactory front end.

Sharing the same 10ft (3.05m)

wheelbase as its Silver Shadow contemporary, along with its mechanicals, the Camargue cost some £10,000 more than its Corniche stablemate but at 2.6 tons (2,641kg) it was some 200lb (90kg) heavier although in compensation it was rather roomier inside.

Still waters: the Camargue roughly doubled in price from £22,700 in 1977 to £48,000 in 1984. This is a late example. (LAT)

The Camargue looked rather better from the back than the front. Unlike its Corniche stablemate, the model name was not displayed on the bootlid. (LAT)

The Camargue's interior with its unique instrument panel and aircraft-style instruments. Rolls-Royce's split-level air-conditioning was fitted from the outset. (Rolls-Royce)

The doors were of considerable width, which greatly eased access to the interior – which was unique to the model. It was luxuriously trimmed and the back seat with separate squabs was a significant 8½in (21.6cm) wider than the Corniche's, making it possible to squeeze in an extra passenger if the need arose. A further benefit was a larger boot.

An even more significant difference was the fitment of the new split-level air-conditioning system, an impressively elaborate design and, arguably, the model's most important feature. It would be extended to the Corniche in 1976 and to the Silver Shadow II in 1977. The controls were positioned in the centre of the dashboard, which also differed from that fitted to the Corniche and Silver Shadow. Although appearing to be wood, it was actually a veneer attached to an alloy base. Also styled by Pininfarina, the instrument panel used angular black frames for the dials, and endowed the cockpit with the look more of a light aircraft than a luxurious road-bound motor car.

Top speed was about 120mph (190kph) and this big car – it was 6ft 3in (1.90m) wide – rode and handled well, although commentators found that the power steering still suffered from the vagueness they had experienced on the Silver Shadow. This failing would not be resolved until the arrival of the Shadow II's more precise rack-and-pinion steering two years later.

Unfortunately the Camargue also lacked some of the refinement that might have been expected of a model at this price. When the perceptive technical editor of *Autocar*, Jeff Daniels, drove what he conceded was a pre-production model, he reported that the new Rolls-Royce did not match the vibration, noise and harshness criteria by which such cars were judged. "This is not to say [it] is noisy in absolute terms: at 70mph (112kph) it is virtually noiseless", he reported at the model's launch. "But in terms of its own class there is a disappointing build-up of noise from that point on, both road rumble and a

Rolls-Royce Camargue 1975–1986

ENGINE:
V8, alloy block, alloy heads

Bore x stroke	104.1mm x 99.1mm
Capacity	6750cc
Valve actuation	Pushrod
Compression ratio	8:1
Carburettors	Solex 4A1*
Power	Not disclosed

*First 60 cars twin SU HD8

TRANSMISSION:
Rear-wheel drive
Three-speed automatic with torque converter
Final drive ratio: 3.08:1

SUSPENSION:
Front: Independent, wishbone and coil spring
Rear: Independent, semi-trailing arms and coil springs. Revised (to Silver Spirit type) in March 1979
Automatic hydraulic height control

STEERING:
Power-assisted recirculating-ball; rack-and-pinion from February 1977
Turns lock-to-lock: 3.5

BRAKES:
Front: Hydraulic disc
Rear: Hydraulic disc
Power assistance from two engine-driven hydraulic pumps

WHEELS/TYRES:
Steel disc wheels
HR70–15in

BODYWORK:
Steel and aluminium unitary-construction two-door coupé

DIMENSIONS:

Length	16ft 11½ in (5.16m)
Wheelbase	10ft 1in (3.05m)
Track - front	5ft 0in (1.52m)
- rear	4ft 11in (1.49m)
Width	6ft 3in (1.90m)
Height	4ft 9in (1.40m)

WEIGHT:
46.2cwt (2,347kg)

PERFORMANCE:
Not road tested by any motoring magazine
Top speed (claimed)   119mph (186kph)

PRICE INCLUDING TAX WHEN NEW:
£29,250

NUMBER BUILT:
Rolls-Royce: 530, Bentley: 1, Total: 531

Buying Hints

1. As the Camargue is, like the Corniche, Shadow-based, the same mechanical check points apply.

2. An exception is the Solex 4A1 carburettor which replaced the original twin SUs after the first 60 Camargues had been completed. The shortcomings of this instrument, which was also fitted to Corniche from 1977, are chronicled on page 106.

3. Bodily the coupé shares the same steel structure as its parent and the large doors are, likewise, aluminium. Rust protection was very effective and corrosion is not a problem.

4. The Camargue tends to attract far lower prices than the Corniche although it was considerably more expensive in its day. Its looks are still not to everyone's tastes, but its handling is considerably better.

measure of wind noise, and at 110mph (177kph) voices must be raised slightly to converse." These shortcomings were not to be eliminated from the production versions.

Launched into a world reeling from the effects of soaring oil prices, the Camargue's fuel consumption of around 11mpg (25 litres/100km) probably didn't over-worry its potential buyers, and it established a solid, if modest, customer base.

But from the very outset Rolls-Royce had decided that its performance needed to be superior to that of the other models. Therefore after the first 60 cars had been

What's in a name? (iii) The Camargue

The Camargue took its name from the lovely region of lakes, marshes and wasteland on the French Riviera between the Grand Rhône and the Petit Rhône about 50 miles (80km) from Marseilles. It is the home of small black bulls and where local herdsman rode half-wild horses. The company hammily evoked this in its publicity for the car, proclaiming: "These horses of the Camargue possess a natural taste for freedom and a life in the wild, and are renowned for their stamina and vivacity – qualities which epitomise the top-of-range Rolls-Royce..." The first Rolls-Royce to be associated with the Camargue area of the French Rivièra was the Silver Ghost.

Pininfarina – the Italian connection

Arguably the best-known of the Italian styling houses, Turin-based Pininfarina was established in 1930 by Batista 'Pinin' Farina. The son of a coachbuilder, Farina was just 27 when he started his business and whilst he bodied many Fiats and Alfa Romeos, he was best known for his work for Lancia. But it was not until the post-war years that he achieved international recognition, notably for his lovely Cisitalia coupé of 1948 that was soon afterwards displayed in the New York Museum of Modern Art. He went on to reach an agreement in 1956 with Enzo Ferrari, giving his company exclusive rights to style and body the sensational sports cars from Modena.

Pininfarina, as his name was spelt from 1960, was well known within Britain's car industry, having been responsible for styling BMC's corporate mid-sized saloons of 1958/59, its Austin A40 of 1958 and the BMC 1100 which became the UK's best-selling car in the 1960s. Following his son Sergio's work for Rolls-Royce on the Camargue, the company was appointed to engineer the Bentley Azure, the open version of the Continental, a contract that continues to this day.

The Pininfarina-bodied Bentley T-Series produced for financier James Hanson (later Lord Hanson), and displayed by the Italian company at the 1968 motor show. (LAT)

completed, the usual twin SUs carburettors were replaced by a single four-choke downdraught Solex 4A1 unit. How measurable an improvement this effected was not to be revealed, as Rolls-Royce never made the model available to motoring magazines for independent testing and evaluation.

Because the Camague, like the

Corniche, was built in London by Mulliner Park Ward, the manufacturing process was elaborate and time-consuming and as with the Corniche it took six months to complete each car. The shells were first assembled at Pressed Steel's Cowley factory, with the work being completed at Hythe Road. They were then dispatched to Crewe for priming and painting where

their mechanicals were added. It was then back to Willesden for trimming and finishing. As in the case of the other Crewe products, the doors, bonnet and bootlid were made of aluminium.

The Camargue received the front spoiler and rack-and-pinion steering of the Shadow II in 1977 and, in the following year, changes were made to

Left: The Camargue's back seats. A spotlight and a floodlight were set into each rear quarter panel. (LAT)

Right: Originally Mulliner Park Ward was credited on the Camargue's body plate but from 1978 Crewe took over production and the wording was altered accordingly. (LAT)

the manufacturing processes to improve build quality. In consequence the Mulliner Park Ward element was removed from the assembly sequence. Instead of the body panels being assembled at Cowley, from autumn 1978 this stage in the manufacturing process was taken on by Motor Panels in Coventry. It was responsible for the upper portion of the body which was then welded to the lower section and floorpan. The completed shells were then dispatched to Crewe where they were rustproofed, painted and the cars completed.

In 1979 the Camargue, along with the Corniche, received the revised independent rear suspension intended for the new Silver Spirit saloon of 1980. That year about two cars were being produced each week, but demand began to slow by the mid-eighties, with output dropping to about 20 examples a year. The end was in sight, and Rolls-Royce ceased to list the Camargue early in 1986. By this time the price stood at £83,122. In March it announced that the Camargue would be discontinued the following year, there still being some 20 examples under completion, mostly for America. This included 12 limited edition cars, identifiable by a Bentley Turbo style of alloy wheel with a RR centre, and by enhanced interiors. Total production amounted to 531 cars, making the Camargue – the low-volume Phantom lines excepted – the rarest and most expensive Rolls-Royce of the post-war years.

The Silver
Spirit series

The Silver Spirit was announced in October 1980, just as a second and ultimately more serious downturn in the world economy was about to take effect. If the company's previous experiences of recession were anything to go by, it would have weathered the ensuing financial storm. But in the event Rolls-Royce and Bentley production halved, from 3,203 cars built in 1980 to 1,551 in 1982.

The new model was essentially a

rebodied Silver Shadow and it thus inherited, in essence, a substructure, running gear and engine conceived in the fifties. It also arrived at a time when the motoring marketplace was becoming more competitive. Rolls-Royce had always recognised Mercedes-Benz as a formidable competitor and it continued to be so. But from the seventies onwards another West German make, BMW, was also offering an impressive range of well-engineered, lighter, more

The Silver Spirit (right), introduced in 1980, here with its Silver Shadow and Silver Cloud predecessors. (LAT)

Above: The Silver Spirit was, in essence, a rebodied Silver Shadow with revised independent rear suspension. (LAT)

Left: Rear-three quarter shot of an early Silver Spirit: from inside, the car doesn't feel as bulky as it appears from outside. (LAT)

Right: The dashboard was essentially carried over from the Silver Shadow although the central digital display was new. (LAT)

economical and faster cars. As the stature of both rivals grew, their most prestigious models, the S-Class and 7-series respectively, began to offer very real alternatives to 'The Best Car in the World', at a fraction of the cost.

Crewe had a very real problem in that since the war it had, in reality, only offered a single model in the luxury field which by its nature was a limited one and particularly vulnerable to the fluctuations of the global marketplace. Worse, Rolls-Royce lacked the financial resources to match the research and development undertaken by its German rivals, although it strove to do so.

As time went on, superlative build quality was just not enough and what once had been proclaimed as strengths were, in the longer run, to become limitations. By the nineties the production of Rolls-Royce cars had dropped to levels not experienced by the company since pre-First World War days. Only the revival of the Bentley marque from the mid-eighties onwards had helped maintain this albeit limited production and prevent the onset of severe financial problems.

The Silver Spirit had cost a modest £28 million to develop and it had an overall length of 17ft 3in (5.26m), consumed fuel at the rate of 12 miles per gallon (23 litres/100km), weighed 44.2cwt (2,245kg), and purchasers would collect little change from a £50,000 cheque. The Spirit was designed to have a manufacturing life of at least 10 years, but there could have been few in 1980 who would have prophesied that the model was destined to survive for no fewer than 18 years in all.

Some 19,000 examples of the Spirit and its Bentley-badged derivatives were produced over this period. This was around half the number of the Silver Shadow line built over the previous 15 years, which underlines the erosion of the marque's appeal.

Work on what was coded the SZ project had begun in 1972. Whilst the mechanicals, with the exception of the rear suspension, were essentially

Fritz Feller 1925–1990

With the Silver Spirit's lines to his credit, the Austrian-born Fritz Feller, was, very unusually, a mechanical engineer who made a mid-career change to replace John Blatchley as Rolls-Royce's chief stylist.

A native of Vienna, Feller came to Britain as a 14-year-old schoolboy refugee in 1939. Two years later, in 1941, he joined Rolls-Royce at Derby as an engineering apprentice and subsequently graduated to aero-engine design. He worked on the Avon jet unit but in 1952 he moved to Crewe. From 1964 Feller undertook pioneering work on what proved to be a stillborn two-stage Wankel diesel engine and he was awarded the Thomas Hawksley Gold Medal in 1970 for a lecture he presented on the subject.

With John Blatchley's impending departure and with his Wankel work at an end, Feller convinced his masters of his stylistic abilities although their apprehension was reflected by the fact that the appointment was initially a temporary one.

His first assignment was to work with Pininfarina on the Camargue but he is forever identified with the Silver Shadow's Silver Spirit successor of 1980. He declared on its announcement: "Nothing in this life is so dull and miserable as the 'average' and 'mean'... Once we regard dreams as a waste of time, magic also dies. That is why Rolls-Royce motor cars must always remain true to our best traditions."

His work was destined to endure for 18 years but illness forced him to take early retirement in 1984 and he died in February 1990 at the age of 64.

those of the 1977 Silver Shadow II, the body was wholly new. John Blatchley had retired in 1969 and, as the accompanying notes indicate, his place was taken by Fritz Feller, who was accorded the title of chief engineer of styling and future projects.

Feller's intention was to produce a car that was not only lower and wider than the angular Shadow but one which would also embody a more pleasing rear profile. This was to be coupled with some 30 per cent more glass and a lower waistline. The look slowly evolved and it was not until 1975/76 that what was allotted the Style F designation was finally approved. The first experimental car was on the road in November 1977, and bore a remarkable similarity to the finished product, the most distinctive stylistic feature of which was a completely re-thought front end.

This was dominated by the famous

Rolls-Royce radiator, this being 1in (2.54cm) lower and 3.6in (9.1cm) wider than the Shadow unit. Also, for safety reasons, its contours had an element of curvature, while legislation also required that the Silver Lady mascot should no longer be spring-loaded on a dummy radiator cap.

Technical director John Hollings recalled in 1981 that this was one of the first safety features to be tackled during the Silver Spirit's gestation. "The European regulations now forbid sharp 'exterior protrusions' and the Flying Lady was considered too dangerous to pedestrians and cyclists. We therefore devised a method of making her retract into the radiator shell when tilted more than 30°. This was appreciated by the authorities but they did insist that she should also retract if struck from directly above." To retrieve the retiring lady, she could be manually lifted back into position and so seal the radiator aperture – which, it should be noted, was not the radiator proper.

Although the Spirit retained, like the Shadow, twin headlights these were contained within rectangular transparent covers which at their extremities wrapped around the front wings and incorporated the sidelights and indicators. They closely adjoined either side of the squatter radiator, accentuating the fact that the new car was lower and wider than its rather upright predecessor.

The Spirit's interior was some 3in (7.6cm) wider than the Silver Shadow's. It still had the aura of a gentleman's club and the burr-walnut veneered dashboard was essentially that of its predecessor although it now featured an outside temperature display and a 12-hour clock.

The principal difference was the introduction of separate back seat squabs in place of a bench seat; there was slightly less rear headroom and some 1½in (3.8cm) more kneeroom, but the space available was not overly generous. Still, the long-wheelbase version redressed matters, with an extra 4in (10cm) of rear floor space.

As already mentioned, the new rear suspension had been quietly introduced on the Corniche and Camargue in March 1979. Suspension finesse was an area where the Silver Shadow had been found wanting, particularly following the 1968 arrival of Jaguar's acclaimed XJ6 saloon, selling on its launch at a third of the Rolls-Royce's price. With a brief to improve handling, ride and comfort, and to suppress vibration, the Crewe engineering team retained the essentials of the Shadow's semi-trailing-arm layout. However, the arm pivots were more inclined, which permitted a more pronounced change in camber as the wheels rose and fell over uneven surfaces; at the same time the dampers were repositioned.

Decibel levels were further reduced by the introduction of two additional cross tubes to the suspension subframe, even if they appeared to be somewhat makeshift in appearance. Otherwise the sophisticated self-levelling and high-pressure hydraulic

Rolls-Royce Silver Spirit
1980–1996

ENGINE:
V8 alloy block and cylinder heads

Bore x stroke	104.1mm x 99.1mm
Capacity	6,750cc
Valve actuation	Pushrod
Compression ratio	9.0:1
Carburettors	Twin SU HIF7*
Power	Not disclosed

*Bosch K–Jetronic fuel injection from October 1986 and MK Motronic fuel injection and engine management system from 1989 model year

TRANSMISSION:
Rear-wheel drive
Three-speed automatic with torque converter to 1991 model year; thereafter four-speed
Final drive ratio: 3.08:1. From 1987 season: 2.69:1

SUSPENSION:
Front: Independent, wishbone and coil spring
Rear: Independent, semi-trailing arms and coil springs. Automatic hydraulic height control. Adaptive suspension from 1990 model year.

STEERING:
Power-assisted rack-and-pinion
Turns lock-to-lock: 3.25

BRAKES:
Front: hydraulic disc
Rear: hydraulic disc
Power assistance from two engine-driven hydraulic pumps. ABS from 1987 model year

WHEELS/TYRES:
Steel disc wheels
235/70HR x 15in

BODYWORK:
Steel and aluminium four-door unitary-construction saloon

DIMENSIONS:

Length	17ft 3in (5.25m)
Wheelbase	10ft 0in (3.00m)
Track – front	5ft 0in (1.52m)
– rear	5ft 0in (1.52m)
Width	6ft 2in (1.88m)
Height	4ft 10in (1.47m)

WEIGHT:
44.1cwt (2,245kg)

PERFORMANCE:
(Source: *Autocar*)

Max speed	119mph (191kph)
0–50mph (0–80kph)	7.3sec
0–60mph (0–100kph)	10.0sec
0–70mph (0–112kph)	13.4sec

PRICE INCLUDING TAX WHEN NEW:
Standard wheelbase £49,629

NUMBER BUILT:
Silver Spirit: 8,129
Silver Spirit II: 1,152
Silver Spirit III: 211
Silver Spirit (1995–1996): 122
Bentley Mulsanne: 482
Total: 10,096

Rolls-Royce Silver Spur I/II/III and Silver Dawn
1980–1998

As Silver Spirit except:

ENGINE:
Light-turbocharged 300bhp V8 in Silver Spur III for 1997 model year

TRANSMISSION:
2.69:1 rear axle ratio

DIMENSIONS:

Length	17ft 7in (5.35m)
Wheelbase	10ft 4½in (3.16m)

WEIGHT:
44.7cwt (2275kg)

PRICE INCLUDING TAX WHEN NEW:
£56,408

NUMBER BUILT:
Silver Spur: 6,238
Silver Spur II: 1,658
Silver Spur III: 430
Silver Spur (from June 1995): 507
Silver Dawn: 237
Bentley Mulsanne L: 49
Total : 9,119

braking system were perpetuated although a minor change was a switch from brake fluid to mineral oil, this being cheaper and not hygroscopic – meaning that it did not absorb water.

The front suspension was, by contrast, essentially carried over from the Silver Shadow II, and thus was the compliant system which had been in use since 1972.

Similarly the Spirit's 6.7-litre V8 was essentially inherited from its long-lived predecessor. However, in March 1980, some eight months prior to the

The Silver Spur, the long-wheelbase version of the Spirit, was announced simultaneously and perpetuated the Everflex roof of its Shadow predecessor. (LAT)

The long-wheelbase body was also available on the Bentley Mulsanne. (LAT)

Missed opportunity?

In 1990 BMW entered into what proved to be a loss-making jointly-financed aero-engine venture with Rolls-Royce plc. Soon afterwards, in recession-hit 1992, its executive chairman, Eberhard von Kuenheim, held protracted discussions with Vickers, owner of Rolls-Royce Motor Cars, with a view to acquiring the business. A deal was agreed whereby BMW would purchase 60 per cent of the car company, with Vickers and Rolls-Royce plc taking 20 per cent apiece. But the German firm pulled out at the eleventh hour because it was financially stretched in building a new American factory, at Spartanburg, South Carolina, and it feared having to make many redundancies at Crewe. In retrospect Rolls-Royce would have been a better acquisition than its calamitous purchase, two years later, of the Rover Group. And although BMW finally acquired the Rolls-Royce name in 1998, it was not in quite the circumstances it had envisaged...

Spirit's announcement, the engine's compression ratio had been raised to 9:1, along with attendant changes to the carburettors, with the intention of improving fuel economy. The GM400 three-speed automatic transmission was likewise retained.

The long-wheelbase car was announced simultaneously with the standard version and accorded the Silver Spur name, the line being instantly identifiable by its Everflex fabric-covered roof and extended rear side windows. This was possible because, unlike the lwb Shadow, which had been laboriously and individually extended by Mulliner Park Ward, its successor's substructure and body were individually tooled by Pressed Steel.

The wisdom of this decision was

Robert Jankel Design of Weybridge, Surrey, was responsible for Rolls-Royce's original stretch limousine, announced in February 1984. Effectively a Silver Spur with a new 3ft/914mm centre section, it initially had six doors although a four-door configuration was later standardised. (LAT)

Interior of the luxurious Jankel stretch limousine, with colour television, VHS recorder and radio cassette player – all for £140,000! (LAT)

reflected by the fact that the Silver Spur proved to be very much more popular than its predecessor, which had accounted for a mere 15 per cent of total production, and suggests that customers may have found the Spirit a little cramped for those passengers confined to its otherwise well-upholstered back seat. In all, 6,240 Silver Spurs were to be produced over the following 12 years, compared with 8,126 Silver Spirits that were built

over a similar period.

There was a shift in marketing emphasis when it came to the name of the Bentley version of the Spirit. If Silver Cloud and Shadow precedent had been anything to go by, the famous winged-B radiator badge would have adorned a car carrying the dispiriting 'U' initial. Against a background of rapidly diminishing sales, the Bentley was instead accorded the Mulsanne name, after

the straight at Le Mans where the marque had achieved so many of its victories in the twenties.

A useful by-product of the revised Rolls-Royce radiator was that the Bentley radiator cowl could be fitted without any changes being made to the bonnet pressing – although conversely the shallow vee of the radiator shell required a different curved front bumper. This rationalisation supposedly removed

Lean Crewe

New production facilities were introduced at Crewe in 1995. But they would not have been been possible without a ground-breaking labour agreement introducing flexible working practices, made in the dark days of 1991. This resulted in Japanese-style team working and 'lean production' methods and in 1995 this led to the culmination of a £200 million investment programme at the factory. This was familiar territory to the then chief executive Chris Woodwark, who had worked for British Leyland and its successors between 1971 and 1993, and seen how Honda's input to that business had transformed its efficiency and the build quality of its cars.

In 1991 it took Rolls-Royce some two months – 61 days, to be precise – to build a single car. In 1996 it was 30 days, and by 1998, when the more production-friendly Silver Seraph was introduced, the figure was down again, to 17.5 days. At the heart of the new procedures was a computer-controlled production line to replace the previous manual system, operating in conjunction with a conveyor which transported bodies around the factory. Automation was thereby introduced to body assembly, engine installation, painting and wood machining.

All the same, in 1996 director of production John Fowler was at pains to point out that robots were only used in less than one per cent of assembly so the hand-crafted element of the cars was not jeopardised. It still took 150 hours to complete each car's interior woodwork, and one man spent 27 hours, spread over 23 days, making one of the two picnic tables. And although the Bentley radiator shells were made of chrome-plated brass pressings, the famous Rolls-Royce one was manually soldered together from 22 separate pieces of stainless-steel sheet. Each took six hours to complete although this procedure was discontinued in 1997 with the impending demise of the Silver Spirit line. And another sign of the times was that the body coachlines, hitherto the work of a skilled artisan with a steady hand and a long-haired brush called a fitch, were by 1996 being painted by a machine.

replacement would be obtainable at any local drug store. Further to this, US bumpers now incorporated Menasco struts to produce a 2¾in (7cm) deflection in the event of a 5mph (13kph) impact; outwardly these bumpers fortunately did not much differ from the British and European versions.

There were even more radical changes beneath the bonnet. From January 1980 those Silver Shadow IIs for sale in California had been fitted with a Bosch K-Jetronic mechanical fuel-injection system because the required emissions levels could not be met using twin SU carburettors. Utilising the manifold created for the Corniche/Camargue's single four-choke Solex carburettor, the injected engine was standardised, from April 1981, on all US-market Silver Spirits, in conjunction with a catalytic converter.

So that the model could run on 91 octane unleaded fuel, the compression ratio was dropped to 8:1, with the result that the engine's power output fell by some 15 per cent. All these modifications resulted in a reduction of the Spirit's top speed of about 15mph (24kph), from 120mph (193kph) to around 105mph (170kph) – although this was considered to be academic in view of the fact that there was a 55mph (88kph) maximum speed limit in force throughout America.

By the end of 1981, the first full year of production, the export scene looked particularly encouraging. Of the 2,967 Silver Spirits produced, 1995 cars had been sold overseas, compared with 1,548 of the Shadow line in 1980. Of these, a substantial 80 per cent, or 1,197, went to the United States and Canada.

In January 1982 chief executive George Fenn predicted that exports were expected to reach a record that year with North America again likely to emerge as the company's largest market. In view of this, he planned to increase production by between five and seven per cent, with most of the extra cars to be sold abroad.

In the event Fenn and his team had

the price differential and both cars sold for the same figure of £49,629. One casualty of the new front was the winged-B mascot, still a feature of the T2 Bentley, which was deleted for safety reasons – although it could be added by the owner, as an accessory. The long-wheelbase equivalent of the Spirit was also offered in Bentley guise, when it became the Mulsanne L. In retrospect this can be seen as the first modest step along a road that lead to the rehabilitation of the marque. Otherwise the cars were essentially similar to the Silver Spirits, for the time being at least.

With America Rolls-Royce's largest export market, the company could not ignore the increasingly stringent emissions, safety and other regulations that had begun to emanate from that country in the sixties. The most significant outward manifestation of this was that the US-market Spirit lost the distinctive and stylish rectangular headlamps covers that so contributed to the model's frontal appearance. In their places were four recessed angular and standardised sealed-beam headlight units, US law requiring that in the event of a headlamp's failure, a

The Silver Spirit II arrived for 1990. Outwardly similar to its predecessor, more apparent was the introduction of a new leather-bound steering wheel and an electronic gear selection display. (LAT)

The rear compartment of a 1990 model-year Spirit II: note the bucket-type seats. (LAT)

Mulliner, Park Ward

Although it bears the same name as its Willesden-based predecessor, the now Crewe-domiciled department is not concerned with the construction of coachwork but with the enhancement of the interiors of existing bodyshells to customers' individual requirements.

The move came in January 1992 and the business relaunched in July 1993 to coincide with the 1994 model year, RR showing a car distinguished with extras supposedly worth £36,000 at that year's Frankfurt Motor Show.

In addition to the production of the Silver Spur III Limousine, MPW was – and continues to be – responsible for introducing such features as special trim and upholstery, fax machines, telephones, television and navigation systems to the interiors of both Rolls-Royce and Bentley models. More practically, it can also fit bulletproof glass and can incorporate necessarily-confidential anti-terrorist features.

By 1996 some 40 per cent of Crewe's products were being personalised in this way by a 250-strong workforce. That year came a separation of the H. J. Mulliner name from the Park Ward one, thereby unscrambling, at least on paper, the 1961 merger: henceforth the Mulliner name would be used for customised Bentleys and the Park Ward label attached to specialised Rolls-Royce cars. The MPW department is thus well positioned to enhance the niche models on which the company is increasingly dependent, under the umbrella of what is now called a 'Personal Commissioning Service'.

A 7.2-litre Silver Spirit?

As is well known, Rolls-Royce's long-running oversquare V8 engine originally appeared in 1959 with internal dimensions of 104mm x 91mm and a capacity of 6,230cc. In 1970 this was enlarged to 6,750cc by increasing the stroke to 99mm and the V8 retains this displacement in its much-revised current form. However, in the seventies Rolls-Royce made plans to again increase the engine's size, this time to 7,269cc. This was achieved by stretching the stroke yet again, to 106mm.

The unit, using the Solex 4A1 carburettor to be fitted to the Corniche and the Camargue, was used in the last of the experimental Silver Shadows, built in 1974. In 1977 this car attained a speed of 127mph (204kph), some 10mph (16kph) faster than the production 6.7-litre Shadow II. Subsequently the bigger engine was used in experimental Silver Spirits, but in the end Rolls-Royce decided not to proceed with a 7.2-litre car because, although the engine was marginally more economical than the 6.7-litre unit, it was not an opportune moment to introduce a larger-capacity engine in the face of rising petrol prices. It was just as well, since the downturn of the early eighties was just around the corner...

misread the depth of the transatlantic recession and the strength of the pound. Even so the 2,489 cars that left Crewe that year was some 600 fewer than the 1981 figure. The company's Vickers parent saw the Rolls-Royce group's profit fall to below £20 million and chief executive David Plastow purged some of the top management – although Fenn kept his job. There were also cuts made to the skilled workforce. One casualty was the architect of the Silver Spirit project, technical director John Hollings. He was replaced by Mike Dunn, who arrived at Crewe in 1983 as engineering director after a distinguished career with Ford. As a result of these reductions in the workforce, the slimmed-down Crewe operation was able, from 1983, to reduce its break-even figure from some 2,800 cars a year to 2,000 cars.

One of the 1983 executive intake was 37-year-old Peter Ward, who joined Rolls-Royce as sales and marketing director from Peugeot-Talbot. He later gave *Autocar* a rare insight into the workings of Rolls-Royce, when he revealed that on arrival he had found "a divided and dispirited company... there had been high levels of redundancy and, naturally, the cars weren't selling." Unhappily the corporate hierarchy had been split in two, with the sales and manufacturing divisions barely on speaking terms. "I believe much of the recession redundancies were caused by the company being led by the manufacturing and engineering requirements, without that being tempered by the marketing side who knew what the world needed at that time", Ward commented.

The 1983 Geneva Motor Show saw the appearance of a supplementary Silver Spur which came with an electric division and permitted the fitment of separate air-conditioning systems. To increase rear accommodation, a bench seat was introduced to replace the upholstered squabs fitted to the original Spur. At £68,278, the new arrival cost some £5,000 more.

But in 1983 production dropped

Fuel injection arrived for the 1987 season. This is a 1989 Silver Spur and the presence of a Silver Cloud II is a reminder that the company's long-running V8 engine had first appeared in that model back in 1959. (LAT)

again, by another 500 units, to 1,568 cars, in order to allow for the disposal of vehicles left over from the previous year. This was undertaken against a background of dealer discounting, an unusual state of affairs at the top end of the market. As it happened, 1983 proved to be the low point of the decade and output rose, with 2,201 vehicles leaving Crewe in 1984 – albeit with a £4.5 million loss still being recorded. This was the year that marked the start of the Bentley revival, but at this stage over 90 per cent of production, or 1,933 cars, were Silver Spirits.

It was in February 1984 that Rolls-Royce announced a six-door version of its long-wheelbase model. The Silver Spur limousine had 3ft (91.4cm) added to its wheelbase, the conversion being the work of Surrey-based Robert Jankel Design, run by the creator of the flamboyant Panther retro sports cars.

The new model was intended to give Rolls-Royce a share of an unlikely sector, namely the so-called 'stretch limousine' market, exemplified on the other side of the Atlantic by the elongated Cadillacs and Lincolns which were required transport for film stars and their entourage. In due course the concept proved to be surprisingly successful. Prices began at a formidable £140,000, which was about twice that of the Silver Spirit, and a total of 16 were produced between 1982 and 1985. Having proved the viability of the idea, Rolls-Royce decided to take over their construction and the stretch-limos were thereafter built by Mulliner Park Ward.

The MPW cars were even longer than the originals, with 3ft 6in (1.06m) added to the wheelbase, but had four rather than six doors. Demand was brisk, for a car which cost £182,571,

and in the four years between 1984 and 1988 a total of 84 were completed.

The broader sales picture was also improving. In June 1984 the company announced that it had sold over 300 cars to its dealers worldwide, which was the highest monthly figure for two years. The total for the year was eventually 2,203 cars, which helped to

move the company decisively back into the black, with a £12 million profit.

Rolls-Royce built its 100,000th car in August 1985 and produced a limited edition of the Silver Spur in commemoration. Confined to just 25 cars, and named the Centenary model to commemorate the 100th anniversary of the invention of the motor car – which Britain erroneously celebrated in 1985, rather than 1986 – it possessed such special features as veneered door panels and a miniature cocktail bar built into a special central console.

As the international financial climate continued to improve, sales rose, and they jumped 7.9 per cent to 2,377 cars in 1985. Profits were also on the up and amounted to £14 million. In 1986, America consolidated its position as the company's largest single market, when sales reached 1155 cars compared with 808 bought by British motorists. In all 2,603 vehicles were sold worldwide, a 9.5 per cent increase on the previous year.

The 1987 season saw, at long last, the arrival of fuel injection for Crewe's entire range, with the exception of the Phantom VI. "More development work has been carried out on that engine in the past three years than in the whole of the preceding 22", Peter Ward announced, and the venerable V8 had indeed been subjected to a radical revision, reducing the number of component parts by some 40 per cent.

Technical director Mike Dunn's contribution was immediately apparent, and changes included lower-friction pistons to improve fuel economy, and revised cylinder heads. Rolls-Royce claimed a 22 per cent increase in power and a 16 per cent improvement in fuel consumption at 56mph (90kph). Anti-lock brakes arrived at the same time, and there were also restyled seats and improvements to the air-conditioning.

January 1987 saw further corporate changes with Peter Ward, who had become managing director in the previous October and was largely credited with the successful revival of the Bentley marque, becoming chief executive.

In September 1989 the first major revisions to the two lines were announced, with the Silver Spirit, Silver Spur and Mulsanne all being accorded the 'II' suffix. Whilst the interiors benefited from a redesigned and more ergonomic dashboard and yet further improvements to the air-conditioning, the most significant feature was the introduction of a Crewe-developed 'Automatic Ride

Control' which, the company claimed, eliminated the need to compromise damper settings. The system adapted in $\frac{1}{100}$th of a second to changes in road conditions, automatically selecting the appropriate 'comfort', 'normal' or 'firm' damper mode. This was achieved via a microprocessor and what Rolls-Royce described as "vertical, longitudinal and lateral accelerometers to monitor acceleration, road surface condition, braking and steering changes". It thus swiftly and unobtrusively adapted to driving conditions from a smooth highway to a rough country lane with such speed that the driver was unaware of the changes being made.

The Spirit/Spur II's electronically-controlled adaptive suspension with three-position solenoid-adjustable Boge dampers. Shown in red, they are concentric with the front springs. (Rolls-Royce/LAT)

Simultaneously, and following their arrival on the Bentley Turbo R in 1985, alloy wheels were fitted to a Rolls-Royce for the first time – Limited Edition Camargue excepted. Wider, at 6½in rather than 6in, the 15in spoked wheels were specially designed for Rolls-Royce and those fitted to the Silver Spur had painted nave plates keyed to the body colour.

These revisions underlined the increasing popularity of the long-wheelbase Silver Spur, which was by then outselling the Silver Spirit. By the time the range was again facelifted in 1993, in all 1,658 of the larger model had been sold, against 1,152 Silver Spirits.

More significant in a corporate sense was 1990, because that year Bentley production overtook, by 214 cars, Rolls-Royce output. The

On the independent rear the Boge units replaced the Girling gas struts and springs which in their turn had in 1980 taken over from the Silver Shadow's levelling rams and shock absorbers. (Rolls-Royce/LAT)

expanding Bentley range was to move decisively ahead throughout the decade and even though there was some cross-pollination of technology to endow Rolls-Royce with more of a performance image, demand for the Silver Spirit line declined, year on year, in its wake.

Meanwhile the German competition remained as strong as ever, and a resurgent and now Ford-owned Jaguar provided a further challenge, as did Toyota's newly-conceived prestige marque, Lexus, that had appeared in 1988. Against this background, Rolls-Royce was once again destined to enter choppy financial waters as the world economy took another nose-dive in 1990, just as the effects of Peter Ward's stewardship of the business appeared to be bearing fruit. In 1989 the Crewe workforce had risen to 4,500 with 300 extra workers taken on that year, as production reached 3,274 cars, just 73 away from the 1978 record. Alas, a slump in sales in 1991 conspired to push the

business deeply into the red, to the tune of £100 million. This was followed by a £30 million loss in 1992 although the company returned to the black in 1993.

It was 1983 all over again although worse in 1991 when output dropped by half to 1,620 cars; 1992's figure of 1,258 was a low for the decade. In due course production would pick up but it never returned to the 2000-plus cars completed annually in the 1980s.

In February 1991 Peter Ward took over the previously dormant post of chairman, and 1,700 jobs were cut with a further 970 redundancies following in 1992. This was the time when, it will be recalled, Mulliner Park Ward was closed and transferred to Crewe. The cost was £14.6 million in redundancy charges. However, the much slimmed-down company was able to revise its break-even figure in 1992 to about 1,350 cars a year, compared with the previous figure of 2,000.

With Vickers itself moving into the red, there were reports of it wishing to dispose of Rolls-Royce or else find a partner to share its all-important development costs. But in April 1992 Sir David Plastow, who had become chairman in 1987, reported that this dialogue was at an end. In fact Vickers had nearly sold Rolls-Royce to BMW, but the German company had withdrawn at the eleventh hour (see box). Plastow left Vickers later in the year and was replaced as chief executive by Sir Colin Chandler, formerly head of export services for the Ministry of Defence. Slowly the market began to pick up in 1992, with 1,378 cars sold.

With the impending demise of the Phantom VI in 1992, in September 1991 Rolls-Royce, determined not to abandon this modest although profitable market, introduced its Touring Limousine at the Tokyo Motor Show. Whilst the Phantom had been built by the London-based Mulliner Park Ward, what was in effect an enhanced Silver Spur was one of the first products of the division's new Crewe home.

The wheelbase was increased by 2ft (61cm), but unlike previous stretches

Driving a Spirit or Mulsanne

The Spirit series defies easy generalisation, if you're talking about the driving experience, because over the 18-year-life of the range the cars improved so much, increment by increment, that an early Rolls-Royce Silver Spirit is a very different beast from a late Bentley Turbo.

There are certain constants, all the same: as with the Shadows, an up-high driving position shrinks what is quite a bulky car, so that – again – the Spirit and its Bentley siblings are not intimidating cars to drive. Also common to all cars is an American-style foot-operated parking brake with manual release; with automatic transmission, such a device is no big deal.

Early carb-fed Silver Spirits and Mulsannes are not hugely different in feel from a late Shadow. The performance – and its silkily unobtrusive delivery – is pretty much the same; the steering, although blessed with a little more feel, is still light enough to demand that the slender-rimmed wheel be carressed rather than aggressively gripped; despite better-controlled suspension, the ride remains cossettingly soft and prone to slight wallowing when caught out by an undulating surface; the laws of physics continue to mean that throwing one of these heavy cars into a roundabout will see it roll more than say a Jaguar, with a concomitant squealing from the tyres.

Injected cars, in comparison, come alive. The engine is more immediately responsive, with definite get-up-and-go both in low-speed kickdown and mid-range part-throttle acceleration. This extra zing is emphasised by an exhaust system that allows the engine to sing rather than, as before, mute out its operation. It doesn't make the V8's soundtrack intrusive: it merely provides a pleasing edge of refined urgency.

The so-called 'heavy rack' introduced on the Bentleys in 1989 and later fitted to the Rolls-Royces is another undoubted advance – to the point where it's not uncommon for it to be retro-fitted to cars with the original 'light' steering. Mated to a thick-rim wheel, it has a lot more beef, and for the first time you feel that it would not be pointlessly indecorous to adopt a slightly more press-on style of driving.

What all this means is that a later normally-aspirated car sends out completely different messages from a more lazy first-generation model. It will feel more instant, subtly more vocal, and less of an alien experience to someone more used to BMWs, Jaguars and the like. Try one of these late cars and its strong performance may well have you feeling that the extra cost and extra operating expenses of a Bentley Turbo aren't worth entertaining.

the four-speed 4L80E unit from the same manufacturer. Its fitment had been foreshadowed on the Bentley Continental R.

The second generation Spirits and Spurs were replaced by the III-series family in August 1993. This once again confirmed the customer preference for the longer car, to the extent that the regular-wheelbase Silver Spirit continued to sell in diminishing numbers and was discontinued in 1997.

The company had spent £30 million on the mechanicals and, in particular, on the venerable 34-year-old V8, with the intention of improving fuel consumption. Larger inlet ports and exhaust valves were introduced to improve breathing whilst a new plenum chamber and a ram-pipe induction system was intended to better the unit's low-speed torque; there was also a new Bosch M3.3 engine management system. A further effect of these modifications was that emissions were improved. Outwardly the cars resembled their predecessors but inside there were new seats and headrests and driver and passenger airbags were standardised.

In May 1994 the benefits of the Bentley Turbo programme were extended, for the first time, to Rolls-Royce. Intended as a limited-edition model, the Flying Spur, with a claimed top speed of 140mph (225kph), was described as "the fastest Rolls-Royce motor car ever". Indeed, a factory declaration that it was able to attain 60mph (100kph) in seven seconds proved to be slightly pessimistic: Autocar managed 6.9 seconds!

Powered by an engine said to produce 50 per cent more output than the normally-aspired unit, outwardly the model's revised front air dam and its Flying Spur badging were the only giveaways to what lurked beneath the bonnet. Additional modifications included further refinements to the Shift Energy Management system, to provide the appropriate automatic gearchanges to complement the driving style of individual drivers.

the extra space was introduced behind the back doors, which meant they could be retained unchanged. The space was taken up by extra side windows and the result was almost two extra feet of leg room. A large glass moonroof was also introduced over the rear seats. Rolls-Royce predicted that it would sell some 25 examples a year, but in the event it sold rather more and 99 cars had been completed by the time production ceased in 1994.

Over the winter of 1991/92 the three-speed GM400 automatic gearbox, introduced on the left-hand-drive Silver Shadow in 1966, was finally discontinued and replaced by

Above: The Flying Spur of 1994 was the first turbocharged Rolls-Royce – and the fastest Rolls-Royce, being capable of over 140mph (225kph). The alloy wheels shod with whitewall tyres differed from those of the Silver Spur. (LAT)

Extensive use of wood characterises this 1994 Flying Spur. Although a dashboard plaque suggests that only 50 Flying Spurs were being built, in the event 133 had been completed by the time that production ceased in 1995. (LAT)

Intended for a relatively short life, with only 50 examples to be produced for European markets, the newcomer clearly struck a chord, as the final total ended up at well over double that figure, at 133 cars, by the time the line was discontinued in 1995. This certainly confirmed the viability of a turbocharged Rolls-Royce.

To the surprise of many, in January 1995 Peter Ward suddenly resigned after 12 years with the company. He had made little secret of his opposition to a possible sale of Rolls-Royce to BMW, (see Chapter 8) following an agreement made in December 1994 for the German company to supply engines for the next generation of models. Ward's

place as chief executive was taken by Chris Woodwark, who had previously held a similar position at Cosworth Engineering – Rolls-Royce's Vickers parent having in 1990 purchased the famous Northampton-based racing-engine business.

In the month after his appointment Woodwark confirmed what had been apparent for some years, namely that "one of the major features of Rolls-Royce Motors Cars now and in the future is niche models." And so, sadly, it has proved to be.

Whilst the 1993 changes had concentrated on improving the cars' mechanical components, the modifications made to the 1996 range, announced in June 1995, were

principally styling alterations undertaken at a cost of £25 million. At this point the models lost their numerical suffixes.

The aim of the modifications was to endow both the Rolls-Royce and Bentley with a sleeker appearance, and most significantly the radiators on both cars were reduced in size and the famous Spirit of Ecstasy mascot diminished by some 20 per cent. In addition the front bumper and spoiler were integrated into the body and the same went for the rear bumper and valance. There were also changes made to the front side windows with the removal of their quarterlights, a feature which dated back to the Mark VI Bentley.

Buying Hints

1. Your most important consideration is that whilst it is possible for the enthusiastic amateur to cope with the refined simplicity of the pre-1965 models, and a mechanic may able to cope with the Shadow family, the 1980/98 Silver Spirit/Mulsanne line is simply too complicated for the average garage. They require specialist attention and equipment and are most definitely not a DIY proposition!

2. As the Silver Spirit/Mulsanne is based on the Silver Shadow, which had been almost completely 'de-bugged' by the time it ceased production in 1980, these Rolls-Royces and Bentleys are probably the most reliable Crewe cars of the post-war years.

3. The adoption of mineral oil in place of brake fluid for the hydraulics of the ride height control and brakes means that these cars are less liable to leak than their predecessors, a major plus. Checks for the high-pressure system are as for the Shadow series.

4. What visible body problems you're likely encounter will probably be confined to rust around the rear wheelarches and in the region of the rear valance. The latter can be missed because it is to be found directly beneath the bumper. Be warned that rust can also spring up where the front wing joins the sill, along the spot-welded join.

5. Older cars may suffer from some underside body ailments. The rear crossmember can split by the propshaft, and the floor can split at the rear where the exhaust mounts; you may find a spreader plate has been fitted here. Additionally the rear spring mounting 'pots' can corrode. A further point vulnerable to rust on neglected high-mileage cars is the forward body outrigger. You should also use an inspection lamp to look above the front subframe to see if there are accident-induced creases in the front longeron.

6. Surprisingly, the Shadow/Spirit family is prone to noisy differentials that cannot be drowned out by turning up the volume control on the radio! Should the seller do precisely that, be suspicious. If you've got the slightest doubts about the example you're contemplating, drive it at approximately 37mph (60kph) and listen. If there is a whine from the rear, there's no alternative but to have a new diff fitted – and the parts alone cost some £3,500.

7. Whilst the air-conditioning unit is particularly reliable, the hoses serving it are rather elongated, and can weaken, necessitating replacement. Regular maintenance is also important.

8. These cars tend to change hands at regular intervals and a ten-year-old example might have had around five or six owners.

9. As on all previously models, a full service history is essential and these cars tend to cease being attended to by factory-approved dealers at around 60,000 miles (100,000km). Providing they've thereafter been tended by a Rolls-Royce and Bentley specialist that's fine, but it has to be on a regular basis.

10. The service interval on these cars is 6,000 miles (10,000km) but there's a really big service due every 48,000 miles (80,000km) when the brake calliper seals, hoses and belts are replaced and you won't get much change from around £1,200. There's another one at 96,000 miles (155,000km), which is a hydraulic overall. The cost? Some £3,000, plus VAT.

11. The V8 is a robust, reliable unit but, given a choice, which is preferable, the pre-1987 carburettored cars or their fuel-injected successors? Whilst the twin SUs have the virtues of relative simplicity, fuel injection means better cold starting, more engine power and improved mpg.

12. Fuel consumption is an important consideration. You'll experience around 12–15mpg for town driving but on long runs the upper teens are perfectly attainable.

Once again the company grasped the nettle of fuel economy, with the introduction of further revisions to the cylinder heads and the management system. This produced a claimed 12 per cent improvement in consumption and a modest increase in overall performance.

Inside there was an electrically-adjustable steering wheel linked to the four seat and mirror memory positions. Rear passengers also benefited from having their own air-conditioning controls. Rolls-Royce was also recognising that its customers required interiors to suit their own particular needs and tastes and of the 516 Silver Spirits produced in 1995, some 30 per cent passed through the Mulliner, Park Ward division where their upholstery and trim were duly enhanced.

The 1996 Geneva Motor Show was the venue chosen by the company to unveil its latest limousine, which it named the Park Ward after the coachbuilding company with which it

had for so long been associated. It prophesied that buyers would have "wisdom and insight that sets them apart from their peers"; such fortunates would also require well-lined pockets, as exercising these virtues would have cost them a cool £210,854. Like the Touring Limousine, 2ft had been added to the Park Ward's wheelbase, but this time the additional side window was introduced between the doors, instead of being behind them.

During chief executive Chris Woodwark's time at Crewe, Japanese 'lean production' techniques (see box) were introduced, sweeping away many of the by then sadly outdated practices initiated by Henry Royce himself. When Woodwark moved on in 1997, his place was taken by Graham Morris, who was fresh from a spell in Germany as sales and marketing director of Audi.

Production rose to a high for the decade in 1997, when 1779 cars were built – although the Silver Spirit only

accounted for 350 of them; group profits rose to £85 million, mainly thanks to burgeoning Bentley sales.

With high-performance motoring now having been extended to the previously rarefied Rolls-Royce arena, for 1997 – in response to customer demand, said the company – the long-wheelbase Silver Spur was given 300bhp or so of 'light turbo' engine, as used in the Bentley Brooklands.

At this point the unblown Silver Spur was renamed the Silver Dawn. This name had been revived for US-market Silver Spirits with effect from the 1995 model year, it having been originally applied to the initially-export-only Rolls-Royce version of the Bentley Mark VI. At the same time the short-wheelbase Rolls-Royce chassis, along with the Silver Spirit name, was discontinued, although a swb car was still available in the form of the Bentley Brooklands.

The blown engine was also extended to the Park Ward and to a supplementary and more modest

The Silver Spirit/Spur III arrived for the 1994 model year. Once again external changes were modest although inside there was a redesigned instrument panel and a new steering wheel. (LAT)

stretch limousine, the awkwardly-named Silver Spur with Division, which arrived in September 1996. This had just 14in (35.5cm) added to its wheelbase.

The 1998 season cars were identifiable by their blue enamel – rather than black – badges and a revised three-tone interior available optionally at no extra cost. Prices now stood at £123,258 for the Silver Dawn, with the Silver Spur costing a further £30,679. Both models finally ceased production in 1998, the low-volume Park Ward lines excepted, when they made way for their Silver Seraph replacement. But by then Rolls-Royce had a new owner and a new chapter in the company's history was about to begin.

The Bentley *revival*

The Royal Albert Hall provides a very British backdrop for the Mulsanne Turbo, introduced in 1982; the painted radiator shell was the only significant indication of what lurked beneath the bonnet. (Rolls-Royce)

In reviving the Bentley marque in the 1980s, Crewe was turning back the clock to the years between 1946 and 1959 when production of cars bearing the famous winged 'B' had dramatically outpaced that of Rolls-Royces. But from 1959 onwards one of the most famous names in British motoring history was progressively downplayed by its owner. The Mulliner-bodied S-series Continental coupé, which was not replaced on its 1959 demise, was the last purpose-designed Bentley.

In retrospect the 1980 arrival of the Mulsanne, the Bentley version of the Silver Spirit, can be seen as the faltering beginnings of the marque's

The Turbo's interior was essentially the same as the standard Mulsanne's. There was the option of cloth upholstery which some commentators preferred to the more traditional leather as it prevented the driver from sliding sideways under cornering. (LAT)

revival. This was followed in 1982 by the faster, outwardly similar Mulsanne Turbo. Bentley production began, slowly, to increase and the all-important Turbo R arrived in 1985.

As mentioned in the last chapter, 37-year-old Peter Ward had been appointed Rolls-Royce's sales director in 1983 and Mike Dunn became his

engineering opposite number. As the accompanying notes indicate, neither was steeped in the traditions of Crewe – quite the reverse, in fact. Ward arrived via British Leyland and Peugeot-Talbot whilst Dunn's technical credentials had been honed at Ford, where he had overall responsibility for the Ford Sierra: a

The Bentley Eight of 1984 was essentially a no-frills Mulsanne with this distinctive wire-mesh grille which was intended to evoke memories of the twenties. The presence of a 1924-based Bentley, now a twin-turbocharged 8 litre was an evocative reminder of such days. (LAT)

greater contrast to the Bentley and Rolls-Royce marques is difficult to imagine.

Both brought with them a greater sense of pragmatism, in that the company began to gear its thinking to the requirements of the market rather than producing cars and expecting the public to respond, just because they were products of a famous factory.

Three years after his arrival, Dunn shared with the readers of *Motor* the philosophy he encountered on arrival at Rolls-Royce Motors. There was, he said, a "tradition for developing cars until they were ready for production – that was a fairly relaxed process. The only deadlines that were kept were for meeting emissions standards." This leisurely approach was to be replaced by a ferment of activity as the Bentley line was nurtured and expanded whilst still retaining the essentials of the quality for which Crewe was justifiably world famous.

By combining the Bentley's performance image with traditional lines and a luxurious interior, the company was able to attract a younger type of owner-driver who would never have contemplated buying a Rolls-Royce. Such was the success of the strategy that in 1990 Bentley production outstripped that of Rolls-Royce for the first time; that trend has been maintained ever since. In short, Bentley has provided Rolls-Royce with its corporate salvation.

A modest 58 examples of the T2, the Bentley version of the Silver Shadow, had been sold in the three years prior to the Silver Spirit's arrival. This compared with 10,566 examples of the Silver Shadow and Silver Wraith IIs, but its Mulsanne successor very nearly did not happen. As Rolls-Royce candidly admitted in a 1984 press release: 'when sales of Bentley-badged variants of Rolls-Royce models fell to around five per cent... *the company thought seriously about dropping the name* (author's italics).

To have come close to extinguishing one of the most famous marques in British motoring history seems an unbelievable admission, particularly

Peter Terry Ward, born 1945

Peter Ward not only ran Rolls-Royce during some of the most traumatic years in its history; he is also widely credited with the revival of the Bentley marque which he undertook in tandem with technical director Mike Dunn (see p134). Ward arrived at Crewe as sales and marketing director in 1983, became managing director of that division in 1984, managing director two years later, chief executive in 1987, and chairman in 1991. He left the company in 1995, following the decision to purchase BMW engines for the next generation of models and became chairman and chief executive of Cunard Line.

Entering the motor industry as Standard-Triumph's service liaison officer, he left in 1973 to join in-house British Leyland's Jaguar Rover Triumph division as parts sales manager. A move to Unipart followed two years later and in 1977 he was made sales director. In 1979 he became managing director of Talbot's Motaquip parts operation, before joining Rolls-Royce in February 1983. He was the first man in the company's history to have worldwide responsibility for sales. "We must accept there are no instant remedies, no crock of gold, no untapped market for Rolls-Royce and Bentley motor cars just around the corner", Ward told the company's in-house *Journal* in 1984. In a bid to exploit the "unexplored potential" of the American market, model-year

changes, as practised by the rest of the industry since the twenties, would be introduced.

"Rolls-Royce Motors was founded on certain principles that get quoted and requoted", he added more pointedly. "Over the years I believe that the company may have strayed from some of them and, in a sense, marked time. The Rolls-Royce motor car will only become an anachronism if we stand back with a complacency and expect customers to beat a path to our door. Then I, Mike Dunn and the rest, will be totally guilty of letting the company down – and that is something we are determined will not happen."

Peter Ward, architect of Rolls-Royce Motors' survival strategy in the 1980s. (Rolls-Royce)

because demand for the model was so low precisely because the company itself had sought to dilute its image. The situation was succinctly summed up by sales director Peter Ward. "Despite all that tradition and heritage a Bentley was no more than a

badge-engineered Rolls-Royce," he told *Autocar* in 1987. "The heritage was being thrown away."

There were, in fact, mitigating reasons for downplaying the legendary name. When Rolls-Royce collapsed so spectacularly in 1971,

Although the Turbo R of 1985 was outwardly similar, the suspension was much tauter than the original and the car was the first Rolls-Royce product to be fitted with alloy wheels. (LAT)

Bentley Turbo R
1985-1997

ENGINE:
V8 alloy block, alloy heads
Bore x stroke   104.1mm x 99.1mm
Capacity   6,750cc
Valve actuation   Pushrod
Compression ratio   8:1
Carburettor   Solex Type 4A1*
Turbocharger   Garrett AiResearch TO4
Power   298bhp** at 3,800rpm
                       (unoffical)
* Bosch KE-Jetronic fuel injection from October 1986, MK Motronic fuel injection and management system from 1989 model year and Zytec EMS3 from 1996 model year
** Offically quoted at 385bhp from 1996 model year

TRANSMISSION:
Rear-wheel drive
Automatic, three-speed with torque converter to 1991 season, thereafter four-speed
Final drive ratio: 2.28:1; 2.69:1 from 1992 model year

SUSPENSION:
Front: Independent, wishbone and coil spring
Rear: Independent, semi-trailing arms
Automatic hydraulic height control

STEERING:
Power assisted rack-and-pinion
Turns lock-to-lock 3.4

BRAKES:
Front: Hydraulic disc
Rear: Hydraulic disc
Power assistance from two engine-driven hydraulic pumps. ABS from 1987 model year

WHEELS/TYRES:
Cast aluminium alloy
255/65VRR15

BODYWORK:
Steel and aluminium unitary-construction four-door saloon

DIMENSIONS:
Length   17ft 3in (5.25m)*
Wheelbase   10ft 6in (3.20m)*
Track - front 5ft 0in (1.52m)
       - rear   5ft 0in (1.52m)
Width   6ft 2in (1.88m)
Height   4ft 10in (1.47m)
* Until 1995, thereafter 17ft 7in (5.35m) with 10ft 4½ins (3.16m) wheelbase

WEIGHT:
44.3cwt (2,252kg)
1996: 48.6cwt (2,470 kg)

PERFORMANCE:
(Source: *Autocar*)
Max speed   143mph (230kph)
0–50mph (0–80kph)   5.2sec
0–60mph (0–100kph)   7.0sec
0–70mph (0–112kph)   9.4sec

PRICE INCLUDING TAX WHEN NEW:
£79,397

NUMBER BUILT:
Short-wheelbase: 4,115
Long-wheelbase: 930
Alternative figures are 4,663 and 1,508, or 5,187 and 2,034! These variations exist because of the difficulty of accounting for the quantities of small runs of niche models within the donor line.

Bentley Continental R
1991 to date

ENGINE:
V8 alloy block, alloy heads
Bore x stroke   104.1mm x 99.1mm
Capacity   6,750cc
Valve actuation   Pushrod
Compression ratio   8:1
Engine management   Bosch K-Motronic*

Turbocharger   Garrett TO4B
Power   360bhp at 4,200rpm
                       (estimate)**
* Zytec EMS3 system from 1996 season
**385bhp at 4,000rpm (from 1995 model year, official)

TRANSMISSION:
Rear-wheel drive
Four-speed automatic with torque converter
Final drive ratio: 3.017:1. From 1992 model year 2.69:1

SUSPENSION:
Front: Independent, wishbone and coil spring
Rear: Independent, semi-trailing arms, coil springs
Automatic hydraulic height control

STEERING:
Power-assisted rack-and-pinion
Turns lock-to-lock: 3.2

BRAKES:
Front: Hydraulic, ventilated disc
Rear: Hydraulic, ventilated disc
Power assistance from two engine-driven hydraulic pumps. ABS standard

WHEELS/TYRES:
Cast aluminium alloy
255/60 ZR16

BODYWORK:
Steel and aluminium two-door unitary-construction coupé

DIMENSIONS:
Length   17ft 5in (5.30m)
Wheelbase   10ft 0in (3.04m)
Track - front 5ft 9in (1.75m)
       - rear   5ft 9in (1.75m)
Width   6ft 7in (2.00m)
Height   4ft 8in (1.42m)

WEIGHT:
47.6cwt (2,420kg)

Michael Ronald David Dunn, born 1935

Mike Dunn, head-hunted for Rolls-Royce, joined the company in February 1983 and was its engineering director for nine years, leaving in 1992. During this period he was responsible for the Bentley Turbo R and, in particular, the Bentley Continental R. Unknown to the public, he also developed the Silver Spirit's SX successor which was eventually sidelined. He is one of Britain's leading automobile engineers.

Educated at Bablake School, Coventry, Dunn attended Birmingham and Sheffield universities and joined Ford as a graduate engineer in 1955. Seven years later, in 1962, he left to become chief engineer of Alvis, replacing his father, appointed in 1950, who had joined the company in 1922. There he was responsible for ensuring that the last Alvis, the TF, was the fastest and most powerful car of its line, and for designing its stillborn unitary-construction TA30 successor.

In 1967 Mike Dunn became a director and chief engineer at Leyland Motors, moving on to be chief engineer of its bus and truck division. Rejoining Ford in 1973, he progressively became Chief Engineer, Advanced Technology, at Cologne and the director of product development with overall responsible for the Sierra. It was inevitable that the arrival at Crewe of such a man would be greeted

with apprehension by the 'old school' of engineers. In 1985 Dunn admitted this to Daniel Ward of *Motor*:

"The custodian of the Rolls-Royce character was a man called 'Mac' MacCraith Fisher, chief engineer motor cars. [He had joined Rolls-Royce in 1942, and was subsequently development engineer for suspension and steering, chief development engineer in 1959, and assistant chief engineer in 1965]. He had been very protective of the Rolls-Royce character – he was very good on refinement. I brought in a different culture. The concern here was that I would disregard all the good points on the cars. They knew my preference would be for a responsive car like a Porsche 911. The concern was that I would spoil the cars. 'Mac' didn't want to see it happen...what has happened is that I have come to appreciate the cars' good points."

With a development team expanded from 135 to 180, 'Mr Sierra' introduced tough Ford-inspired cost-control targets and a 10 per cent reduction in the parts count. At this stage Rolls-Royce's V8 engine contained 1200 components. In 1986 this was reduced by 400. An improvement in fuel consumption and weight reduction were twin priorities. Then there was a reduction in the lengthy time in producing prototypes which was necessary

in order to be responsive to market demand...

But how did Rolls-Royce compare with Ford? "I loved working at Ford. The real criteria is 'Do you want to go to work in the mornings?' I always have. This is just different."

On leaving Crewe in 1992, Mike Dunn became chairman of MGA Developments, which specialised in the production of prototypes for the motor industry. He subsequently became a consultant and lecturer at Loughborough University.

Engineering director Mike Dunn, who with Peter Ward, jointly steered the Bentley revival. (Rolls-Royce)

managing director David Plastow decided it was wisest to concentrate all corporate resources on a single brand, that of Rolls-Royce. North America was regarded as offering the greatest potential and this approach was clearly preferable on a continent where the Bentley name played a very second fiddle to that of Rolls-Royce.

Nevertheless, Plastow could see a performance agenda might one day have some appeal. In 1974, the year after BMW had introduced its pioneering and all-too-ephemeral 2002 Turbo, he suggested, in consultation with chief engineer John Hollings, that the company investigate the possibility of

developing a turbocharged car.

In consequence a rather down-at-heel works Silver Shadow was dispatched to Broadspeed Engineering, previously known for its turbocharged Ford Capris and Opel Mantas – as well as, of course, its racing Minis. Broadspeed duly turbocharged the Shadow, the car was

A bonnetful of engine: the Turbo R's power unit. This is the fuel-injected version introduced for the 1987 model year. (LAT)

Starting point for the Continental R, the Project 90 concept announced at the 1985 Geneva Motor Show, shown here in company with an S-type Continental by H. J. Mulliner, the last Bentley to have a purpose-designed body. (Rolls-Royce/LAT)

evaluated at Crewe, and then it returned to Ralph Broad's premises, where, after slumbering under a dust sheet, it was ultimately broken up. This was the starting point for what in 1982 emerged as the Mulsanne Turbo.

The experiments did not end with this Silver Shadow. In 1976 further work was undertaken by Broadspeed on D-1, the prototype Bentley-radiatored Camargue, when a turbocharger was fitted. However, this unit was removed at the beginning of 1977 and replaced by a Garrett AiResearch unit. All this work, subsequently followed through in-

house by Rolls Royce's Advanced Projects office, proceeded as a low-key feasibility exercise and proved that the rugged V8 could be reliably turbocharged – D-1 being finally scrapped in 1982 after covering some 250,000 miles (400,000km) in all.

Plastow believed that this might have formed the basis of a Bentley version of the Camargue. But market research revealed that sales of a turbocharged Bentley could be as high as 150 a year, and this was beyond the capabilities of Mulliner Park Ward. Nor did such a model chime with an expensive low-

production top-of-range car such as the Camargue. In any case, Rolls-Royce didn't have a performance image in the way Bentley did, even if that image had been allowed to become dormant. The only possible way forward, therefore, was to base the new car on the Mulsanne four-door saloon.

"There was considerable heart-searching about the marque's future, but decisions were reached then to use the name for the Mulsanne Turbo", Ward later recalled. The project was given the corporate green light in January 1981, which proved to be a year when just 120 Bentleys were built.

The model duly made its debut 14 months later, in March 1982, at the Geneva Motor Show. There was a historical bonus to the project because it revived memories of the legendary supercharged 4½-litre Bentley of 1929/31 (see box) and a 1929 example was duly displayed on the stand at the Swiss event alongside the Mulsanne Turbo.

Outwardly there could be little doubt that this was a rather special Bentley because the radiator shell was painted body-colour, rather than being chromium-plated. Interestingly, this idea dated back to 1977, when the experimental Z-3 Silver Spirit had received this treatment. Less apparent but nonetheless significant was that, instead of the exhaust pipes emerging from either side of the tail, they were concentrated on the right-hand side. The only other giveaway was the 'Turbo' name affixed to the nearside of the bootlid and further discreet badging low on the front wings.

Introducing a turbocharger under the already crowded Bentley bonnet was something of an achievement and did great credit to Broadspeed and to the Crewe team which effected the production conversion. Had this been a new car, the V8 would have been fitted with one small turbocharger per cylinder bank, in the style of the Maserati Biturbo. But the Mulsanne's restricted engine compartment meant that the only available space was the front offside corner, which dictated the fitment of a large single unit. The aim was to achieve a 50 per cent increase in torque and power without increasing engine speed. Garrett AiResearch therefore came up with its TO4 unit. This necessitated moving the power steering pump to the left to make room for the big blower, which was fed from each cylinder bank via new exhaust manifolds.

The basic layout and plumbing still bore some Broadspeed echoes, the turbo being mounted upstream of and blowing through the carburettor. Instead of the customary SUs, the engine employed a Solex 4A1 of the

Glory days: Bentley's sporting heritage

When in 1982 Rolls-Royce awoke Bentley from its slumbers, it was able to draw on a racing and performance heritage created by Britain's most revered and successful sports cars of the inter-war period. For although the Cricklewood-based Bentley Motors only existed for the 12 years between 1919 and 1931, it won the famous Le Mans 24-hour race on no fewer than five occasions.

The cars were the creation of the modest, conservative but formidably able Walter Owen Bentley, an engineer who made engine reliability the key tenet of his design philosophy. This automotive creed was triumphantly vindicated by the marque's outstanding racing successes. And like Rolls-Royce, 'WO' only built his cars in chassis form, to be bodied by specialist coachbuilders.

His first model, a 3-litre powered by a four-cylinder single-overhead-camshaft engine, reached the public in 1921 and an example was entered in the first Le Mans race of 1923. To the surprise of Bentley and the staff of his small North London factory, it took fourth place. The following year another 3-litre was driven to victory, and the model was again triumphant in 1927.

That year the 3-litre was

replaced by a 4½-litre car which won the 1928 event. But the two subsequent victories of 1929 and 1930 were achieved by a 6½-litre six-cylinder model introduced in 1926 and conceived by 'WO' as a challenge to the Rolls-Royce Phantom I. The marque's reputation was further enhanced by the arrival, in 1931, of its splendid 8-litre derivative, a town carriage which had Rolls-Royce's new Phantom II in its sights.

When the depression took its toll on Bentley's well-heeled clientèle, Napier, Derby's great rival from pre-war days, negotiated to buy the company but Rolls-Royce, fearing a challenge to its pre-eminent position, stepped in with characteristic ruthlessness and acquired Bentley, on 20 October 1931, via a sealed bid of £125,175. W. O. Bentley joined Rolls-Royce but only stayed until 1935. The Cricklewood factory had been closed down, and in 1933 production restarted at Derby although all subsequent Bentleys were based on Rolls-Royces. However, the new generation of cars to be produced under Volkswagen's ownership will, for the first time for some 70 years, be mechanically unrelated.

And VW has seen a Bentley-badged car make a return to Le Mans in 2001...

type used on the Corniche and Camargue, on the grounds that it could accept more air/fuel mixture at high pressure. The carb was housed within a central air box which unequivocally spelt out the word TURBO on its roof. The turbocharger blew at the rate of 7psi, although this was only attained at 3,000rpm, and instead of boost spiralling upwards thereafter it actually tailed off. In

consequence there was plenty of low-down torque.

Rolls-Royce jokingly claimed that the power developed by the 6,750cc unit with an 8:1 compression ratio was "sufficient, plus 50 per cent". As ever, if you didn't know what 'sufficient' was, the description was meaningless. Fortunately the veil was at last lifted on the V8's true output in 1982, no less than 23 years after the

The Bentley Mulsanne S which replaced the original Mulsanne in 1987. It inherited the Turbo R's alloy wheels but its chromed radiator shell indicates an unturbocharged engine. (LAT)

The interior of this 1991 model-year Turbo R still features a steering-column gearchange, but note that the dashboard now has a rev-counter and that there is a thicker-rimmed sports steering wheel, along with more supportive sports seats. (LAT)

engine's debut – but it wasn't Rolls-Royce spilling the beans. To gain Type Approval for the Mulsanne Turbo in Germany the company was required to reveal the power developed by the Silver Spirit/Mulsanne. This was given as 148Kw at 4,000rpm – translating as 198bhp. In turn the output of the Turbo was declared as 222Kw at 3,800rpm – making a robust if not exceptional 298bhp.

This extra power demanded some changes to the transmission and the torque converter was uprated to have six rather than the usual three driving lugs. The sturdy GM400 automatic transmission was more than able to cope with increased power: in America it was even used on trucks! However, the shift points were tweaked to cater for the increased oomph. A higher final-drive ratio of

2.7:1 instead of 3.08:1 was chosen, the halfshafts were increased in diameter from 1in to 1.3in (2.54cm to 3.4cm), and the universal joints uprated.

The intensely cost-conscious nature of the project and the tight time schedule were reflected in the fact that no changes were made to the suspension. The only concession was to fit uprated VR-rated tyres to cater

From 'Blower' Bentley to Mulsanne Turbo

With the arrival of the Mulsanne Turbo, Rolls-Royce was reviving the memory of the 4½-litre supercharged Bentley. Initiated by racing driver Tim Birkin, who had won Le Mans for Bentley in 1929, and financed by heiress the Hon Dorothy Paget, it was a concept borrowed from Grand Prix racing. To qualify for Le Mans, 50 of these cars, the minimum required, were built between 1929 and 1931 – not by Bentley but by Birkin and Paget, at premises in Welwyn Garden City.

The supercharger is, in effect, an engine-driven compressor which forces the petrol/air mixture into the cylinders and the additional boost that results increases the amount of power developed.

But the 'blown four-and-a-half' was created in the face of W. O. Bentley's fierce opposition, as the model's potentially greater performance was mitigated by the risk of unreliability which challenged the premise on which the marque's reputation had been built. He believed, he later wrote, that "the supercharger applied to the Bentley engine was, by its nature, a false inducer. When we wanted higher performance, we increased the engine size..."[1]

Interestingly, in light of future developments, when in 1932 Rolls-Royce was experimentally developing the first of its Bentleys, a 2.6-litre single-overhead-camshaft Roots-supercharged engine was conceived as a possible power unit, but did not reach production. Royce was concerned by the lack of refinement and Ernest Hives, like Bentley, bridled at the prospect of unreliability. A mildly-tuned 20/25hp Rolls-Royce unit was used instead.

The supercharger reigned supreme on racing cars until the early fifties. In 1968 BMW wanted to increase the competitiveness of the engine of its 2002 saloon in Group 5 racing and turned to the turbocharger, a concept that had been around since 1905.

Developed for aero engines and diesel engines on both sides of the Atlantic during the thirties, in 1958 AiResearch of Arizona began the production of its turbochargers and one of its units was briefly offered on Oldsmobile's compact F-85 Jetfire of 1962.

As the supercharger, the turbo is an induction air compressor although it rotates courtesy of the engine's otherwise wasted exhaust gases, and so does not absorb power. On the debit side is a characteristic throttle lag, to which is coupled the corrosive effect of the gases on the rotor – the Bentley's turbine turns at some 80,000rpm, it should be recorded.

Nevertheless, in 1973, BMW launched its 2002 Turbo, which was Europe's first turbocharged road car although it was withdrawn after 10 months because of lack of demand as its arrival coincided with the first global oil-price hike. However, the concept soon returned, thanks to the efforts of Porsche and Saab, and has been with us ever since.

When David Plastow initiated the turbocharging of the Rolls-Royce V8 engine it was in the knowledge that the company already had experience of such forced induction on its B-series range of military and commercial engines as well as on its multi-fuelled military K-series flat-six unit of the 1960s.

Although the conversion was initially undertaken by the now defunct Broadspeed Engineering, the work soon gathered pace from 1979 onwards under a factory team led by Jack Read. The turbocharged engine was not only extended to Bentley but later to Rolls-Royce. However, on the Bentley Arnage, its BMW V8 was turbocharged by racing-engine specialist Cosworth, owned between 1990 and 1998 by Rolls-Royce's Vickers parent and now in the hands of Volkswagen.

[1] W O by W. O. Bentley (Hutchinson, 1958)

The original 'Blower' Bentley. This 4½-litre car is one of three entered in the 1930 500 Miles Race at Brooklands where, driven by Eddie Hall and Dudley Benjafield, it was placed second. This was the last occasion in which the supercharged Bentleys appeared as a team. (Author's collection)

for speeds in excess of 130mph (210kph). This was to accommodate the Turbo's claimed top speed of 135mph (217kph), a considerable improvement on the 119mph (191kph) attainable by the Mulsanne saloon. The 0–60mph time, meanwhile, was shaved by three seconds from ten to seven seconds. Inevitably, though, fuel consumption was prodigious and the Turbo's thirst of 12.1mpg (23 litres/ 100km) compared with 14mpg (20 litres/100km) for the normally aspirated car.

"If fuel costs don't matter, the Bentley is immensely attractive and enjoyable", commented *Autocar*, while feeling moved to stress that at £61,744 – £6,504 more than the mainstream Mulsanne – the Turbo was over twice the price of a Mercedes-Benz 500SEL, a car which with a top speed of 145mph (233kph) was also significantly faster.

Because of the missing ingredient of suspension modifications, the boulevard ride was felt to be too soft, there being excessive body roll and a tendency for the big saloon to bottom

on poor roads. Nevertheless, the Bentley Turbo generated considerable interest and, above all, sales – once production had begun in September 1982, some six months after the model's debut. Rolls-Royce had expected to sell about 100 examples a year but in the event more than double that number of cars – 202 in the first year and 209 in the second – left the Crewe works. Total production eventually amounted to 519 cars, of which 24 were based on the long-wheelbase Mulsanne L.

The response to the Turbo, despite its limitations, made Rolls-Royce realise that it had awakened a slumbering giant. "The market was ripe for picking", Ward later reflected, and the company proceeded to devote much of its limited resources in that direction. In 1984 Bentley sales accounted for 22 per cent of production and customers worldwide were facing a five to six month waiting list for their cars.

Peter Ward recognised that the Turbo gave "younger businessmen an opportunity to move up to Bentley, probably for the first time." With the

The Continental R which revived the concept of the purpose-designed Bentley. Introduced in 1991, it is still in production. (LAT)

economy beginning to gather momentum during the Thatcher years, the five-star yuppie now had the ultimate alternative to the otherwise ubiquitous Porsche 911 and its variants. Ward indicated that the company was now determined to upgrade the famous name and not to repeat the understated themes of the past. "The marque's tradition and history are impressive. We shall ensure that potential customers are aware of Bentley as a separate identity and not simply a name on a radiator."

In July 1984 came the Bentley Eight which, significantly, was priced at under £50,000. The intention was to allow prospective customers to trade up from a Mercedes-Benz or Jaguar. At £49,497 the Eight cost noticeably less than the Mulsanne's £55,240 and the model was instantly identifiable by its new bright-mesh sports grille with its echoes of the twenties. Replacing the distinctive chromium-plated vertical slats that had been a feature of the marque since 1930, in truth it sat uneasily between the two rectangular headlight units.

An unprecedented number of 17 body colour and trim options were offered on the Bentley Eight, the intention being for owners to personalise their cars. There could now be little doubt of marque's identity because the Bentley name was repeated on both the front wings and the model name also appeared on the boot lid. Mechanical changes were confined to stiffer front suspension and there was a revised dashboard of straight-grain walnut veneer. Sales were, at this stage, restricted to the British market.

As noted in Chapter 6, the arrival of the Eight coincided with the Bentley Corniche being renamed the Continental. But these models were all variations on existing bodyshells. What Bentley needed was its own stylistic identity and the first step towards this was seen at the 1985 Geneva Motor Show. Project 90 was a mock-up of a Bentley coupé in the spirit of the legendary H. J. Mulliner Continental of the fifties. The work of British designers John Heffernan and Ken Greenley, who already had the lines of Panther Solo sports car of 1984 to their credit, the idea was to gauge public reaction to the concept.

Time had been of the essence. The former industry stylists, then both

What's in a name? (v) A question of labels

In the days of the original Bentley company, the colour of the enamel used on a car's radiator badge, and sometimes repeated on the petrol tank badging, provided an indication of its mechanical specification. The practice has since been revived and was first applied to the Bentley Brooklands of 1992, which was accorded a green badge.

The 3-litre of 1921, the first of the line, featured a blue badge, and the desirable 100mph (160kph) Supersports version of 1925–27 used a so-called green label. The same colour also featured on the Speed Model of 1928–30, the more potent version of Bentley's 6½-litre.

The revised Bentley Arnage of 2000 was distinguished by the Red Label name which first appeared on the 3-litre Speed Model of 1924–29 vintage. The original BMW-powered Arnage was simultaneously given the Green Label name.

Modern Bentleys now have different-coloured enamels in their radiator badges, reviving a practice introduced by the original Bentley company. (LAT)

Royal College of Art lecturers, had been approached early in 1984 by Rolls-Royce's product planning director, John Stephenson, and given three months to complete their work. "We decided not to do a boring Euro-design but develop the Mulliner theme," Heffernan told *Motor*. "I have always been a great fan of the R-type Bentleys and this car is evocative of the past."

After completion by Worthing-based International Automotive Design, the black-painted GRP concept had been altered following its showing at an all-important American customer styling clinic, Heffernan revealed. The initial transatlantic response was, he said, that "it looked too much like a Lincoln, so the three-quarter shape was altered."

The public reaction at Geneva was duly reported by the weekly motoring press. *Autocar* referred to it being "the talking point of the Show" but *Motor* cautioned that it had broken cover "to a mixed reception". However, Rolls-Royce was sufficiently confident to press ahead, and Project 90 paved the way for the arrival of the Continental R six years later.

Work on the car began in earnest in 1986, the year in which the Rolls-Royce Camargue flagship coupé ceased production. There could now be no doubt that what resources the newly-renamed Rolls-Royce Motor Cars possessed would first be directed to the consolidation of the growing popularity of the existing Bentley line.

Project 90 was not the only exciting Bentley offering at the 1985 Geneva show. There Rolls-Royce unveiled the Turbo R, the 'R' suffix signifying 'roadholding'; the Mulsanne name was deleted. Outwardly similar to its predecessor and with essentially the same engine, the car featured all-important chassis modifications.

Although some work was already underway on suspension changes, those finally adopted were much more radical, following Mike Dunn's appointment as Rolls-Royce's new

The Continental's dashboard is peculiar to the model, with a console that extends to the rear passengers. Leg room at the back is at a premium, as this photo shows. (LAT)

engineering director. He had arrived at Crewe early in February 1983, just after the Mulsanne Turbo had entered production. As Dunn later recalled, in that key year "engineering was directed to improve the handling of the car to match or beat the best of competitive luxury cars whilst retaining the unique refinement and character of the Mulsanne Turbo".[1]

At that point what was to emerge as the Turbo R had only 10 per cent greater roll stiffness. "Are you serious?" was Dunn's response to the Crewe engineer who proposed this. Dunn immediately revised the target to 50 per cent and ended up with front and rear anti-roll bars stiffer by 100 per cent and 60 per cent respectively. The damping was also beefed up, particularly on the rebound, and at the rear the suspension subframe was anchored by its own hard-rubber-bushed Panhard rod to eliminate rear-end steering. Greater resistance was introduced to the power steering by the introduction of a 50 per cent stiffer torsion bar.

More apparent were the new German Ronal aluminium wheels, the first occasion that such items had ever appeared on a Rolls-Royce product. The wheels were shod with huge Pirelli P7 tyres, and when *Motor* came to test the Turbo R it recognised that whilst these covers gave the car its grip they were also a factor in generating fierce body shake. Dunn and his team had been the first to recognise this deficiency and the model was soon fitted with bespoke Avon covers that were intended to remedy the problem. The much-improved handling also showed up the limitations of the original seats, which were now not as supportive as they might have been.

Priced at £61,744, the Turbo R was the most expensive model in Crewe's range but was destined to be the most numerically successful Bentley of its day, with 5,187 examples completed by the time its production ceased in 1996. A further 2,034 were based on the long-wheelbase Mulsanne L.

Driving a turbocharged Bentley

The point about incremental differences over the years transforming the product is as true of the turbocharged Bentleys as it is of lesser models in the Silver Spirit range.

Crushing performance effortlessly delivered is a constant, but early carb-fed cars are slightly slower and have a minimal but still noticeable lag before the turbo cuts in. With largely unmodified suspension, these first models also have a softer and less well-controlled ride than might be felt appropriate for a car of such performance.

Fuel injection improves both performance and responsiveness and another development milestone, anti-lock braking, gives yet more reassurance to the press-on driver. Suspension was stiffened for the Turbo R, giving it a sporting firmness but perhaps depriving the chassis of a degree of finesse. That was provided by the 1989 introduction of 'active ride' suspension. The arrival of the four-speed gearbox with its floor change further sportified the turbo cars, and the last Turbo S benefited from the extra power thanks to the fitment of an intercooler.

Driving an all-bells-and-whistles early 1990s Turbo R is certainly a profoundly impressive experience. Sublimely refined, the big turbocharged V8 offers an annihilating performance without any effort on behalf of the driver: the hewn-from-the-solid muscle punches the car seamlessly forward with such reserves that at 80mph the Bentley is barely turning over, the rev-counter reading a piffling 2,000rpm.

The four-speed gearbox shifts with imperceptible smoothness, the brakes are a paragon of progressiveness and undramatic efficiency, and the chassis with its adaptive damping has a combination of resilience and control light years ahead of that on an early Spirit. Better still, the steering has a weight and precision to match.

The result is a car of crushing competence, delivering everything one could possibly wish of a high-performance luxury saloon, but with the crucial difference that this seductive cocktail of virtues is presented with total unobtrusiveness: everything happens without the slightest ripple of disruption to the Bentley's calm but cruise-missile-rapid progress.

Dial in the exquisite fit, finish and quality of materials that you have a right to expect – the push-pull chrome knobs for the ventilation eyeballs are just one delicious detail amongst many – and you have what is surely the ultimate in four-door saloons.

The Turbo R was soon outselling the Mulsanne Turbo, which ceased production in 1985. In October 1986 the Turbo R, along with the rest of the Bentley/Rolls-Royce range, received fuel injection and anti-lock brakes for the 1987 season. Inside there were much needed slimmer front seats with fully adjustable head restraints. At the same time, in a bid to increase Bentley's penetration of the American market, the Bentley Eight was also modified to meet US legal requirements.

The 1988 model year saw the mainstream Bentley saloon redesignated the Mulsanne S. Outwardly similar to its predecessor, inside it now featured a rev-counter and a central console, to underline

the marque's refound sporting character.

In mid 1988 changes were made to the front of the Turbo R with the arrival of twin round headlamps and a deeper front air dam, along with steel sill extensions and a rear skirt. The new lamps were subsequently, in January 1989, extended to the normally aspirated Mulsanne S and the Eight, where they seemed in greater visual sympathy with the mesh radiator. These front-end changes further underlined the subtle differences between Bentley and its Rolls-Royce stablemate.

Then at the 1991 Geneva Motor Show came the Continental R coupé which was the production version of Project 90 exhibited at the same

venue six years previously. Basing it on Turbo R mechanicals, Crewe's engineers had been required to achieve a 10 per cent improvement in the performance on the Turbo R. This meant a top speed nudging the 150mph (240kph) mark with 0–60mph acceleration reduced to around six seconds. This was quite a brief for a car that turned the scales at 47.7cwt (2,422kg).

Bodily the latter-day Continental echoed its famous predecessor of 1952–59 but then its stylist, Ivan Evernden, had been constrained by having to retain the original Bentley radiator. Heffernan and Greenley had not been so restricted and so the radiator shell had been reduced in height to harmonise with a body that

The Bentley Brooklands replaced the Eight and Mulsanne for the 1993 season. It has the round headlamps introduced on the Turbo R for the 1989 season. (LAT)

Buying Hints

1. As these cars are closely related to the Silver Spirit, the same remarks apply to blown Bentleys. However, there are a few points that specifically relate to the Turbo and Turbo R lines.

2. Examples made prior to the 1986 model year, when fuel injection arrived, are fitted with the same Solex carburettor used on the Camargue and in addition to the aforementioned difficulties, whilst cold starting does not present a particular problem, hot starting is more problematic. It will probably take six to eight turns of the key to get the engine to fire, not a major problem but an annoyance nonetheless. In these circumstances you are far better off with the fuel-injected cars, which have no such problems.

3. The turbocharged engine is virtually indestructible and does not suffer from any significant peccadilloes, apart from the above. A worn turbocharger could be betrayed by oily hose connections; removing the inlet pipe could confirm this, if the pipe is badly oiled-up inside. With the engine off, you should be able to spin the turbocharger by hand; if not, it has seized...

4. Be prepared to replace the rear tyres every two years. The 15in and 17in covers were specially made for the cars and retail at around £300 apiece. The brakes also have a hard time, so you must be prepared to spend some money if the previous owner(s) didn't.

---

could as a consequence be about 1in (2.5cm) lower than that of the Mulsanne saloon. This contributed to a 0.36 drag coefficient.

The interior was new and deliberately distanced from that of the saloons. A new dashboard repositioned all the instruments in front of the driver, and in a radical break with tradition the central console was extended to the rear compartment. It also housed the automatic gearlever, transferred from the steering column where it had resided since 1952.

There was also a change of transmission, with the long-running GM400 three-speed automatic gearbox being replaced by a 4L80E four-speed unit, also by General Motors, with a choice of sports and economy settings – the gearlever incorporating a switch which allowed the driver to change setting at will. A flick of the control resulted in the gearbox working harder and simultaneously tightening up the suspension. The new 'box would be introduced across the Bentley and Rolls-Royce range over the period of

the 1991/92 winter.

Top speed was a limited 145mph (233kph) which was achieved by a combination of the more aerodynamically-efficient body lines and changes made to the V8 engine. One radical modification contemplated was the fitment of more efficient four-valve cylinder heads developed by Cosworth and publicly displayed by them in 1989. In the event these were not used but the Crewe/Northampton dialogue led to Rolls-Royce's Vickers parent acquiring Cosworth in 1990. A worthwhile purchase it proved to be, not only for its Formula 1 and IndyCar units but also for its patented aluminium engine-casting business.

In the event less radical changes were made to engine, namely a more efficient induction system which occupied less space than its predecessor and the fitment of a new Bosch K-Motronic fuel injection. These produced what pundits estimated at 360bhp, or 30bhp more than the Turbo R's output.

Rolls-Royce planned to build 70 Continentals a year and the

allocation for the first two seasons was sold before production began early in 1992 – with the car selling at the time for £175,000, making it by far and away the most expensive Crewe model. The Continental R remains in production at the time of writing.

The Continental's arrival coincided with the impending transfer of Mulliner Park Ward to Crewe. Its manufacture was accordingly relatively straightforward, in that the bodies were produced by Park Sheet Metal in Coventry and they were then delivered to Crewe for completion.

The beautifully-appointed grand tourer was acclaimed for its silence and refinement; as a long-legged intercontinental sporting coupé, criticisms were mostly confined to the lack of room for rear passengers and to the ride. Also the car seemed less than happy in the rain, which suggested a need for traction control.

But in 1992, the year in which the Continental entered production, and after nine years at Crewe as engineering director, Mike Dunn took early retirement. He was replaced by Antony Gott, who had joined Rolls-Royce from Lotus as senior engineer in 1982; in 1997 he would be promoted to director of engineering.

In the meantime the Bentley saloon line was continuing to evolve and in September 1992 the Mulsanne and the Eight were replaced by a single £91,000 model named the Bentley Brooklands. The chrome radiator was now a thing of the past, replaced by the Turbo's painted shell, and the unblown engine was the established fuel-injected unit. There were new 15in alloy wheels, and instead of the usual radiator badge of a silver 'B' set against a black background, there was a green badge which harked back to the marque's origins (see box) when the make was a familiar sight at Brooklands. Inside, the automatic gear lever followed Continental precedent and was transferred to the central console, whilst the door interiors featured a unique hide finish.

The Brooklands was the first model

Rear view of the Brooklands: the alloy wheels suit it well. (LAT)

to be produced under a Japanese-inspired team-based manufacturing process (see box). This new discipline, with its accent on flexible working practices, allowed Rolls-Royce to respond speedily to the individual requirements of customers.

With the passing of the years the Continental has benefited from the updates introduced on the saloons. For 1994 came the extensively revised V8, while inside so-called seatbelt 'presenters' were fitted which automatically proffered the belt to anyone who sat down in a seat. New, wider alloy wheels completed the package.

The 1995 season saw the arrival of the limited-production higher-performance Turbo S saloon: with the V8 having been re-engineered to include a liquid-cooled intercooler

and a new management system derived from Formula 1 technology; it was capable of 155mph (249kph). Externally there was a lower-profile version of the Bentley radiator grille and wraparound bumpers integral with the front airdam and rear fairing.

The 'S' engine was simultaneously extended to a Continental S, sold alongside the Continental R; just 18 examples were built in 1994 and 1995. This engine was also fitted to the convertible version of the Continental called the Azure and introduced at the 1995 Geneva Motor Show.

Chief executive Chris Woodwark recognised that Bentley owners were more interested in engine output than their Rolls-Royce counterparts so, for the first time for 45 years, Crewe no longer relied on the teasingly discreet

response 'adequate' to questions regarding the power output. It officially revealed that the 'S' unit developed 385bhp, and pushed out a massive 553lb ft of torque in the 2,000rpm–3,450rpm rev range.

If the method of building the Continental R was relatively straightforward, this certainly did not apply to the Azure. As with the closed car, the shell began life at Park Steel Metal in Coventry, but it was then sent to Italy, to Pininfarina in Turin, for fitment of the power-operated hood assembly and for painting. The body was then returned to Crewe for trimming and final assembly. As with the Corniche, the Azure was

The Azure of 1995 is effectively a convertible version of the Continental R and is a joint manufacturing venture with Pininfarina. (LAT)

noticeably heavier than its closed equivalent, to the tune of 3.14cwt (160kg); this was as a result of reinforcing the rear floorpan, which was endowed with deeper and stronger sills, and beefing up the A-posts and the screen header rail. The body was claimed as a consequence to be 25 per cent more rigid than the Corniche line it replaced.

Although resembling the coupé, practically all the panels on the Azure were new and this was reflected in an announcement price of £215,000, some £27,000 more than the closed car. Inside the layout resembled that of the coupé although the front seats came from BMW's 8-series. This reflected an agreement signed in 1992 whereby BMW would supply parts and technology to Rolls-Royce. Again, the Azure remains in production at the

time of writing.

The Azure shared the 1996 Geneva show stand with the fearsome short-wheelbase Continental T. With the 400bhp engine and a claimed top speed of 155mph (249kph), with a 0–60mph time of 5.8 seconds, the 'T' was, the company said, "the fastest Bentley yet." Shorter by 4in (10cm) than the standard car, at £215,000 it was about the same price as the Azure. As well as being lighter than the regular Continental, it was also wider, on account of its flared wheelarches and purposeful five-spoke alloy wheels. These concealed micro-alloy disc brakes, revised suspension, and electric traction control as standard. Inside there was an engine-turned aluminium dashboard with echoes of the twenties, and to underline that this was a car which meant business, a large red starter-button.

Also introduced at this time was the Turbo R Sport saloon. Aimed at German buyers, it shared the Continental T's alloy wheels and

inside carbon fibre replaced the traditional burr walnut, while a state-of-the-art navigation equipment and entertainment system were standard. The short-wheelbase version was discontinued in 1996, leaving the long-wheelbase R – no longer known as the RL – as the sole representative of the line.

With the new Bentley Arnage waiting in the wings, the Mulsanne saloon was reaching the end of the line. The R was replaced for 1998, its last season, by the RT, powered by the Continental T's 400bhp engine governed down to 150mph (241kph). It was instantly identifiable by the return of the wire-mesh radiator grille used on the Bentley Eight. The package was completed by the fitment of five-spoked alloy wheels.

Changes had also been made to the Brooklands, the cheapest model in the range, and the only saloon to retain the short wheelbase. For 1997 it received the 300bhp light-turbo engine also used in the Rolls-Royce Silver Spur. Capable of 140mph

(225kph), it was 4mph (6.4kph) faster than the normally-aspired Bentley, which now ceased production. For the final 1998 season it inherited the Turbo's uprated suspension and mesh radiator, and became known as the Brooklands R.

Superlative standards had been maintained to the very end of the line, Steve Cropley of *Autocar* reporting that the Brooklands R "provided a stern test of the Bentley's key luxury car qualities, like seat and low-speed ride comfort, smoothness and light throttle opening... In every facet it excelled". It was also, he said, "freer from rattles and creaks than any Bentley I've ever been in". The car was, however, in need of a "new, more rigid, better packaged body".

The 17-year-old Mulsanne line finally ceased production in December 1997 but not before the last 100 Turbo RTs had left the works in bespoke Mulliner form, a specification that was also extended to the final Brooklands cars.

Compared with the ageing saloon,

the Continental R line was only seven years old, a mere stripling in Crewe terms. The '98 London Motor Show saw the arrival of an uprated Continental T with boosted turbocharger output and a remapped engine management system. These combined to produce an extra 20bhp, giving 420bhp in all. Top speed was increased to a quoted 170mph (273kph) and the 0–60mph figure was shaved to a claimed 5.7 seconds. At the same time the 'T', in common with the Azure, gained a stainless-steel grille.

The Paris Motor Show of 1998 was chosen as the venue for the arrival of the Continental SC, or Sedanca Coupé, with targa-style detachable roof. Perfected in conjunction with Pininfarina, some £12 million had been expended on its development. The cost to the customer? A cool £245,000, precisely £100,000 more than the Arnage saloon...

So ended the first momentous stage of the Bentley revival. With considerable ingenuity and – at least

An Azure on home ground in the French Riviera. Its magnificently appointed interior maintains the combination of walnut veneer and leather upholstery that reaches back to Rolls-Royce's Edwardian origins. (LAT)

in the early days – a very tight budget, Rolls-Royce management had since 1982 revitalised the marque. For this great credit must go to the Peter Ward/Mike Dunn partnership, whose initiatives have been perpetuated by their successors. The last word in this remarkable renaissance must go to Ward who in 1987 summed up the essence of the Bentley revival: "In the old days Rolls-Royce traded on repeat business. The recession and the collapse of the Middle East market showed how shaky that could be. By creating a new image for Bentley, we spread our base... most Bentley sales have been conquest ones."

[1] Proceedings of the Automobile Division, Institution of Mechanical Engineers, 1987

The Silver Seraph
and Bentley Arnage

The BMW-engined Rolls-Royce Silver Seraph, introduced in 1998, received a mixed reception, certainly as far as its packaging was concerned. All-important improvements were made for the 2000 season and these included a stiffer body structure. (Rolls-Royce).

The Silver Seraph launched in March 1998 has the distinction of being the last Rolls-Royce to be born of British parentage. For just five months after its arrival the world-famous name was acquired by the German-owned BMW company. And instead of being powered by Crewe's seemingly indestructible V8, the new model used a V12 BMW unit. In doing so it became the first Rolls-Royce to employ a proprietary engine.

But the Seraph's launch, and that of its Bentley Arnage stablemate, was insensitively timed and became unnecessarily entangled with the untidy disposal of Rolls-Royce Motors Cars to the highest bidder. The packaging and performance of both models were the subject of criticism; sales suffered. The BMW-engined Arnage was discontinued in 2001, although the Red Label version continues, whilst the production of the Silver Seraph will cease in 2002.

The protracted nine-month takeover battle, finally resolved in July 1998, saw Volkswagen, which had gained control of the company, obliged to relinquish the Rolls-Royce

name to BMW. Despite the two-way split following the 1971 collapse of the company, the rights to the famous name were held by Rolls-Royce plc, the aero-engine arm of the original Rolls-Royce concern. It favoured BMW over Volkswagen, and decided that while Volkswagen might have purchased the Rolls-Royce works it did not have entitlement to the name. VW was thus left with Bentley and the Crewe factory, so after a 67-year association the two marques are, once again, in separate ownership.

A new BMW-designed Rolls-Royce, scheduled to appear on 1 January 2003, is to be produced at a purpose-built factory in West Sussex. Meanwhile at Crewe Volkswagen has initiated a £500 million investment programme, output is scheduled to increase to 10,000 cars per annum, and a new medium-sized saloon is due for a 2002 launch.

The arrival of the BMW-powered cars was the final expression of the predicament in which Rolls-Royce's Vickers parent found itself in the recession-hit early nineties. As recorded in the previous chapter, it tentatively put the loss-making Rolls-Royce Motor Cars up for sale in 1991 but by the following year Vickers was disingenuously referring to it as "a core business" after its secret plan to sell the company to BMW had fallen through. It therefore decided to retain the company and wait for better times. Yet doing so meant replacing the ageing Silver Spirit and its even older V8 engine, at a total cost of £200–£300 million, of which the new power unit would account for about £40 million. But Vickers was only in a position to contribute £100 million from its own coffers.

The BMW/Vickers dialogue bore some fruit because in February 1992 news broke that the German company had agreed to supply Crewe with a number of usually unseen minor components, namely airbags, electric seat mechanisms and gearbox controls. These were items which would have been costly for Rolls-Royce to initiate for its relatively small volumes. A further element of

Rolls-Royce Silver Seraph
1998 to 2002

ENGINE:
V12 alloy block, alloy heads	
Bore x stroke	85mm x 79mm
Capacity	5,379cc
Valve actuation	Single overhead camshaft per bank
Compression ratio	10:1
Engine management	Bosch Motronic 5.2.1
Power	322bhp at 5,000 rpm

TRANSMISSION:
Rear-wheel drive
Five-speed automatic with torque converter
Final drive ratio: 2.93:1

SUSPENSION:
Front: Independent, wishbone and coil spring
Rear: Independent, wishbone and coil spring.
Computer-controlled adaptive electro-hydraulic dampers, automatic ride-height control with automatic load compensation

STEERING:
Power assisted rack-and-pinion
Turns lock-to-lock: 3.55

BRAKES:
Front: Hydraulic, ventilated disc
Rear: Hydraulic, ventilated disc
Hydraulically-operated brake servo with anti-lock control

WHEELS/TYRES:
Cast aluminium alloy
235/65 R16

BODYWORK:
Steel and aluminium four-door unitary-construction saloon

DIMENSIONS:
Length	17ft 8in (5.39m)
Wheelbase	10ft 2in (3.11m)
Track - front	5ft 3in (1.60m)
- rear	5ft 3in (1.60m)
Width	7ft 0in (2.15m)
Height	4ft 11in (1.51m)

WEIGHT:
46cwt (2,338 kg)

PERFORMANCE:
(Source: *Autocar*)
Max speed	137mph (220kph)
0–50mph (0–80kph)	
0–60mph (0–100kph)	7.1sec
0–70mph (0–112kph)	

PRICE INCLUDING TAX WHEN NEW:
£155,000

NUMBER BUILT:
Still in production

Bentley Arnage
1998 to 2001

ENGINE:
V8, alloy block, alloy heads	
Bore x stroke	79mm x 92mm
Capacity	4,398cc
Valve actuation	Twin overhead camshaft per bank
Compression ratio	8.5:1
Engine management	Bosch M5.2.1
Turbochargers	Twin water-cooled, low inertia
Power	350bhp at 5,500rpm

TRANSMISSION:
Rear-wheel drive
Five-speed automatic gearbox with torque converter
Final drive ratio: 2.69:1

SUSPENSION:
Front: Independent, wishbone and coil spring
Rear: Independent, wishbone and coil spring
Computer-controlled adaptive electro-hydraulic dampers, automatic ride-height control with automatic load compensation

STEERING:
Power-assisted rack and pinion
Turns lock-to-lock: 3.55

BRAKES:
Front: Hydraulic, ventilated disc
Rear: Hydraulic, ventilated disc
Hydraulically-operated brake servo with anti-lock control

WHEELS/TYRES:
Cast aluminium alloy
255/55 R17

BODYWORK:
Steel and aluminium four-door unitary-construction saloon

DIMENSIONS:
Length	17ft 8in (5.39m)
Wheelbase	10ft 2in (3.11m)
Track - front	5ft 3in (1.60m)
- rear	5ft 3in (1.60m)
Width	6ft 3in (1.93m)
Height	4ft 11in (1.51m)

WEIGHT:
45.3cwt (2,302 kg)

PERFORMANCE:
(Source: *Autocar*)
Max speed	150mph (241kph)
0–50mph (0–80kph)	4.8sec
0–60mph (0–100kph)	6.3sec
0–70mph (0–112kph)	8.1sec

PRICE INCLUDING TAX WHEN NEW:
£145,000

NUMBER BUILT: Still in production

technical co-operation was aimed at the solving of engineering problems in the areas of body acoustics, vibration and rigidity.

This immediately generated speculation that BMW was emerging as Rolls-Royce's eventual purchaser. But when questioned by *Autocar* on the subject, a senior BMW executive stonewalled. "We're not interested in buying Rolls-Royce, even if we could", he said. "Why should we be? What does Rolls-Royce have to offer BMW?" However, in May 1993, the German car maker acquired a new chairman, 45-year-old Bernd Pischetsrieder, who was to take a very different public stance on the matter.

One corporate initiative that did reach the public eye was a design exercise for a 'Junior Bentley' convertible, called Project Java – a name that had previously been applied to an experimental Austin-based Bentley saloon of 1962. The new Java was a very definite crowd-puller at the 1994 Geneva Motor Show and was a joint project between the chief stylist at Crewe, Graham Hull, and Warwick-based Design Research Associates, run by former Rover Group styling chief Roy Axe.

With a hybrid Cosworth 3.5-litre V8 engine under its bonnet, the Java attracted intense interest and approval at Geneva and was subsequently displayed throughout the world, including at the famous Pebble Beach concours d'élégance in America. Chairman Peter Ward maintained that it could have entered production although at a cost of some £200 million. "If a partnership opportunity came along that was right, we'd certainly look at it very seriously..."

Work was in the meantime proceeding on the Silver Spirit/Mulsanne replacement and the project had already passed through a number of evolutionary phases since engineering director Mike Dunn had joined the company in 1983 with a brief to design the car.

The choice of engines remained at the heart of the concept and in 1994 Vickers began to talk to a number of

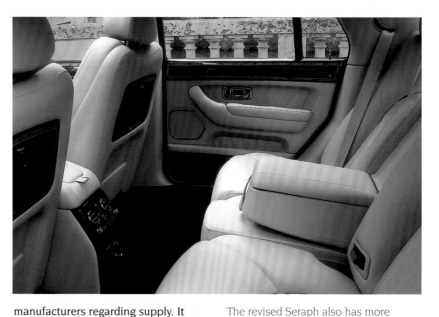

manufacturers regarding supply. It came down to a choice of American or German engines: no Japanese units were contemplated. Ford's then-experimental 'modular' V12 and General Motors' Northstar V8 were the first to be eliminated, and in November 1994 news broke that there was a choice of two potential suppliers, both of which were German. Predictably, they were Rolls-Royce's long-time rivals, namely Mercedes-Benz and BMW, both of whom possessed engines of sufficient size and technical ability to power 'The Best Car in the World'.

In due course Mercedes-Benz emerged as the favourite but, in December 1994 Vickers decided in favour of BMW. Its chairman, Sir Colin Chandler maintained that price had been the deciding factor but, unknown to the public, BMW had acquired a doughty champion in the shape of Sir Ralph Robins, who had joined Rolls-Royce as an aero-engine development engineer in 1955, and was now chairman of the Derby-based business. His intervention proved decisive.

Not only had Rolls-Royce plc signed a contract with BMW in 1990 for a joint aero-engine research and development programme, but significantly the firm, although corporately divorced from Rolls-Royce Motor Cars since 1971, retained the

The revised Seraph also has more headroom and legroom for rear passengers when compared with the original. (Rolls-Royce)

The Mayflower connection

The Silver Seraph was the first beneficiary of a new £40 million body plant Rolls-Royce built from the money it saved from not developing its own engine. Established in conjunction with the Mayflower Corporation, it filled the space previously occupied by the engine-building facility that was transferred to Cosworth. However, this activity has, since 1999, returned to Crewe.

Panels were produced at Mayflower's Coventry plant, formerly Motor Panels, and thus the one-time producer of body parts for the Camargue. Crewe having styled the then unnamed Silver Seraph, the body and its new substructure were prepared for production in Coventry, so breaking an association of 50 years with Pressed Steel – now the body-manufacturing section of the Rover Group.

Antony David Gott, born 1956

Rolls-Royce and Bentley's current chief executive is Antony Gott who joined the company in 1984. Holding a BSc in business administration, Tony Gott joined Tube Investments as a development engineer but after a year switched to the motor industry and moved to a similar position at Lotus. He was promoted senior engineer in 1982.

Two years later he joined Rolls-Royce as senior design engineer, becoming senior project engineer and then general manager of strategic planning before being made project director for the Rolls-Royce Silver Seraph and Bentley Arnage in January 1994. Promoted in 1997 to the Rolls-Royce board, in January 1999 he became acting chief executive on Graham Morris's departure; his appointment as chief executive was confirmed in April 1999.

rights to the prized name. With these factors in mind, Sir Ralph was destined to play a similarly pivotal role when the car company was sold to Volkswagen four years later.

Having won this 1994 contest, BMW emerged as the firm favourite to be Rolls-Royce's eventual owner, but only when Vickers was ready to sell it. Earlier in that year BMW had purchased the Rover Group from British Aerospace and the articulate, anglophile Bernd Pischetsrieder was now a significant force within the British motor industry.

As a result of this arrangement, BMW's newly-introduced 5.4-litre V12, then being used in the 750i, would find its way under the bonnet of the projected Rolls-Royce whilst a newly-developed BMW V8, turbocharged by in-house Cosworth Engineering, would power the sportier Bentley. Rolls-Royce chairman Peter Ward announced that the first recipient of the latter unit would be a production version of the Java concept car, to be based on a BMW 5-series platform.

But Ward resigned in January 1995, confirming speculation that he had

been against the BMW agreement and the element of control that went with it. He would have preferred the power unit to have been supplied by a British manufacturer. Java was then sidelined in the summer by his successor, Chris Woodwark, although BMW's position as supplier of engines for the next generation of cars was assured.

Even then it did not mean the end of Rolls-Royce's own V8 because it would continue to power the Bentley Continental line. Beyond this, as will emerge, it has since acquired an extended lease of life. However, in 1995 its production was transferred from Crewe to Cosworth's Northampton factory, so leaving room for a revised production line.

Work in the meantime was proceeding on the Silver Spirit replacement, under the P3000 coding.

After a five-year absence, the Rolls-Royce Corniche reappeared in 2000 as the convertible version of the Silver Seraph. Once again, 'retro' styling elements are apparent. However, production ceases in 2002, after only three years. (Rolls-Royce)

BMW: From Dixi to Rolls-Royce

As is the case with Rolls-Royce, BMW – standing for the Bavarian Motor Works – began the production of aero engines during the First World War. This is why the famous BMW blue-and-white quartered badge is a representation of the blur of an aeroplane propeller.

After the war BMW was able to retain its design team but it needed to diversify. In 1923 it started to produce motorcycles and in 1928 it acquired the Eisenach-based Dixi company which had just begun to build the British Austin Seven under licence. BMW quickly introduced a sporting ingredient to its products and the advanced 328 sports car of 1936 was light years ahead of Britain's traditional open two-seaters.

But the ending of the war saw Eisenach trapped behind the Iron Curtain in East Germany and it was only in 1952 that BMW car production restarted, in Munich. In the meantime its pre-war 2-litre 327 model had formed the basis of the new British marque of Bristol, the 400 model of 1947 being put into production with the help of ex-BMW engineer Fritz Fiedler.

During the 1950s BMW's car production was divided between two extremes: its prestigious 500-series cars, which sold in penny numbers, on one hand, and the high-volume/low-profit Italian Isetta bubble car it produced under licence on the other. A cash crisis in 1959 and an impending take-over by Mercedes-Benz was averted with financial support from the secretive Quandt family, which is still the majority shareholder. This was coupled with the arrival, in 1962, of a new 1500 model, tailor-made for the young executive, and the first of a new generation of distinctive, impressively engineered sporting saloons from which the company's ensuing prosperity derived.

some 1.5cwt (74kg) heavier.

Like the Silver Spirit, it was styled in-house and was the work of Graham Hull. He had not hesitated to draw on the company's recent past and, in particular, the Silver Cloud of 1955 which he regarded as the best-looking of the Crewe Rolls-Royces. The result was a 'retro' look with echoes of the Cloud and a 'bow wave' line running down the car's tapering flank. This is what Hull described as "yacht aesthetics." He also spoke of "an air of mystery" being created by a broad C-pillar which concealed the heads of the rear passengers.

The all-important radiator, complete with its disappearing Silver Lady, was visually downplayed and was more integrated into the car's nose than its predecessor. The lines of the now pressed rather than handmade shell were accordingly smoother and less clearly defined.

Despite the slightly longer wheelbase, there was about 1in (2.54cm) less legroom for back-seat passengers, who seem to have experienced a raw deal from Rolls-Royce packagers over the years. The difference in length was made up by the presence of a larger boot than previously.

The familiar rather upright driving position was maintained whilst the seats were new and, as ever, upholstered in the finest Scandinavian leather, chosen because of the absence there of barbed wire to damage the hide. Tradition was similarly maintained with the new and beautifully veneered dashboard but a more cost-conscious era was reflected by the fact that some of the minor switches hailed from the 7-series BMW. A miniature console at the rear contained not only the air-conditioning outlet ducts but also — a sign of the times — twin cup-holders.

The 5.3-litre alloy V12 engine, courtesy of the BMW 750i, and with single overhead camshafts operating two valves per cylinder, was essentially the same as in the German car although Crewe claimed that it had been tuned to produce more

After Mike Dunn's departure in 1992, the task of developing the new models fell to Antony Gott, who in April 1996 was appointed project director.

Then in the following year, on 26 October 1997, *The Sunday Times* broke the soon-to-be-confirmed news that Vickers was planning to auction Rolls-Royce – "which would command opening bids of £400 million". Ford and Ferrari were mentioned as having joined the race for what was the last significant British car company in indigenous ownership. Once again it was widely expected that BMW would emerge as the likely victor, as its engines were already powering experimental versions of the impending Rolls-Royce and Bentley.

Then, to the great surprise of the industry and commentators alike, and with corporate ownership still unresolved, Vickers scheduled the new cars for launch in the spring of 1998. In a break with past precedent, it was planned to solely announce the new Rolls-Royce at the March 1998 Geneva Motor Show, so that it would not be overshadowed by the more popular Bentley, whose announcement would follow at the end of April, two months later.

The Silver Seraph was the first wholly new model since the arrival of the Silver Wraith 52 years before. This was not only because the long-running V8 had been finally sidelined: the substructure of its Silver Spirit predecessor, which dated back to the Silver Shadow of 1965, was finally banished and replaced by a new underframe some 65 per cent stiffer, co-engineered with the Mayflower Corporation.

At £155,000 the Seraph cost £31,742 more than its predecessor; it was 3.9in (10cm) longer, with a 2.1in (5.5cm) increase in wheelbase, and was wider and, at 45.3cwt (2,302kg),

torque. The Rolls-Royce name was thus noticeably absent from the plastic engine cover which twice proclaimed the words 'Silver Seraph'. There could indeed be no doubt of the unit's origins, as each induction manifold was marked 'BMW'. Although the stated output of 322bhp was rather less than that of the turbocharged V8 of the Flying Spur, its refinement and smoothness were readily apparent. A 0–60mph time of 6.9 seconds was four seconds quicker than the Silver Spur, and top speed was a governed 140mph (225kph).

Drive passed through a ZF five-speed adaptive automatic gearbox and generated 361lb ft of torque – compared with 552lb ft produced by the turbocharged V8 used in the Spur.

Suspension was by all-round coil springs and wishbones, a change from the rear semi-trailing arms that had featured since 1965. This was combined with all-round hydraulic adaptive damping. The braking was particularly good, thanks to the 12.7in/12in (32.4cm/30.5cm) discs.

Autocar later compared the Silver Seraph with the BMW 750iL (with which it shared the same engine), Daimler's Super Eight, the Lexus LS400 and Mercedes-Benz S500, all of which were less than half the price of the Rolls-Royce. In awarding the accolade of 'The Best Car in the World' to the S500, it declared that, despite Crewe's limited resources, it had done "a competent job" with the Seraph. But although it "motored down the highway, oblivious of the outside world, crushing every bump in its path", the journal felt that "even those defenders of the faith had to concede that something has been lost with the new model".

Whilst refinement should have been taken as read, the new Rolls-Royce proved to be noisier than all its rivals and the magazine had severe

The Bentley was reworked with the arrival of the Red Label version of 2000; instead of using the Arnage's BMW V8, its is powered by Crewe's trusty turbocharged V8. (Rolls-Royce)

reservations about the packaging: "...you have to ask how it is possible for so large car to have so small an interior.... Tall drivers struggle to slide behind the wheel and then have to get used to a cramped driving position. Rear passengers find the cushion has been lowered so far in the interests of headroom that comfort can't be taken for granted. It also feels big and heavy, lacking body control and high speed ride composure compared with the others".

Some four weeks after the Seraph's launch, on 30 March 1998, Vickers announced that it had agreed in principle to sell the business to BMW for £340 million. A month later it duly

From Beetle to Bentley

On 10 April 1945 a few soldiers of the American 102nd Infantry division entered the town of KdF-Stadt (Strength-through-Joy Town) some 50 miles (80km) east of Hanover. There on the banks of the Mittelland Canal, they discovered a massive car factory, three quarters of which had been damaged by Allied bombing. It was the home of the KdF-Wagen, more generally known as the Volkswagen, the German's People's Car conceived by Adolf Hitler, developed by Ferdinand Porsche's Stuttgart-based Design Bureau, and intended to sell for RM1,000 (£85). Anyone who predicted the ensuing success of this car would make Volkswagen Europe's largest motor manufacturer and the eventual owner of Rolls-Royce's esteemed Bentley marque, and its Crewe factory, would have been regarded as a prime candidate for the Funny Farm!

Yet this is precisely what has happened.

Volkswagen production began in the renamed town of Wolfsburg under British army control but in 1948 the company was returned to German ownership. General manager Heinz Nordhoff turned the VW, which the world knows as the Beetle, into a global car, just like the Model T Ford that inspired its creation. It was succeeded in 1974 by the Golf, and at the time of writing the latest generation of the line remains the Continent's most popular model.

In 1993, Ferdinand Piech, who also has the distinction of being Ferdinand Porsche's grandson, became Volkswagen chairman. He not only revitalised the business but also broadened its marketing base with the purchase, in 1998, of no fewer than three prestigious European sporting marques. First, in February, came Lamborghini, to be followed by Bentley in July and Bugatti in September. Not only is there likely to be a mechanical relationship between this trio of makes, but Le Mans also beckons. It should be remembered that in 1963–72 Piech worked for the family firm and had overall responsibility for the mighty Porsche 917 that in 1970 gave the company its first Le Mans victory...

Rolls-Royce cars under licence from BMW until 31 December 2002. BMW for its part made it clear that there was no question of Rolls-Royce production being moved abroad: the cars would be built in a purpose-designed factory at an undisclosed location.

Then on the following day chief executive Graham Morris, only 16 months in the job, resigned – although he agreed to stay on until the end of the year until a successor was found. "Everyone at Crewe wanted Rolls-Royce to stay together, and we'd all been working towards that. So when the split came I felt that I'd been compromised", he later told *Autocar*. This corporate upheaval could do nothing to aid sales of the Seraph or the Bentley Arnage that followed it at the end of April.

Although both shared essentially the same bodyshell, the Rolls-Royce and the Bentley were quite different in character. Gott and his team had developed them simultaneously and in parallel so that one could not be regarded as the parent of the other. As with the Mulsanne of 18 years before, Rolls-Royce chose a Le Mans name for its new Bentley – although Arnage is in fact the slowest corner on the Sarthe circuit. Priced at £145,000, the new Bentley cost £10,000 less than the Seraph but with a governed top speed of 150mph (241kph) it was 10mph (16kph) quicker and significantly faster through the gears.

Using the same bodyshell as the Rolls-Royce, the Arnage differed externally only by the painted Bentley radiator shell with its mesh grille, and by its distinctive style of alloy wheel. But from thereon the two cars diverged. Under the bonnet was the 4.4-litre twin-turbocharger V8 used in normally-aspired form in the BMW 540 and 740 saloons. With four valves per cylinder and twin overhead camshafts per cylinder bank, the unit developed 350bhp at 5500rpm, which was some 28bhp more than the larger-capacity V12. Little wonder the model's quoted 0–62mph (0–100kph) time of 6.2 seconds was some 0.3 of a second faster than the Seraph's.

confirmed the sale but had not reckoned on the determination of a surprise contender, namely Volkswagen's chairman, Ferdinand Piech, to secure the business. It had offered a significant £90 million more, to the tune of £430 million. BMW, however, would not notably increase its bid and Vickers announced that it had agreed in principle to sell the company to the latecomer. This was confirmed on 5 June, despite an eleventh-hour attempt by a consortium of British enthusiasts, led by barrister and avowed Eurosceptic Michael Shrimpton, who wished to prevent what they regarded as a gilt-edged British institution falling into German hands.

The sale was duly secured on 3 July and two days later BMW announced that it was terminating engine supplies. Yet there was to be a significant twist to the transfer of ownership because, as will have been apparent, Vickers did not own the rights to the Rolls-Royce name. This was retained by Rolls-Royce plc although Bentley did not enjoy such protection.

Once again RR chairman Sir Ralph Robins moved to the fore and, on 28 July, the company sold the rights to the Rolls-Royce name to rival bidder BMW for £40 million. The matter was finally resolved that day between Piech and Pischetsrieder on a Bavarian golf course, with the result that Volkswagen retained the Bentley name and the Crewe factory. The deal also included Cosworth Engineering. VW would continue to manufacture

As befitted a performance car, the Arnage's dashboard was very different from that of the Rolls-Royce, featuring five dials instead of the Rolls-Royce's two, including a tachometer. The lavishly upholstered interior also differed, with the front seats providing much improved support.

The change for the automatic gearbox was floor-mounted, and the five-speed 'box was adaptive, with the computer's memory logging how the driver behaved and adjusting the gearbox's actions accordingly. It was a similar although outwardly less apparent story as far as the chassis was concerned: the suspension was stiffer, with uprated anti-roll bars and dampers, and the handsome alloy wheels were shod with bigger tyres.

The year 1998 would go down as the most traumatic in the company's history, the 1971 bankruptcy excepted. Demand for the Silver Seraph, in particular, suffered in the upheavals and Rolls-Royce sales slumped by 299 cars, from 1,918 sold in 1997 to 1,619 in 1998. The result was a loss of £122 million.

In January 1999, when Tony Gott took over as chief executive, about 100 workers were told to remain at home because of a lack of demand. By the end of the year Rolls-Royce sales were down by a substantial 30 per cent: just 444 Seraphs were sold. Bentley purchases were, as ever, greater and marginally reduced to 1003 from 1019 cars. Losses again rose, this time to £136 million.

Although commentators had clearly enjoyed the Arnage, there had been criticism that the blown BMW V8 did not provide quite the performance and, above all, the character of its predecessors. *Autocar* spoke for many when it wrote: "There isn't quite the old V8 feeling of effortless abundant torque; to go so fast this unit needs half a second to produce boost, and for its engine/transmission relationship to get sorted out."

The now Volkswagen-owned company took seriously these criticisms, of a model after all powered by an engine emanating from its BMW rival, and in September 1998, just six months after the Arnage's launch, it begun to rethink its specifications. The outcome was the arrival, at the Frankfurt Motor Show in September 1999, of the supplementary Arnage Red Label — with the BMW-powered original

renamed the Green Label for 2000 but discontinued in the following year.

The principal difference between the two was that the Red Label used the ageing but apparently still competitive V8, the production of which reverted to Crewe. Further work was undertaken on the engine so that it could meet future emissions requirements without a loss of power, resulting in 400bhp at 4,000rpm – some 50bhp more than the smaller-capacity BMW unit. The outcome was that the Red Label's torque figure of 619lb ft at 2,150rpm was in excess of any comparable car of its day. Its adoption also meant a reversion to the earlier four-speed gearbox.

Outward changes were mainly confined to a deeper front spoiler and 18in wheels in place of the Arnage's 17in ones. Modifications were also made to the suspension and traction control, while the Bentley's monocoque was stiffened by introducing a cast-alloy brace in the engine bay and reinforcing the

The Bentley Continental T for 2001, in Monaco Yellow with Personal Commission interior: yours for £233,355. (Rolls-Royce)

The West Sussex connection

As mentioned in the Introduction, Henry Royce spent the last 15 years of his life, from late in 1917 until his death in 1933, at 'Elmstead', a house located in the coastal West Sussex village of West Wittering. Aided by a small team of designers, Royce's creativity was maintained and world-famous cars and aero engines continued to emanate from this unlikely rural location.

When BMW secured the rights to the Rolls-Royce name in 1998, it required a new factory in which to build its cars and looked at possible sites in Oxford, Crewe, Derby and...West Sussex.

In May 2000 the news broke that it was planning to build the new factory near to the Goodwood racing circuit in West Sussex, only about 20 miles (32km) from where Henry Royce once worked. The site is a 30-acre (12.2 hectares) disused gravel pit in the south-east corner of the Goodwood estate owed by the Earl of March. The intention, declared project director Karl-Heinz Kalbfell, was to create "the world's most exclusive car manufacturing plant" and architects Nicholas Grimshaw and Partners came up with a headline-grabbing scheme. Adventurously the eight acre (3.2 hectares) £60 million works would be partially submerged and its roofs topped with grass and moss to harmonise with the local environment. This would require the excavation of some 492,100 tons (500,000 tonnes) of gravel.

The plant would be capable of building 1,000 cars a year, the equivalent of five cars every day, and would house a 30-strong design team. In all some 350 jobs could be created. Visitors would enter via a glass-fronted courtyard so that they could view craftsmen at work. It was hoped that skilled labour could be recruited from yacht-builders and Formula 1 constructors in the area. Bodies, built in Germany, would be painted and trimmed on the premises, and those cars destined for overseas customers dispatched from neighbouring Southampton. The nearby circuit could be used for testing.

Such was the scheme as it was announced. But the Environment Agency's concerns regarding

flooding, following the heavy rains over the winter of 2000/01, and highlighted by the factory's unconventional design, caused some delay. However, BMW received the green light in the summer of 2001 and work on the project began immediately. If all goes accordingly to plan, Rolls-Royce production should begin there in January 2003.

An architect's drawing of the proposed partially concealed Rolls-Royce factory near Goodwood, West Sussex, intended for completion in 2003. Note the specially constructed lake in the left foreground which would receive rainwater from the 'living green roof'. (BMW Group)

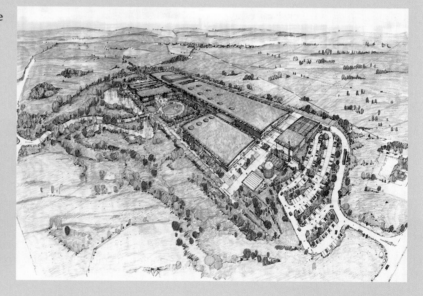

transmission tunnel and floorpan. These ministrations produced some 20 per cent greater stiffness than on the original Arnage.

Inside a radical rearrangement of the furniture meant revised seating which provided 2in (5.1cm) more legroom and 1in (2.54cm) more headroom, achieved by lowering the floor and reshaping the backs of the front seats.

These modifications resulted in a faster, more accelerative car with a top speed of 155mph (249kph), rather than a governed 150mph (241kph) and a 0–60mph figure of 5.9 seconds, compared to the BMW-powered Arnage's 6.3 seconds. At £149,000, the revised saloon cost £4000 more.

The Silver Seraph was similarly improved for the 2000 season although it retained its BMW V12

power unit. Revisions to the body structure resulted in a 65 per cent stiffer hull in a bid to reduce road-generated sound. Careful attention was also paid to the door seals to cut down on wind noise. Like the Bentley, the Seraph also benefited from improved rear accommodation with more headroom, legroom and kneeroom. In short, it was a much improved product.

Since the 1995 demise of the Shadow-derived Corniche there had been no Rolls-Royce convertible. In January 2000 this was remedied when an open Corniche version of the Silver Seraph was launched at the Los Angeles Motor Show. Whilst the lines of the second-generation model were related to the recently-introduced saloon, Graham Hull introduced an element of individuality, particularly around its rear, and declared a latter-day debt to Hooper's outstanding stylist Osmond Rivers.

Unlike the saloon the Corniche does not rely on the BMW V12 but like the Red Label Bentley has reverted to the Crewe-built V8 – developing 325bhp in the light-turbocharged format used. The logic of using the Crewe V8 is that the Corniche is built on the Bentley Azure floorpan. Rolls-Royce claims a top speed of 135mph (217kph) and a 0–60mph time of eight seconds. The Corniche's current price of £212,765 places it as the most expensive model in the RR range.

The company chose the 2000 Geneva Motor Show to unveil the long-wheelbase version of the Seraph, although it ceases production in 2002, which it named the Park Ward. With 9.8in (25cm) more between the wheel centres, it provided rear passengers with some much needed legroom.
It was planned to make only 60 cars a year.

In June came a heavily revised two-seater Continental T, the work of the Bentley Special Commission department. Priced at £300,000, some £66,000 more than the standard 'T', its new front bumper, air dam and sills spelt improved aerodynamics to reflect that the blueprinted V8 with revised management system now had 440bhp on tap. Inside was an engine-turned dashboard and quilted leather upholstery and the space previously occupied by the rear seats now contained a set of matching custom-built luggage bags.

In August came news that a Bentley State Limousine was being built for HM The Queen for her Golden Jubilee, which falls in 2002. This will be the

first occasion on which the monarch has officially used the make.

Volkswagen chose the 2000 British Motor Show to announce that it was investing £13.3 million in a new wood and chrome shop to be built at Crewe. A further £56 million was to be spent at the site for plant and equipment for the assembly of the new Mid-Sized Bentley, coded MSB, the exterior styling of which was signed off in December 1999. The new Bentley intended for 2002 will be smaller, lighter and will cost some £75,000, around half the price of the Arnage – which is destined to survive until at least 2006. It will be joined in about 2005 by a coupé which will be Crewe's first four-wheel-drive car.

In 2000 came the second phase of a £3 million design centre. This is headed by Dirk van Braekel, who replaced Graham Hull in March 1999 as Bentley's new styling supremo, arriving at Crewe from Skoda where he is credited with the lines of the Octavia and Fabia. A 40-strong team was responsible for the new Bentley's interior styling, which was approved during the year 2000.

In the meantime Volkswagen continues to build the Silver Seraph for BMW until 2002. If all goes according to plan, come 1 January 2003 BMW will have departed with the Rolls-Royce name, the Spirit of Ecstasy mascot and the famous radiator for a purpose-designed new factory (see box) to be located near Goodwood, West Sussex.

BMW had not wasted any time in beginning work in Germany on the next generation of Rolls-Royces, and at the end of 2000 test 'mules' began to appear on German roads. The Anglo-German model, coded RR01, is accordingly slated for a launch on New Year's Day 2003 and is to have an aluminium spaceframe chassis, using technology pioneered on BMW's Z8 roadster of 1999. At an estimated weight of 2,000kg, or 39.4cwt, the new car will be some 5.9cwt (300kg) lighter than the Silver Seraph and its sophisticated chassis will permit a variety of body styles, with coupé and convertible versions able to be

produced with relative ease.

The British element is provided by the design of the saloon bodywork, the responsibility of a small team headed by former Pininfarina stylist Ian Cameron. With Crewe out of bounds, the work was undertaken in a former Barclays Bank building off London's Bayswater Road and was completed by December 1999. The intention is to match Mercedes-Benz's prestigious new Maybach brand and Volkswagen's impending Bentley line. RR01 will be powered by a V12 engine but, unlike the Seraph, will be of a unique 6.8-litre capacity with bespoke twin-cam cylinder heads and developing some 450bhp. It will be matched to a new ZF six-speed automatic transmission.

In short, the car should be lighter, roomier and faster than the current Rolls-Royce. The world will be waiting and watching for the next instalment in this fascinating story...

And finally

Two final twists to the extraordinary saga of Vickers' 1998 sale of Rolls-Royce and Bentley did not emerge until the following year. In February 1999 Bernd Pischetsrieder, who at the eleventh hour had snatched Rolls-Royce from Volkswagen, was ousted from his job, the victim of a boardroom wrangle relating to his ill-fated purchase of the Rover Group. But soon afterwards he joined Volkswagen and is currently tipped to succeed Ferdinand Piech...

Then, in September of the same year, and just 15 months after it had disposed of the two car companies, Vickers itself was sold...to Rolls-Royce plc for £576 million, just £120 million more than it had received from Volkswagen. After 171 years, one of Britain's most famous industrial names was no more whilst those of Bentley and Rolls-Royce survive, albeit in German ownership.

Clubs, Acknowledgements & Bibliography

Clubs

If you run one of these cars, or are contemplating their purchase, then club membership is a must. The Rolls-Royce Enthusiasts' Club caters for Rolls-Royces of all ages, and post-1933 Bentleys, and in addition to the usual full calendar of events and high quality magazine, it stages ten or so technical seminars a year. These are held at the Club's headquarters, The Hunt House, High Street, Paulerspury, Northampton NN12 7NA. Related models such as the Bentley Mark VI/R-type and Silver Wraith are grouped together, as are the Silver Shadow and T-series, Silver Spirit and Mulsanne and so on. Owners of coachbuilt cars also have their own seminar addressed by specialists in their respective fields, namely a panel beater, woodworker and trimmer. There is also a used-car inspection service for members. Additionally, owners can obtain details of their car's history from the original factory Chassis Cards and Build Records carefully preserved at Paulerspury.

A similar search facility is provided by the Bentley Drivers' Club of 16, Chearlsey Road, Long Crendon, Aylesbury, Buckinghamshire HP18 9AW. It serves all owners of cars with winged 'B' badge, from the original Cricklewood-built cars to the current Bentley Azure. Members are also able to benefit from spares schemes, advice and the occasional technical seminar.

Acknowledgements

My thanks to Warren Allport, who so diligently chronicled Rolls-Royce affairs for *Autocar* over a 20 year period, for putting me right on some specific details of this story although I need hardly add that I alone am responsible for any conclusions drawn.

The Buying Hints for the respective models are the outcome of talking to Rolls-Royce and Bentley owners and specialists over many years although I am particularly grateful to Tony Worthington of Phantom Motors of Crondall, Farnham, Surrey (tel: 01252 850231), who has some 40 years experience of both marques, for his help in this regard.

Cars for driving impressions were kindly provided by RR&B Garages of Bromsgrove (tel: 01527 876513), Royce Service & Engineering of Ashtead (tel: 01372 276546), London's Frank Dale & Stepsons (tel: 0208 847 5447), and Phantom Motors. The author very much appreciates the generosity of these well-regarded specialists in making available their cars, and for the additional advice they have given on ownership practicalities.

Most photographs are from the archive of LAT Photographic, Somerset House, Somerset Road, Teddington, Middlesex TW11 8RU. Details of the photo-library's services are available on 0208 251 3000.

Performance figures in the data sections are quoted with acknowledgement and thanks to *Autocar* magazine, inheritor of the *The Autocar* and *The Motor* titles.

Books

A-Z of British Coachbuilders (Bay View Books, 1997), Nick Walker

Bentley – The Cars from Crewe (Dalton Watson, 1988), Rodney Steel

Rolls-Royce (Octopus, 1982), Jonathan Wood

Henry Royce - Mechanic (Rolls-Royce Heritage Trust Historical Series No 12, 1989), Donald Bastow

Hives, The Quiet Tiger (Sir Henry Royce Memorial Foundation, Historical Series No 7, 1985), Alec Harvey-Bailey

Hives' Turbulent Barons (Sir Henry Royce Memorial Foundation, Historical Series No 20, 1992), Alec Harvey-Bailey

Rolls-Royce - The First Cars from Crewe (Rolls-Royce Heritage Trust Historical Series No 23, 1997), Ken Lea

Rolls-Royce The Classic Elegance (Dalton Watson. 1987), Lawrence Dalton

Rolls-Royce and Bentley Experimental Cars (Rolls-Royce Enthusiasts' Club, 1986), Ian Rimmer

Rolls-Royce and Bentley The Crewe Years (Haynes, 1999), Martin Bennett

The Rolls-Royce Silver Dawn & Silver Wraith (Complete Classics Publication, 1998), Bernard L. King

The Rolls-Royce Wraith (John M. Fasal, 1986), Tom C. Clarke

The Rolls-Royce and Bentley, Vols 1/4 (Motor Racing Publications, 1984, 1985, 1999), Graham Robson

Silver Ghosts and Silver Dawn (Constable, 1970), W. A. Robotham

Twenty Years of Crewe Bentleys 1946-1965 (The Bentley Drivers' Club, 1973)

Magazines and publications

The Autocar (now *Autocar*); *Autocar & Motor*; *Journal* [House magazine of Rolls-Royce Motors]; *The Motor* (latterly *Motor*); Proceedings, Automobile Division, Institution of Mechanical Engineers; Rolls-Royce Enthusiasts' Club *Bulletin*

Index

*Pages numbers in **bold** refer to illustrations*

Rolls-Royce marked the end of its association with Crewe by launching the Last of the Line Silver Seraph for the valedictory 2002 model year. A total of 170 are to be built, with 45 retained for the home market. Unique features include interior enhancements and a duo-tone livery in the Silver Cloud idiom. The usually black Rolls-Royce radiator badge, which is repeated on the rear quarter panels and boot lid, reverts to the red enamel of the pre-1933 era. In addition, the Spirit of Ecstasy mascot design's featured on the wheel knave plates. A similarly enhanced version of the Corniche is to be produced.